INSPIRE / PLAN / DISCOVER / EXPERIENCE

VENICE
AND THE VENETO

DK EYEWITNESS

VENICE
AND THE VENETO

CONTENTS

DISCOVER 6

EXPERIENCE 70

NEED TO KNOW 250

Left: Colourful buildings of Burano
Previous page: Church of Santa Maria della Salute
Cover: Ornate palazzos line the the Grand Canal

DISCOVER

The islands of Venice

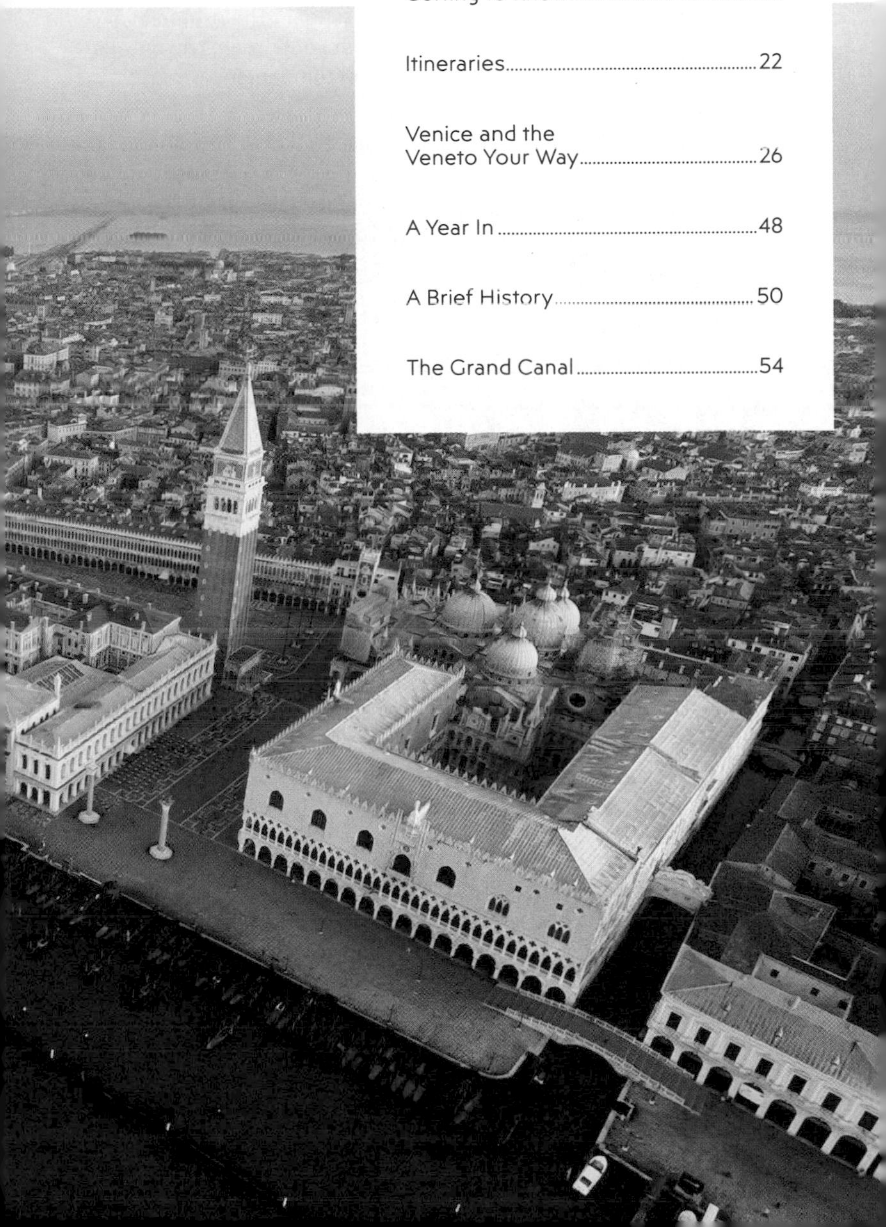

WELCOME TO
VENICE AND
THE VENETO

Incredible architecture and astounding collections of priceless art. Charming *campi* and a magical maze of canals. Rolling hills, medieval towns and meandering wine routes. Whatever your dream trip entails, this DK Eyewitness Guide is the perfect travel companion.

① Squero San Trovaso, a gondola boat yard in Venice.

② Sunset in the Dolomites.

③ Colourful houses line the canal on the island of Burano.

④ Busy *osterie* spill on to a cobbled square, Venice.

Venice is a labyrinthine, dreamlike city. It is also an extremely fragile one, with rising waters and mass tourism endangering its fragile microcosm. Yet you can still enjoy its many wonders without leaving a trace: so put down your selfie stick and respect the city and its inhabitants. Sure, Venice is home to myriad must-see sights; its ostentatious basilica, opulent palazzos, and acclaimed art galleries such as the Accademia and Peggy Guggenheim Collection. But this tiny city also squeezes an immense store of heritage into its hidden corners and sleepy *sestieri*, where you'll find yourself far from the crowds of San Marco.

Meanwhile, the Veneto mainland is a heady mix of bucolic valleys and medieval towns. Verona offers archaeological history and a generous dose of romance, while fun-loving

Padua is home to an ancient university and a chapel filled to the rafters with Giotto's frescoes. Beyond, vineyards stripe the hillsides, and the picturesque pastel-hued towns that hug the shores of Lake Garda offer relaxation and endless watery pursuits, while to the north stand the precipitous peaks of the Dolomites.

Although a relatively small region, Venice and the Veneto can easily overwhelm. We've broken the region down into easily navigable chapters, with detailed itineraries, expert local knowledge and comprehensive maps to help plan your perfect trip. Whether you're staying for a weekend, a week, or longer, this DK Eyewitness guide will ensure that you see the very best the area has to offer. Enjoy the book, and enjoy Venice and the Veneto.

REASONS TO LOVE
VENICE AND
THE VENETO

Superb Roman ruins, romantic towns, lakeside adventures and delectable cuisine, all washed down with a glass of one of the region's sublime wines; the reasons to love this corner of Italy go far beyond the busy streets of Venice.

1 CARNEVALE

Brace yourself for the crowds and let your imagination run riot as you join revellers taking to the streets of Venice dressed in costumes ranging from the Baroque to the bizarre.

PADUA 2

Roman ruins and magnificent squares: the city of Padua has plenty to offer. Head to the Cappella degli Scrovegni (p205) to see Giotto's sublime frescoes dance across the interior walls.

3 ART OLD AND NEW IN DORSODURO

From the Accademia (p140) to the Punta della Dogana (p146), Venice is home to art of all ages. Feeling inspired? Find a shady spot, sharpen your pencil and get sketching.

VALPOLICELLA VINES 4

Explore lush Valpolicella vineyards (p238) and indulge in some of Italy's finest wines. If red is not to your taste, nearby Soave *(p234)* is on hand with refreshing white, amber or rosé varieties.

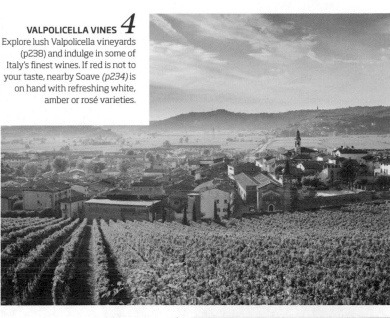

CRUISING DOWN VENICE'S GRAND CANAL 5

One of the world's greatest waterways. Take the slow boat, vaporetto No. 1, and stand on deck for views of lacy façades and life in a city in which everything happens by water.

LOCAL CUISINE 6

Venetian cuisine is centred around the sea. Head to the Rialto Market *(p107)* to gawp at the day's catch before feasting on seafood at one of the city's many fine seafood restaurants.

THE DOLOMITES 7

These majestic mountains are the ideal setting for getting back to nature. Paraglide from their precipitous peaks or ramble through crisp alpine forest while inhaling that fresh mountain air.

CYCLING AROUND LAKE GARDA 8

Miles of dramatic shoreline, a "floating" bike route and pretty stop-off points like the Sirmione Peninsula make Lake Garda *(p230)* an ideal spot for an adventure on two wheels.

9 FAIR VERONA

See a breathtaking show at the world's third-largest Roman Arena *(p223)* or embrace the romance as you peer over the balcony of Juliet's House *(p225)* in search of your Romeo.

10 HIDDEN VENICE

In Venice, hidden treasures, quiet *campi* and green spaces reward those who dare leave the tourist bubble. Go farther still to discover the humble charm of Venice's lagoon islands.

PIAZZA SAN MARCO 11

Venice's must-see square contains so many incredible sights that it takes time to let its beauty sink in. Grab a coffee and let San Marco's colonnaded grandeur wash over you.

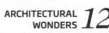

ARCHITECTURAL WONDERS 12

Balanced on oak piles, Venice is a marvel in and of itself. Within it, intricate façades line canals, gilded domes glitter in the sun, and the spires of grand basilicas pierce the heavens.

0 metres 500
0 yards 500
N

Canale delle Sacche

Canale delle

Madonna
dell'Orto

Campo del
Ghetto Nuovo

CANNAREGIO
p154

Gesuiti

TRONCHETTO

Campo San
Geremia

Ca' d'Oro

SAN POLO AND
SANTA CROCE
p98

Campo
della
Peschiera

Santa Maria
Gloriosa dei Frari

Campo
San Pola

Ponte
di Rialto

Canal Grande

SAN MARCO
p72

Campo
Santa
Margherita

Campo
Sant'
Angelo

La
Fenice

Piazza
San Mar

Campo
Santo
Stefano

SANTA
MARTA

DORSODURO
p136

Accademia

Santa Maria
della Salute

EXPLORE
VENICE AND
THE VENETO

This guide divides the six *sestieri* of Venice and the
surrounding Veneto region into nine colour-coded
sightseeing areas, as shown on this map. Find out
more about each area on the following pages.

MURANO

ITALY

SWITZERLAND AUSTRIA HUNGARY
SLOVENIA
CROATIA
Milan • • **VENICE**
• Bologna SERBIA
BOSNIA AND
HERZEGOVINA
FRANCE Florence • **ITALY** MONTENEGRO
*Adriatic
Sea*
• Rome
• Naples
*Tyrrhenian
Sea*
*Ionian
Sea*
*Mediterranean
Sea* Palermo •

SAN
MICHELE

Fondamenta Nuove

Santi Giovanni
e Paolo

CASTELLO
p116

Campo
S Maria
Formosa

Scuola di San Giorgio
degli Schiavoni

San Pietro
di Castello

Basilica di
San Marco

Palazzo Ducale

Museo Storico
Navale

Canale di San Marco

Giardini
della
Biennale

SANT'
ELENA

San Giorgio
Maggiore

THE VENETO

Bolzano ○ ● Cortina d'Ampezzo

THE DOLOMITES
p240

Trento ○ ○ Belluno

Feltre ○

Udine ○

Riva del
Garda ○ ○ Vittorio Veneto

Bassano
del Grappa ○

**VERONA AND
LAKE GARDA**
p216

*Lake
Garda*

Vicenza ○

**THE
VENETO PLAIN**
p186

○ Portogruaro

Treviso ○

Caorle ○

☐ *Area of main Venice map*

Verona ○

Padua ○

**THE LAGOON
ISLANDS**
p172

Mantova ○

Monselice ○

*Golfo di
Venezia*

○ Rovigo

0 kilometres 40
0 miles 40

N
↑

GETTING TO KNOW
VENICE AND THE VENETO

The focal point of Venice is San Marco, home to a whole host of world famous landmarks in one square alone. Beyond Venice's lagoon, wondrous sights, spectacular landscapes and world-renowned food and wine await.

SAN MARCO

PAGE 72

This *sestiere* is considered the hub of Venice, and its eponymously named Piazza sees tourists and the district's wealthy residents sipping coffee side by side surrounded by some of the city's most famous monuments. Designer shops and jewellery stores line the grand streets of Via XXII Marzo while towards Rialto the establishments become a little less exclusive.

Best for
Sightseeing and shopping

Home to
Basilica di San Marco, Palazzo Ducale, Museo Correr

Experience
Climbing the campanile at San Giorgio for sweeping views of the city

PAGE 98

SAN POLO AND SANTA CROCE

These two districts retain a local feel, with resident Venetians still outnumbering tourists as they go about their daily business. Thanks to the Architecture Institute, it's also a popular haunt for students, particularly in the Tolentini area. During the day charming squares teem with gleeful children after the school day is done. At night the area becomes a natural meeting spot and local bars and trattorias spill on to the streets that surround the Rialto Market.

Best for
Gastronomy and art

Home to
Rialto Market, Basilica dei Frari, Scuola Grande di San Rocco

Experience
A post-market cichetto and aperitivo at a market bar

PAGE 113

CASTELLO

Once home to the workers of the Arsenale, to this day Castello retains a grittier ambiance than much of Venice. It is also quieter the further east you go and contains plenty of sleepy squares and green spaces, so rare in the more frequented San Marco area. Via Garibaldi is a magnet for shoppers by day and a popular watering hole in the evening, and the neighbourhood is home to some of the best restaurants in town. In May, Castello springs to life with the Biennale art and architecture international exhibitions.

Best for
Escaping the crowds and exploring quiet squares with a local feel

Home to
San Zaccaria, Arsenale, Santi Giovanni e Paolo

Experience
Getting off the beaten track and discover seldom-visited spots like San Francesco della Vigna and San Pietro di Castello

$\rightarrow$

PAGE 136

DORSODURO

Often compared to New York's SoHo, Dorsoduro is home to galleries galore. Thanks to the university and Architecture Institute, it contains a lively student population, which is centred around Campo Santa Margherita of an evening. The south-facing Zattere is a popular promenade for Venetians, particularly in winter when the tourist crowds have dispersed and once again they have their city all to themselves.

Best for
Art galleries, student haunts and late-night bars

Home to
The Accademia, Peggy Guggenheim Collection, Ca' Rezzonico

Experience
Watching the sunset from the Zattere

PAGE 154

CANNAREGIO

Leafy Cannaregio is something of a paradox, being both a residential neighbourhood, and a major tourist draw. This is mainly due to Strada Nuova, the long street and erstwhile canal that leads from the train station directly to the Rialto Bridge, which is constantly heaving with commuters and daytrippers. There are few squares but two large parks, offering an abundance of space – a rare commodity in this city. And on Fondamenta della Misericordia and Fondamenta de la Sensa, it has more bars and restaurants per metre than anywhere else in town.

Best for
Eateries, bars and quiet green areas

Home to
The Ghetto, Santa Maria dei Miracoli, Ca' d'Oro

Experience
Dining out in style in one of the many fine restaurants that line the bustling Fondamenta della Misericordia, or enjoy a quiet picnic in the relaxed green spaces of Giardini Savorgnan

PAGE 172

THE LAGOON ISLANDS

Decidedly quieter than the city centre, the lagoon islands offer respite from the thronging crowds. Each island has its own charm. While Murano and candy-coloured Burano host plenty of visitors during the day, the isolated reverance of Torcello and San Francesco del Deserto feels a world away from fun-loving Lido, where Venetians flock to in summer months. With beaches in no short supply, it's the perfect spot to enjoy an aperitivo accompanied by sunset views of Venice bathed in a glorious pink glow.

Best for
Beaches, early Venetian settlements and Palladian churches

Home to
Redentore Church, Torcello, Murano, San Lazzaro degli Armeni

Experience
A tour of Murano's Museo del Vetro and see glass-blowers at work

$\rightarrow$

PAGE 186

THE VENETO PLAIN

Far from the bustling crowds of Venice, the towns and cities of the Veneto plain are often overlooked by tourists. But they hide some of the most impressive examples of art and architecture, including Giotto's stunning Cappella degli Scrovegni and Palladio's Teatro Olimpico. From the rough and ready streets of Mestre, Venice's industrial offshoot, to the lush, rolling hills of Conegliano on the Strada del Prosecco Route, via towns that have housed spas since Roman times, this is a fascinating area worthy of an extended visit.

Best for
Archaeological sites, thermal spas and superlative art

Home to
Cappella degli Scrovegni, Teatro Olimpico, Villa Rotonda, Basilica di Sant'Antonio

Experience
A boat trip down the Brenta Canal

PAGE 216

VERONA AND LAKE GARDA

The verdant hills of this region are home to world-famous vineyards producing Valpolicella and Soave. The pace of life is slow in the villages nestled high in the hilltops, while down below, Verona, dating back to Roman times, exudes sophisticated charm. The sleepy towns dotted on the shores of Lake Garda offer plenty of outdoor pursuits both on and off the water.

Best for
Roman ruins, world-class wines and outdoor pursuits

Home to
Verona Arena, San Zeno Maggiore, Sirmione Peninsula

Experience
Circumnavigating the perimeter of Lake Garda by bicycle

THE DOLOMITES

The Dolomites offer a respite from city life and the chance to reconnect with nature. The resplendent peaks of some of Italy's highest mountains can be seen from Venice on clear days, and they offer a dazzling backdrop to a relatively unsullied landscape. Opportunities for adventurous sporting activities abound, but easy walks along gentle trails mean that this region can be enjoyed by visitors of all abilities. And of course, even here among the wood-panelled mountain chalets, it is possible to find wonderful architecture and works of art.

Best for
Breathtaking views, natural wonders, historical sites

Home to
Cortina d'Ampezzo, Titian's Birthplace, Belluno

Experience
Taking a chair lift to reach some of Italy's highest points

←

1 San Marco Campanile.

2 Colourful Burano.

3 The view from the San Giorgio Maggiore bell tower.

4 Visitors exploring the Accademia galleries.

3 DAYS
in Venice

Day 1

Morning Get up bright and early to reach Piazza San Marco (p76) before the crowds descend. Take a moment to admire the grand surroundings before entering the Basilica di San Marco (p78), then head straight next door to the Palazzo Ducale (p82) to admire its magnificent combination of Byzantine, Gothic and Renaissance architecture and explore its dingy dungeons. Refuel with a coffee at the historic Caffè Florian (p89). From here, a short stroll through the busy streets will lead you to the Rialto Bridge (p107). Cross over to get to the famous Rialto Pescheria, also an excellent lunch spot.

Afternoon Make for the San Polo district and the Scuola Grande di San Rocco (p104) with its remarkable cycle of Tintorettos. For a further dose of unforgettable art, head straight to the towering church of Santa Maria Gloriosa dei Frari (p102), which includes two works by Titian and a beautiful triptych by Giovanni Bellini.

Evening Sip on spectacular cocktails at Il Mercante (www.ilmercantevenezia.com), overlooking the Frari, before sampling some authentic Venetian cuisine at one of San Polo's local restaurants (p113).

Day 2

Morning Start the day in the sleepy *sestiere* of Cannaregio at the magnificent Ca' d'Oro (p158), one of the city's most atmospheric Gothic palaces. It's a short walk to the Ghetto (p160) for a tour of the area's synagogues and fascinating museum. There are plenty of great low-key restaurants for lunch (p165).

Afternoon Heading north will take you to the Fondamente Nuove (p166), where you can catch a boat to the islands of the north lagoon. First stop is Murano (p179) for a glass tour, while not forgetting to visit the 12th-century Basilica dei Santi Maria e Donato. Hop back on the vaporetto to the picture-perfect island of Burano. Buy some famous S-shaped biscuits to munch on as you walk around the brightly painted houses and watch lace-makers at work. From here, another boat ride will bring you to the verdant hush of Torcello (p176), not far from the bustle of the previous islands, but at the same time a world away.

Evening Enjoy a delightful dinner at Torcello's family-run Locanda Cipriani (www.locandacipriani.com) before catching the last boat back to the city.

Day 3

Morning Dorsoduro is all about art. Start with the Accademia (p140) and walk among the works of Venetian masters before a short walk east to the Peggy Guggenheim Collection (p144) for some modern greats. Stop here for lunch on the terrace overlooking the pretty garden.

Afternoon Take the waterbus from Zattere to the island of San Giorgio Maggiore (p94). The climb up the bell tower is rewarded with stunning views of the city. From here take a boat to Riva degli Schiavoni (p124) and a walk around the imposing walls of the Arsenale (p130).

Evening Treat yourself to a drink on Danieli's rooftop terrace (p122) followed by dinner in one of Castello's charming neighbourhood restaurants (p125).

$\longrightarrow$

1 Turquoise waters surround the Sirmione Peninsula.

2 Statue of Juliet in Verona.

3 Taking in the view from Col Druscie, Cortina d'Ampezzo.

4 A tranquil canal at sunset, Treviso.

5 DAYS
in Veneto

Day 1

Morning Starting in Padua (p198), marvel at Giotto's lapis-blue frescoes in the Cappella degli Scrovegni before exploring the ancient university grounds. Refuel at the famous Caffè Pedrocchi.

Afternoon Chug down the Brenta Canal (p203) on a half-day cruise, and admire the Palladian villas that line the banks.

Evening Back in Padua, rub shoulders with the locals at one of the city's many excellent drinking holes.

Day 2

Morning From Padua, wind your way along the Valpolicella Wine Route (p238), stopping for lunch at one of the many hilltop *cantine* (tasting rooms).

Afternoon Visit picturesque Peschiera on the shores of Lake Garda (p230), and hire a bike to explore at your own pace.

Evening Head to neighbouring Sirmione Peninsula for fabulous views before embarking on a sunset dinner cruise.

Day 3

Morning Next stop Verona (p220), where you can experience ancient Rome at one of the oldest Roman amphitheatres in the world – the Arena. Grab lunch at one of the many restaurants offering local fare.

Afternoon Walk to Casa di Giulietta and channel your inner Shakespeare as you pen your own love letter with the letter-writing Juliet Club (p225).

Evening Keep the romance alive with a pre-dinner stroll around the lush grounds of Giardino Giusti, then crack open a bottle of Valpolicella while sampling the region's famous *bollito misto*, which consists of mixed boiled meats. Ristorante Greppia serves the best in town (www.ristorantegreppia.it).

Day 4

Morning This morning is all about Andrea Palladio in nearby Vicenza (p190). Visit the illusionary Teatro Olimpico and fall for its *trompe-l'oeil* trickery. After a morning of theatrics, lunch on traditional dishes in the heart of town.

Afternoon Head north to the glamorous mountain resort of Cortina d'Ampezzo (p246), set against the dramatic backdrop of the Dolomites. Hike, or take a cable car up to the peaks for breathtaking views.

Evening Bunk down at one of the *rifugios* (refuges) on Col Gallina or Averau and watch the mountains turn pink at sunset before searching for constellations in the crystalline night sky.

Day 5

Morning Explore the winding streets of Belluno (p247) and admire its magnificent Duomo and Palazzo dei Rettori.

Afternoon Continuing south, stop off at the medieval town of Treviso (p210). Stroll along its willow-lined canals and ancient city walls before visiting the church and chapterhouse of San Nicolò to admire their 14th-century frescoes.

Evening Treat yourself to a reservation at Toni del Spin (Via Inferiore 7) and delight in local dishes such as *faraona alla peverada*, guinea fowl served with pomegranate sauce. Spend the night in the luxury Hotel Relais Monaco (www.relaismonaco.it) to end your trip in style.

Foundations of a Floating City

This breathtaking city is home to a dizzying array of architectural styles and influences, but don't lose sight of the bigger picture. Venetian builders made the impossible a reality by creating structures that float on water. The secret lies beneath the surface: layers of Istrian stone laid on top of closely packed wooden piles plunged deep into the ground. As you stroll through the city's ancient streets and navigate its intricate web of canals, be sure to take the time to appreciate this sheer feat of medieval engineering.

→

Placing the foundations for the new Campanile on Piazza San Marco, 1905

VENICE AND THE VENETO FOR
ASTOUNDING ARCHITECTURE

From Medieval to Neo-Classical, Venice's ostentatious palaces and opulent churches stand as testament to the Serenissima Republic's powerful reign. But the ever-growing number of contemporary marvels speak of a city that, although deeply rooted in its past, is very much focused on its future.

Building Bridges

Iron, wood or stone, bridges are vital links. The Bridge of Sighs *(p125)* is what many come to Venice to see and it does not disappoint, while the Rialto Bridge *(p107)* affords one of the most iconic views of the city. But perhaps most impressive is the Ponte della Libertà, which connects Venice to the mainland by train, car or bus. Nothing compares to the sense of wonder as hundreds of tiny Venetian islands come into view as you speed towards them.

→

A gondolier passing under the Rialto Bridge at sunset

Palazzos and Palladio

Admire the many palazzos that line Venice's Grand Canal *(p54)* for the price of a vaporetto ticket. Among them is the Venetian Gothic style Ca' d'Oro *(p158)*, named for its once shimmering, now faded, gold-leaf exterior. But lavish façades and ostentatious design are prevalent across the Veneto. Tread the boards at Andrea Palladio's Teatro Olimpico *(p194)* in Vicenza, a city defined by his signature style, or admire the many fine Palladian villas that line the Brenta Canal *(p203)*.

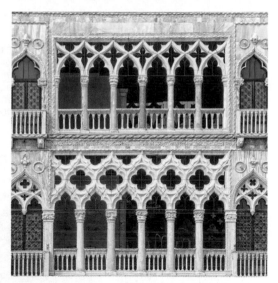

→

Ornate façade of Ca' d'Oro overlooking the Grand Canal

The World in One City

For centuries, Venice linked the Adriatic and the Mediterranean seas to Constantinople, Egypt and Syria, and the influence of these lands can be clearly seen in the city's ancient architecture. Take a tour of the Eastern Med as you explore the ground-floor arcades and open galleries of the Fondaco dei Turchi *(p113)*; gaze upon the crenellations of the Palazzo Ducale *(p82)* and pointed arches of the Basilica di San Marco *(p78)* that mirror those of Egyptian mosques; and lose yourself in the unmistakably Islamic tilework of many a canalside palazzo.

←

One of the magnificent colonnades that surround the Palazzo Ducale in Venice

Modern Marvels

Contemporary structures abound in Venice. Architects such as Tadao Ando, who designed the Teatrino of Palazzo Grassi *(p93)*, Santiago Calatrava, designer of metallic Ponte della Costituzione, and Carlo Scarpa who realised many of the Veneto's most iconic buildings, all left their mark on this ancient city. The Architecture Biennale showcases cutting-edge architectural works from around the globe. For anyone with a penchant for contemporary design and the latest architectural innovations, it's well worth a visit.

→

Bamboo Stalactite by VTN Architects at the Venice Architecture Biennale 2018

THE BUILDING OF VENICE

Venice is built on a patchwork of 117 low-lying islands in the middle of a swampy lagoon. To overcome these extremely challenging conditions, early Venetian builders developed a unique construction technique, building with impermeable stone supported by larchwood rafts and timber piles. This method proved effective and most Venetian buildings are remarkably robust, many having stood for at least 400 years. By 1500 the city had taken on much of its present shape.

THE CAMPO

The fabric of Venice is made up of scores of self-contained island communities, linked by bridges to their neighbouring islands. Each has its own water supply, church and bell tower, centred on a *campo* (square), once the main focus of commercial life. Palazzos, with shops and warehouses at ground-floor level, border the *campo* which is connected to workshops and more humble houses by a maze of side alleys.

↑ Campo San Boldo with its central water well in San Polo

This square, with its central wellhead and its businesslike landward façades, is typical of medieval venetian construction. Ornate decoration on buildings was usually reserved for the canalfront façades.

Campaniles often lean because of slight movement in the subsoil.

Water grilles

Rainwater was channelled through grilles into a clay-lined cistern filled with sand.

Istrian stone, a type of marble, was used to create damp-proof foundations.

Closely packed piles do not rot in the waterlogged subsoil because there is no free oxygen, vital for microbes that cause decay.

↑ Campo Santa Maria Mater Domini, a typical medieval square

THE CAMPANILE FOUNDATIONS

When the Campanile *(p86)* collapsed in 1902, the ancient pilings underpinning the landmark were found to be in excellent condition, after 1,000 years in the ground. All buildings in Venice are supported on oak and pine piles, harvested in the forests of the northern Veneto and shipped downriver to the Venetian Lagoon. Once driven through the lagoon subsoil, they create an immensely strong yet flexible foundation. Even so, there is a limit to how much weight they can carry. The Campanile, its height having been increased several times, simply grew too tall and collapsed. When the tower was rebuilt, larger timber foundations were used.

Did you know?

Despite wooden piles supporting the city for centuries, Venice is sinking by 2mm every year.

Palazzo roofs, built of light, glazed tiles, had gutters to channel rainwater to the well.

Façades were built of lightweight rose-coloured bricks, sometimes left bare, sometimes weatherproofed with plaster.

Bridges were often privately owned and tolls were charged for their use. Originally, none had railings, creating a night-time hazard for the unwary in the dark streets.

Oak piles were driven into the ground before building work began. They rest on the solid caranto *(compressed clay) layer at the bottom of the lagoon.*

Caranto is compacted clay and sand in alternate layers, which provides a stable base for building.

Rowing Around

Set your own pace by taking a stand-up rowing lesson, Venetian style. Explore the city's labyrinthine canals and waterways in the historic centre and beyond with a qualified rower from Row Venice (rowvenice.org). There's even a *cichetto* tour, during which you row to two bars for sustenance. Watch out for low-hanging bridges!

←

Rowing on one of the city's quiet side canals with Row Venice

VENICE AND THE VENETO
ON THE WATER

Whether delivering goods, moving house or simply going to work, much of Venetian life takes place on the water. A gondola or vaporetto ride is a must, but rowing and sailing on the lagoon are also popular pursuits, while the Brenta Canal and Lake Garda offer watery adventures in the heart of the Veneto.

Vaporetto Adventures

Waterbuses *(vaporetti)* chug up and down the Grand Canal and around Venice's lagoon. For tourists, a single ride is €7.50, but there are plenty of travelcard options that make it a convenient and inexpensive way to see the city. Boats fill up fast, especially during Carnevale, but nothing beats cruising along the Grand Canal *(p54)* after a hard day's sightseeing.

ACQUA ALTA

Acqua alta (high water) affects the city from October to March, and is caused by a combination of low atmospheric pressure, strong sirocco winds from the south and high tides. As warning sirens fill the air people head for higher ground, shopkeepers rush to put up protective barriers and street sweepers lay out duck boards. Piazza San Marco is among the most vulnerable spots.

Gondolas Galore

In their heyday gondolas numbered over 10,000. Now around 400 survive. Pick-up points are dotted around the city, with prices set by a consortium. A 40-minute ride for up to six passengers costs €80 (€100 after 7pm). On a tight budget? Take a *traghetto*, a gondola ferry that crosses the Grand Canal, a bargain at just €2.50. If you still haven't had your fill, head over to the Squero di San Trovaso *(p150)* to see where gondolas are made and repaired.

→

A *traghetto* transporting people across the Grand Canal

Setting Sail

Have an experienced sailor take you out on the lagoon in a traditional *bragozzo (www.il bragozzo.it)*, or brave the windswept waters of Lake Garda *(p230)* on catamaran or dinghy. Check out Sailing Du Lac Multisports Centre in Riva del Garda *(www.sailingdulac.com)*.

←

Sailing around the lagoon on a traditional Venetian *bragozzo*

Boating Beyond the City

Venice's patrician families escaped to country estates on the Brenta Canal *(p203)* in summer. Why not do the same? Il Burchiello *(www.il burchiello.it)* includes lunch, villa visits and an overnight stay in Padua. Alternatively, head to Lake Garda *(p230)* for boat trips to Isola Del Garda and Sirmione *(www.sirmioneboats.it)*.

↑ An early morning vaporetto cruise down the Grand Canal

↑ Neo-Gothic villa on Isola del Garda, Lake Garda's only island

Market Fresh

The Rialto's stalls teem with fresh fish and vibrant produce, but colourful markets and *fruttivendolo* can be found all over Venice. Santa Marta has a weekly market every Monday, Lido has one on Tuesdays, and Sacca Fisola on Fridays. Floating fruit and veg vendors are moored in Campo San Barnaba and on Via Garibaldi.

> INSIDER TIP
> **Cheap Eats**
>
> *Cichetti,* Venetian small plates, can be a satisfying meal without breaking the bank. Head to a local bar before lunch or early evening for the best selection.

Tempting displays brim ↑ with fresh produce at Rialto Market

VENICE AND THE VENETO FOR
FOOD LOVERS

While not as renowned for its cuisine as other regions, the Veneto has created some world-famous dishes and, with the Adriatic on its doorstep, seafood takes pride of place. In Venice, Michelin-starred restaurants abound, but even a humble *cichetto* washed down with local wine is a culinary treat.

Fine Dining

Tourist traps aside, Venice is home to some exemplary fine dining restaurants, many of them with a Michelin star. The charming Osteria Da Fiore *(www.dafiore.net)* has long been serving classic Venetian dishes with a twist, while at Il Ridotto *(www.ilridotto.com),* behind Piazza San Marco, fish plays a big part on the menu. Don't miss the bucolic Venissa *(www.venissa.it)* - it has a thriving kitchen garden and even produces its very own white wine.

←

Delicately spiced poached pears with gelato at Da Fiore

TOP 5 · VENETIAN DELICACIES

Seppie in Nero
Cuttlefish cooked perfectly in its own ink.

Sarde in Saor
Fried sardines marinated with onions and currants.

Pasta e Fagioli
A humble dish of pasta and borlotti beans.

Fegato alla Veneziana
Calf's liver, sautéed onions and polenta.

Bigoli in Salsa
Buckwheat pasta served with anchovies.

Cooking Courses

At the Acquolina cooking school *(www.acquolina.com)*, Marika Contaldo offers classes in her wonderful Lido home. Courses include trips to Rialto Market and half-day taster sessions. Further afield, at Villa Quaranta *(www.villaquaranta.com)* in Verona, master the art of making fresh pasta while sipping on a glass of Valpolicella.

↑ Learn how to make fresh pasta from scratch

THE HISTORY OF VENETIAN CUISINE

Venice made its fortune on trade and one of its most important goods was locally produced salt. Used to preserve fish and other food, salt was essential for sailors going on long journeys. Rice was introduced by the Arabs via Spain and has been grown in the Veneto for centuries, while spices such as nutmeg and cloves entered Venetian cuisine via its trade links with the East.

↑ Gelato, the perfect accompaniment to a canalside stroll

Something Sweet

Tiramisù is one of the Veneto's most famous creations: literally meaning "pick me up", you can find this calorific mix of coffee, mascarpone and sponge in most restaurants. Be sure to swing by Gelateria Alaska *(Calle Larga dei Bari)* where they serve unusual flavours like ginger, rose, or orange and rocket, and their chocolate ice cream is the best in town.

La Strada del Prosecco

Linking Conegliano and the rolling hills of Valdobbiadene, this scenic route will take you to some of the best prosecco *cantine* (tasting rooms) in Italy. Start in pretty Follina *(p210)* and head to Cantine Gregoletto *(www.gregoletto. it)* for a wine tasting. It's well worth staying overnight so you can indulge in the fizz: these winding roads are a challenge even when sober.

→

Sunset over the vine-striped hills of Valdobbiadene

VENICE AND THE VENETO
BY THE GLASS

Aperitivo time. As the day slides into evening, local bars spill on to streets already packed with tables, and a palpable energy fills the air. Of course, spritz is the traditional tipple, though cocktails are becoming more popular, but in a region heaving with vineyards, wine will always be the drink of choice.

Did You Know?

The word "spritz" comes from the Austro-Hungarian practice of adding a splash of water to Italian wines.

Venetian Spirit

While classic cocktails are popular in many a Venetian bar, the spritz is ubiquitous all over Italy, and nowhere more so than in the Veneto, where it originated in the 1800s. The two most popular versions are made with Aperol or Campari. The spritz is mixed with prosecco or sparkling water and white wine, and is usually served with an olive and an orange or lemon slice. After a hard day's sightseeing, sit back and enjoy a glass before dinner as you watch the sun set in a pretty piazza. Fortunately the Veneto has plenty, so take your pick.

Wine Tasting on the Valpolicella Route

Heading west from Verona to Lake Garda is the famous Valpolicella Wine Route *(p238)*. Many winemakers also run B&Bs, so you can spend more than a day in the bucolic hills. The Valpolicella Consortium *(consorziovalpolicella.it)* has a handy app to guide you around the many producers. Veronality *(www.veronality. com)* offers an Amarone tour, or for a fully immersive experience, stay on the wine-producing farm Agriturismo San Mattia *(www.agriturismo sanmattia)* just outside Verona.

← Enjoying the elegant and aromatic flavours of Amarone Classico on a Valpolicella vineyard

DRINK

Adriatico Mar
What owner Francesco doesn't know about wine isn't worth knowing. Squeeze into this tiny bar for a viticultural education.

🏠 Calle Crosera, Venice
📞 041 476 4322

Cantinone già Schiavi
An exemplary vintner and popular wine bar.

🏠 Fondamenta Priuli, Venice 🌐 cantina schiavi.com

Il Mercante
By far the best cocktail bar in town.

🏠 Campo dei Frari, Venice 🌐 ilmercante venezia.com

Distinctively orange Aperol spritz and *cichetti* by the canal
↓

Venetian City Vines

Venice was once full of vineyards, but few exist today. Venissa *(www.venissa.it)* on Mazzorbo produces eye-wateringly pricey wines from the local Dorona di Venezia grape. The Laguna nel Bicchiere association *(www. lagunanelbicchiere.it)* teaches the history of viticulture in Venice and promotes wines from the city's few remaining vineyards.

↑ Sampling local wines at Venissa on the island of Mazzorbo, Venice

Get Creative

The Scuola Internazionale di Grafica *(www.scuolagrafica. it)* hosts workshops in everything from printing to calligraphy. Create your own Renaissance masterpiece at the Bottega del Tintoretto *(www.tintorettovenezia.it)* next door to the master's home. Or try out etching, woodcutting and silk-screen printing at DoppioFondo *(www.doppiofondo.org)*.

←

Typesetting and printing at the Scuola Internazionale Grafica

VENICE AND THE VENETO FOR
ART LOVERS

Venice contains incredible artworks in its galleries, churches and museums. Gothic sculpture, Renaissance masters or conceptual art, you'll find them here in spades. Yet the city itself is described as a work of art, so if museums aren't your thing, simply enjoy the colour and beauty to be found on every street.

BEHIND THE MASK

Today, Venetian masks are synonymous with Carnevale, but in the past the city's denizens could spend much of the year in disguise. The simple white *bauta* was the most popular choice. The Plague Doctor mask with its distinctive hooked beak was once worn as protection against the plague, its beak tightly packed with herbs. Other masks stem from commedia dell'arte, with Harlequin a perennial favourite.

Make Your Own Mask

Fancy having a go at making your own Venetian mask? It's great fun and gives you an insight into the complex techniques behind the finished product. One of the best mask shops in town is Ca' Macana *(www.camacana.com)*, which runs classes for large groups and individuals. Over two hours, learn the history of mask-making before decorating your own.

→

An artisan decorating a mask with vibrant colours in his Venice workshop

↑ Piet Mondrian's Composition No. 1, at the Peggy Guggenheim

Museums and Galleries

Venice's Accademia *(p140)* contains jaw-dropping works by the likes of Bellini, Carpaccio, Titian and other masters. The Museo Correr *(p88)* in the Procuratie Nuove offers a history of the city as well as showcasing its greatest artists. For a modern twist, visit Palazzo Grassi and *(p93)* Punta della Dogana *(p146)*, which house a superb collection of contemporary art, while the Peggy Guggenheim Collection *(p144)* is a veritable trove of modern treasures. In Padua, admire the work of Florentine artist Giotto, whose vibrant frescoes adorn the deep-blue walls of the Cappella degli Scrovegni *(p204)*.

HIDDEN GEM
Palazzo Cini

Between the Accademia and the Peggy Guggenheim Collection, the often overlooked Palazzo Cini is packed with artistic treasures by the likes of Botticelli, Giotti and Piero della Francesca.

Immersive Experiences

Who said art should be enjoyed from a distance? Next to the main building, the Teatrino Palazzo Grassi *(p93)* hosts all manner of weird and wonderful performances, from live concerts and experimental soundscapes to video screenings and lectures. During the Art Biennale *(p48)* Venice comes alive with art showcases and exciting interactive exhibits in venues across town.

↑ Music performance at Palazzo Grassi; Set Up music and dance at Punta della Dogana *(inset)*

Beloved Book Shops

Libreria Marco Polo is putting up a noble fight against online behemoths. Its flagship store is on Campo Santa Margherita but it has also opened the first bookstore on the Giudecca *(p181)*. Both branches contain books in English and host literary evenings. Quirky Libreria Acqua Alta *(p127)* has a staircase made of books and cats sleeping in boats piled high with well-thumbed volumes. If it's art books you are after, look no further than Libreria Bertoni *(www.bertonilibri.com)*. It has an excellent range of exhibition catalogues, monographs and discount coffee-table tomes.

$\rightarrow$

Colourful chaos
in Venice's quirky
Libreria Acqua Alta

VENICE AND THE VENETO FOR
BOOKWORMS

The Serenissima was a 15th-century printing powerhouse, producing more books than anywhere else. As such, Venice and the Veneto has spawned more than its fair share of stellar writers, and inspired many more. With literary festivals and events galore, the region is a bookworm's paradise.

TOP 4 NOVELS SET IN VENICE

Don't Look Now (1973)
Daphne du Maurier's chilling short story will make you wary of children in red coats.

The Comfort of Strangers (1981)
Unnamed Venice is the setting for this twisted novel by Ian McEwan.

Death in Venice (1912)
Thomas Mann recounts an older man falling in love with a boy on Lido.

The Aspern Papers
Henry James's 1888 novella is based on the letters between Percy Bysshe Shelley and his wife's stepsister.

Literary Luminaries

Carlo Goldoni's influence on Italian theatre was huge. Visit his small - but perfectly formed - Casa di Goldoni *(p109)* to see where he lived. Famed for his sexual exploits, Casanova wrote *Story of My Life* (1898), an insight into 18th-century life. Visit the Casanova Museum *(casanova museum.com)* to learn more. Another legendary lothario, Lord Byron, spent years in Venice where he found inspiration in many forms.

Tiepolo's *Minuet* (1756), $\uparrow$
inspired by Goldoni's
Commedia dell'arte

Lovely Libraries

As you'd expect of a city famous for printing, Venice has some impressive libraries, none more so than the Biblioteca Nazionale Marciana *(p87)*. Founded in 1537 and housing over 750,000 volumes, it also contains Fra Mauro's famous map of the world and works by Titian and Veronese. Ca' Foscari University's Cultural Flow Zone *(www.unive.it)* hosts exhibitions, workshops and events. The Fondazione Querini Stampalia *(p125)* has one of the best-stocked libraries in town. Take a guided tour of its sumptuous rooms or you can apply for your own card to enter independently.

← Fra Mauro's 1450 map of the world is housed in the Biblioteca Nazionale Marchiana

CONTEMPORARY AUTHORS

As well as enticing writers from around the world, Venice has produced plenty of home-grown talent of its own. Perhaps the most famous Venetian contemporary author is Tiziano Scarpa, thanks to his hugely successful *Venice is a Fish*. He won the prestigious Premio Strega in 2009 for his novel *Stabat Mater,* which tells the story of an orphaned girl who learns the violin under Antonio Vivaldi. Another celebrated writer, Enrico Palandri, lived in London for many years before returning to his native city. Many of his novels have been translated into multiple languages, including *Ages Apart* and *The Other Evening*.

Literary Festivals

Incroci di Civiltà *(www.unive.it)* is organized by Venice's Ca' Foscari University and brings together high-calibre authors from around the world. Recent participants include Jonathan Coe and Ian McEwan. Meanwhile, Verona celebrates all things Shakespeare every April, with talks, guided walks and performances *(shakespeareweek.it)*.

↑ Celebrated Chinese writer Su Tong speaking at the Incroci di Civiltà book festival 2019

Classical Concerts

Opportunities to attend live classical concerts abound in Venice, where many deconsecrated churches house orchestras. The Venice Music Project *(www.venicemusic-project.it)* performs in St George's Anglican Church, San Vidal hosts the Interpreti Veneziani and La Pietà *(p123)* is home to the talented Virtuosi Italiani.

←

Venice Music Project performing at St George's Anglican Church

VENICE AND THE VENETO FOR
MUSIC LOVERS

Birthplace of Vivaldi and Luigi Nono and much loved by both Wagner and Stravinsky, Venice is where opera began. Classical music and opera are still performed all over town, and intimate venues offer a contemporary line-up. Meanwhile, Padua and Verona host big-name artists in super-size venues.

A Night at the Opera

The newly resplendent Teatro La Fenice *(p92)* offers a rich variety of opera and classical performances. During its restoration, Teatro Malibran *(p169)* accommodated performances and continues to work with its famous partner. Once the site of gladiatorial combat, Verona Arena *(p223)* is a magnificent venue for open-air opera. Performances take place from June to September with world-class performers.

INSIDER TIP
Fenice Tickets

Tickets can be pricey. For a discount, ask at the Fenice ticket office for seats with restricted views. The experience is just as breathtaking.

Music Festivals

In Venice, the Venezia Jazz Festival *(venetojazz.com)* is held in venues around the city throughout July, while the Biennale hosts a contemporary music festival every autumn *(www.labiennale.org)*. Also in autumn, Veneto Concertante is a series of classical concerts held in historic locations throughout the Veneto.

→

Jack Savoretti performing at the Venezia Jazz Festival

Live and Loud!

Verona's Arena *(p223)* is a spectacular place to see big-name performers. But smaller venues are championing live music in Venice too. Charming Paradiso Perduto *(Fondamenta della Misericordia)*, Osteria Da Filo *(Calle del Tentor)* and the Venice Jazz Club *(Dorsoduro 3102)* keep contemporary music alive in the city.

←

Famous Italian singer Zucchero wows fans at Verona Arena

Musical Greats

Born in Castello, Vivaldi's baptism records take pride of place in the church of San Giovanni in Bragora *(p129)*. Mozart and Wagner were frequent visitors to the city; visit the Wagner Museum in Venice Casino *(www.casinovenezia.it)*. Other big names include Stravinsky and Venetian avant-garde composer Luigi Nono.

→

↑ Performance of *Turandot* Venice's most famous opera house, La Fenice

Painting of composer and violinist Antonio Vivaldi dated 1723

Pedal Power

The Veneto is cycling-obsessed, producing many a world-class cyclist. Due for completion in 2021, Lake Garda's new floating cycle path hugs 140km (86 miles) of shoreline. With the option to substitute tougher sections with a boat ride, even less energetic cyclists can participate. For something a tad more energetic, why not try some Giro d'Italia climbs *(www.dolomitemountains.com)*.

←

Taking in spectacular scenery by bike, near Cortina d'Ampezzo

VENICE AND THE VENETO FOR
THE GREAT OUTDOORS

With miles of sandy beaches on the Adriatic, dramatic mountain ranges to the north, and rolling countryside in between – not to mention the largest lake in Italy – Venice and the Veneto offer ample opportunities for outdoor activities that will get your heart racing and your adrenaline pumping.

Hiking in the Veneto

Whether it's rolling hills, flat fenland or dramatic peaks, the Veneto is ideal hiking territory. Walk from the centre of Vicenza up Monte Berico on part of the 80km (50 mile) Montegalda-Tonezzo del Cimone route *(www. camminiveneti.it)*. Malcesine *(p232)*, nestled between Lake Garda and the surrounding mountains, is an excellent base from which to explore the area's many scenic trails.

Take to the Skies

For a bird's-eye view of the Dolomites, take to the skies with a trained paraglider (*www.dolomitiskirock.com*). These tandem flights run summer and winter, and offer jaw-dropping vistas of knife-edge peaks and plummetting valleys. If that sounds like too much work, hop aboard a hot-air balloon (*www.voloinmongolfiera. com*) and be swept up and away over the undulating Veneto hills and plains.

↑ Hot-air balloons over the little church of St Johann in Ranui

Majestic Mountains

In summer, hiking and climbing are popular activities in the dramatic Dolomites. The more adventurous can try the *vie ferrate* – routes equipped with cables and fixed anchors to help climbers reach lofty peaks. In winter, take to the pistes: all the major slopes have skiing and snowboarding schools.

←

A climber on an exposed *via ferrata* in the Dolomites

Life's a Beach

Lido has a deceptively leisurely vibe, but it is actually action packed. There's a gorgeous golf club (*www.circologolf venezia.it*) on its southern tip, while just steps from the beach lies Tennis Club Del Moro (*tennisclubcadel moro.com*) with both clay and synthetic grass courts.

↑ Hikers rest up at Rifugio Vicenza in the Dolomites

→

Sunseekers escape the city in favour of relaxing on sandy Lido beach

Green Spaces

Sant'Elena, Giardini and the Giardinetti Reali are the best-known public parks in Venice, but there are many more. Parco Savorgnan is a green oasis just off Campo San Geremia. It has a children's playground and plenty of quiet spots for a picnic or a snooze. Further north is Parco Groggia, which has its own theatre. Giardini Papadopoli is a verdant haven next to Piazzale Roma where kids can let off steam. On the Lido's southern tip is the Alberoni "oasis", with wooded walks and cycle path.

←

Giardinetti Reali on
Riva degli Schiavoni, just
off busy Piazza San Marco

VENICE AND THE VENETO
ESCAPING THE CROWDS

Around 20 million people flock to Venice annually, and the crowds can be overwhelming. Veer off the main drag and venture beyond the centre to find plenty of quiet corners, idyllic villas, green spaces and hidden gems that offer welcome respite from the bustling tourist hotspots.

Island Escapes

Venice's lagoon islands feel a world away from the packed city centre. Sample the local flavours of Sant'Erasmo, known as Venice's kitchen island, or wander the cloistered monastery and serene grounds of tiny San Francesco del Deserto *(p180)* for a contemplative visit.

→

An aerial view of the
island of San Francesco
del Deserto

INSIDER TIP
Dodge the Cruises
Cruises tend to bring the biggest crowds to Venice. Check shipping schedules online *(www.ports.cruises. com)* and plan your visit for quieter days.

Seeking Inspiration

Lord Byron spent several years on San Lazzaro degli Armeni *(p183)*, where he sought inspiration and learned Armenian. Petrarch settled in Arquà *(www.arquapetrarca. com)*, which he described as "rich of green vegetation and full of peace". Gabriele D'Annunzio's muse was Lake Garda, where he made his home near Gardone Riviera *(www.vittoriale.it)*.

→

Colourful buildings reflect the sun in Gardone Riviera

Venice's Serene Sestieri

In sleepy Castello and Cannaregio treasures await those who venture off the beaten track. Independent boutiques and quirky shops line quiet streets and family-run *osterie* serve authentic dishes at, believe it or not, reasonable prices. Here you will find the real Venice.

←

Tree-lined Viale IV Novembre next to Parco delle Rimembranza in Castello

Rural Retreats

Idyllic villas and tranquil escapes abound in the Veneto. In Follina, the gorgeous 14th-century Hotel Villa Abbazia *(www.hotelabbazia.it)* offers elegant luxury in the foothills of the Italian Alps, and Parco Giardino Sigurtà *(p226)* in Valeggio sul Mincio, is a gardener's paradise.

→

Leafy Parco Giardino Sigurtà, a peaceful haven just outside Verona

Go Locavore

Support local business by shopping at local greengrocers, fishmongers and markets. The I & S stall at Santa Marta market (on Monday mornings) sells organic fruit and veg from Sant'Erasmo and has a delightful farm shop in Cannaregio *(www. iesfarm.it)*. The Natura Sì healthfood store *(www.naturasi.it)* satisfies all your eco-friendly desires, while Osteria Zanze XVI *(zanze.it)* meticulously sources local produce to create zero-kilometre cuisine.

$\rightarrow$

Lemon trees and fresh produce for sale at a Venetian street market

SAVE VENICE!

Mass tourism, pollution, rising water levels and wave-induced erosion are just some of the issues that Venice has to contend with. A number of charities, grassroots movements and environmental scientists are searching for solutions to safeguard this most precious of cities. Here's how you can help.

Travel Smart

From the cruise-ship crowds and pollution to *moto ondoso*, the destructive wave action caused by speeding motorboats, the city is under a lot of strain. Consider your transport options carefully to limit your impact, and opt for public transport whenever possible. Cruise ships are a particularly contentious issue. The average cruise liner pollutes as much as do 14,000 cars and damages the already fragile lagoon environment.

↑ No Grandi Navi campaign for a ban on cruise ships entering the lagoon

Shop Local

Whether you want to pick up some Murano glassware, a Venetian mask for Carnevale or some quirky souvenirs to take home, always try to buy the genuine article from a local vendor rather than an imported fake. Check out Gilberto Penzo's model boats *(www.veniceboats.com)*, try on Gondola-shaped shoes at Giovanna Zanella's workshop *(www.giovanna zanella.it)*, or venture under the Rialto arches, where Daniele and Stefano Attombri *(www. attombri.com)* fashion antique Murano beads into stunning necklaces.

←

An artisan carefully moulding molten glass into the shape of a horse at a Murano factory

PRESERVING THE CITY

There are multiple organizations working to protect Venetian heritage as well as its fauna and flora. The largest is Save Venice, whose dedicated team restores architecture and artworks, funded by the generosity of wealthy benefactors.

Get Your Hands Dirty

There are plenty of ways to get involved during your stay. Venice Calls *(www. venicecalls.com)* runs regular graffiti elimination days, as well as canal dredging and beach cleaning. The WWF *(www.wwf.it)* runs fun workshops, nature walks and rubbish collecting parties around the Alberoni dunes on the Lido. Further afield, dust off your binoculars and head to the Po Delta Park *(www. parcodeltapo.org)* to help count birds in one of the area's largest wetlands.

↑ A volunteer painting over unsightly graffiti on a city wall

A YEAR IN
VENICE AND THE VENETO

JANUARY

New Year's Day, Venice Lido *(1 Jan)* Hardy bathers plunge into the Venetian Lagoon to mark the beginning of a new year.

△ **La Regata delle Befane** *(6 Jan)* Coinciding with Epiphany, competitors dress as witches, and give children stockings full of presents.

FEBRUARY

△ **Carnevale** *(10 days up to Lent)* This festival is celebrated across the region, with the most extravagant pageants, concerts and balls.

Verona in Love Festival *(week of Feb 14)* A week of romancing, poetry and love-themed festivity in the city of Shakespeare's star-crossed lovers, Romeo and Juliet.

MAY

Primavera del Prosecco *(May–Jun)* The Prosecco Spring Festival features wine-tastings and vineyard tours along the Strade del Prosecco from Conegliano to Valdobbiadene.

△ **La Sensa** *(1st Sun after Ascension)* A symbolic marriage ceremony between Venice and the sea, with boat races and street celebrations.

JUNE

△ **Venice Biennale** *(Jun–Nov)* The world's biggest contemporary art show takes place in odd-numbered years. In even-numbered years, the city hosts the Biennale d'Architettura.

Vogalonga *(2nd Sun after Ascension)* Hundreds of boats partake in the 32-km *(20-mile)* "Long Row" from Palazzo Ducale to Burano and back.

SEPTEMBER

Regata Storica *(1st Sun)* Venice's favourite regatta recalls the arrival of the Queen of Cyprus in 1489, with a costumed pageant on the Grand Canal.

△ **Venice Glass Week** *(2nd week)* Displays, demonstrations and celebrations of all things glass in Venice, Murano and Mestre.

OCTOBER

Feast of the Must *(1st weekend)* Parties celebrate the completion of the harvest in Sant'Erasmo, with barefoot dancers pressing grapes the traditional way.

△ **Venice Marathon** *(last Sun)* Eight thousand runners take to the streets for the city's annual international marathon.

MARCH

△ **Benedizione del Fuoco** (*Maundy Thursday*)
In Venice, the start of Easter is marked with the "Blessing of Fire", a holy flame lit in the darkness of the Basilica di San Marco after dusk, followed by a sombre procession lighting each candle in the church one by one.

APRIL

△ **Su e Zo per i Ponti** (*1st Sunday*)
A 12-km (7.5-mile) charity fun run through streets of Venice and up and down the city's 45 bridges.
Festa di San Marco (*25 April*) Venice's patron saint is honoured with a gondola regatta. Men cross Piazza San Marco with a rose for their sweetheart.

JULY

Opera Festival (*July–Sep*) A renowned festival of opera staged in Verona's breathtaking Roman Arena
△ **Festa del Redentore** (*3rd weekend*) A boat race, fair and fireworks commemorate Venice's deliverance from the plague in 1576.
Sardellata al Pal del Vo (*last weekend*)
Moonlit sardine-fishing displays take place at Pal de Vo, Lake Garda, then the catch is enjoyed on the lakeshore, accompanied by celebratory fireworks.

AUGUST

△ **Venice Film Festival** (*late Aug–1st week Sep*)
One of the world's most important celebrations of cinema, drawing an array of film stars and paparazzi to Venice's Lido.

NOVEMBER

△ **Festa della Salute** (*21 Nov*) A votive bridge is erected across the Grand Canal so that people can cross to extol La Madonna della Salute for deliverance from the 1631 plague.

DECEMBER

Mercatini di Natale, Venice (*6 Dec*) The city's Christmas lights are illuminated, Campo San Polo becomes an ice rink and squares and palazzos host Christmas markets.
△ **Regata dei Babbi Natali** (*Sun mid-month*)
Rowers dress as Santa Clause and compete on the Grand Canal before taking part in a water parade featuring Santa and his elves.

A BRIEF
HISTORY

From its origins in Roman Venetia to its prosperity during the Renaissance, the history of this slowly sinking city never ceases to fascinate. More than 20 million visitors a year succumb to the magic of this improbable place, where the streets are filled with water and the past is evident at every turn.

Roman Domination

The Veneto took its name from the Veneti, an Indo-European tribe who settled in north eastern Italy around 600 BC. They are also known as Paleoveneti so as not to be confused with modern-day inhabitants of the Veneto. However, by the 3rd century BC, the region had been conquered by the Romans, and the peaceful Veneti citizens of Verona, Vicenza, Este and Treviso granted Roman citizenship. Verona was built as a pivotal base for the ambitious Roman armies as they pushed their empire northwards over the Alps. Roman Venetia, and its capital Padua, thrived for centuries until attacks from Barbarian tribes brought about the fall of Rome in the 5th century AD.

① Ancient map of Venice.

② An 18th-century depiction of Verona's Roman amphitheatre.

③ Byzantine art in the Basilica di San Marco.

④ A manuscript details Venetian ships partaking in the Crusades.

Timeline of events

3rd Century BC
Veneto is conquered by the Romans; Verona, Aquileia, Padua and Latinum founded.

401
Goths invade; the people of Veneto migrate to the lagoon.

421
Refugees build on the islets of Rivo Alto (Rialto) and establish the city of Venice.

639
The Bishop of Altino founds Santa Maria dell'Assunta, Torcello.

828
Venice steals the relics of St Mark; his winged lion is the symbol of the republic.

l'Arena di Verona.

The Founding of Venice

The imperial administration began to crumble. Venice emerged when the Goths invaded and the people of Veneto fled to the lagoon. Legend claims the city was founded on 25 April, St Mark's Day. Trade links with Byzantium were forged, and the city prospered on its salt trade. The first dogo, elected in 697, was a Byzantine magistrate. In 828, the Venetians brazenly stole the relics of St Mark the Evangelist from Alexandria for their basilica. This signalled their ambition to become the foremost city in Christendom. Shortly after, they proclaimed the religious and political independence of the islands – the Venetian Republic.

La Serenissima and The Crusades

The Venetian Republic (697-1797), traditionally known as *La Serenissima*, was primarily a maritime republic. Before long, Venice dominated trade in the Mediterranean and Adriatic seas, as well as commerce between Europe, North Africa and Asia. It provided supplies and shipped Crusaders to fight the Saracens in the Holy Land; most notably in the Fourth Crusade, which culminated, in 1204, with the conquest of the capital of the Byzantine Empire, Constantinople.

> ### WHERE TO SEE ROMAN VENETO
>
> Verona has a higher concentration of ancient Roman sites than anywhere outside of Rome; its Archaeo-logical Museum is full of fine mosaics and sculptures, while Castelvecchio has some very rare early Christian glass and silver. Museums can also be found at Este, Adria, Treviso and Portogruaro, situated near Concordia.

1000

Venice controls the Adriatic coast. The "Marriage of Venice to the Sea" ceremony is inaugurated.

1096–1204

Venice and the cities of the Veneto join the Crusades.

1260–95

Famed Venetian merchant, explorer and writer, Marco Polo, sets off to explore Asia.

1453

Constantinople falls to the Turks, leading to the first Ottoman-Venetian War.

1348–9

The plague, the Black Death, kills half of Venice's population.

1

2

The Golden Age

The Venetian empire reached its zenith around the 15th century, and by the 16th century, Venice had a monopoly on Mediterranean trade and had colonized the whole of North-eastern Italy. As well as great wealth, the region also enjoyed a golden age of art and music – dominated by such innovative painters as Canaletto, Tintoretto, Tiepolo, Titian and Veronese; composers Monteverdi, Gabrieli and Vivaldi; the architect Palladio, and the astronomer Galileo – which was to endure through the Renaissance until the fall of the Venetian Republic.

The Fall of the Venetian Republic

In 1797, Napoleon Bonaparte invaded Venice and brought about the end of the 1,000-year-old City State. Venice and its territories were given to Austria in exchange for Lombardy. Tossed for decades between France and Austria, many disgruntled Venetians joined the vanguard of the revolutionary Risorgimento fighting to unify Italy, and eventually freed themselves from Austrian rule in 1866. The Veneto became part of the Kingdom of Italy four years later.

THE LEAGUE OF CAMBRAI

Keeping hold of such a vast empire meant that Venice was in a near-constant state of war. The League of Cambrai, formed in 1508 by Pope Julius II and the Holy Roman Emperor Maximilian, sacked the cities of the Veneto, but the region remained loyal to Venice's benign rule. The city continued to dominate the Eastern Mediterranean for another 200 years.

Timeline of events

1530
Luigi da Porto of Vicenza writes the original story of Romeo and Juliet.

1489
The king of Cyprus is poisoned after marrying into Venetian nobility.

1639
Plague strikes Venice again, reducing the population to 102,200.

1703
Composer Vivaldi becomes musical director of La Pietà.

1797
Napoleon Bonaparte invades the Veneto; the doge abdicates and the Venetian Republic ends.

Tourism and the 20th Century

With the advent of the Biennale art exhibition in 1895, Venice remained the vanguard of art and architecture. The Lido became a stylish resort, with grand hotel developments along its sandy shoreline, and the Venice Film Festival started in 1932.

During both world wars, Venice was surprisingly unscathed, but fighting took place in the Veneto's mountain passes. In 1966, the city was hit by the worst floods in its history. UNESCO launched its Save Venice Appeal, sparking worldwide concern.

Venice and the Veneto Today

Today, Venice treads a fragile line between living city and floating museum. The flood defences introduced in 2003 are not yet operational. In 2017, UNESCO threatened to place the city on its "in danger" list, due to concerns over cruise ships, mass tourism and damage to the fragile lagoon ecosystem. Now only smaller ships are allowed to dock in Venice, though larger ships are still allowed into the lagoon – but with tourist revenue vital, and with the city 123 cm (48 in) lower in the water than it was in 1900, the future is far from plain sailing.

1 Galileo Galilei.

2 1807 print of Napoleon in Venice.

3 Entrance to the Venice Biennale, 1895.

4 Cruise ship *Seabourn Pride* docked at Stazione Marittima in Dorsoduro.

Did You Know?

Elena Cornaro Piscopia was the first woman to gain a degree. It was from Padua University in 1678.

1846
A causeway connects the city to the mainland and the Italian rail network.

1966
The worst flood in Venetian history. Save Venice Appeal launched; plans for flood gates begin.

2017
The #EnjoyRespect Venezia campaign calls for responsible tourism in the city.

1861
Vittorio Emanuele becomes King of Italy; Venice and the Veneto are freed from Austrian rule five years later.

Looking down the Grand Canal towards Dorsoduro

GRAND CANAL

Known to the Venetians as the Canalazzo, the Grand Canal sweeps through the heart of Venice, following the course of an ancient riverbed. Since the founding days of the empire it has served as the city's main thoroughfare. Once used by great galleys or trading vessels making their stately way to the Rialto, it now teems with vaporetto, launches, barges and gondolas. Glimpses of its glorious past, however, are never far away. The annual re-enactment of historic pageants, showcasing the traditions of the Venetian Republic, brings a blaze of colour to the canal. The most spectacular is the Regata Storica held in September, a huge procession of historic craft packed with crews in traditional costumes, followed by boat and gondola races down the Grand Canal.

The parade of palaces bordering the winding waterway, built over a span of around 500 years, presents some of the finest architecture of the Republic. A roll call of the old Venetian aristocracy, almost every palazzo bears the name of a grand family. Bright frescoes may have faded, precious marbles worn, and foundations frayed with the tides, but the Grand Canal is still, to quote Charles VIII of France's ambassador in 1495, "the most beautiful street in the world".

THE GRAND CANAL

SANTA LUCIA TO PALAZZO FLANGINI

The Grand Canal is best admired from a gondola or a vaporetto. Several lines travel the length of the canal, but only the No. 1 goes slowly enough for you to take in the many spectacular buildings and magnificent palazzos that line this waterway.

The journey from Santa Lucia station to the terminus at San Zaccaria takes about 40 minutes. Nearly 4 km (2 miles) long, the canal is spanned by four bridges, the Scalzi, the Rialto, the Accademia and the Constituzione – known by locals as the Ponte di Calatrava after its designer, Santiago Calatrava. The modern bridge, controversial due to its structural flaws, expensive repair needs and slippery glass surface, links Piazzale Roma and Santa Lucia station.

💬 INSIDER TIP
Vaporetto Tickets

A one-way ticket costs €6.50 and it is valid for 60 minutes. You can purchase a ticket onboard for €1 more, but you must tell the staff immediately upon boarding. Always validate tickets at the machines provided at the vaporetto stop.

Santa Lucia railway station, *built in the mid-19th century and remodelled in the 1950s, links the city with the mainland.*

La Direzione Compartimentale, *the administration offices for the railway, was built on the site of the church of Santa Lucia and other ancient buildings.*

0 metres 50
0 yards 50

N ↑

The busy Scalzi Bridge straddling the Grand Canal

THE SCALZI

The Roman Catholic church of Santa Maria di Nazareth is known today as the Scalzi, meaning barefoot after the supposedly shoeless Carmelites who founded it. Inside is the tomb of Ludovico Giovanni Manin, last doge of Venice, forced to abdicate by Napoleon Bonaparte in 1797 when French troops marched on the city.

Santa Lucia to Palazzo Flangini

Locator Map

Palazzo Flangini *was designed by Giuseppe Sardi, a leading 17th-century architect.*

Palazzo Calbo Crotta *is now the four-star Hotel Principe. Fine antiques that once decorated the palace are in Ca' Rezzonico (p147).*

Santa Maria di Nazareth *is known today as the Scalzi.*

Ponte degli Scalzi

The Grand Canal from Santa Lucia to Palazzo Flangini

Campo San Simeone Grande, *named after the nearby church, overlooks the canal.*

Casa Adoldo *and* **Palazzo Foscari-Contarini**

San Simeone Piccolo, *built in 1738, was based on the Pantheon in Rome. It is open for worship only.*

Palazzo Diedo, *also known as Palazzo Emo, is believed to be the birthplace of Angelo Emo (1731–92), the last admiral of the Venetian fleet.*

Sunrise over the turquoise dome of San Simeone Piccolo

THE GRAND CANAL
SAN GEREMIA TO SAN STAE

Locator Map

This stretch of the canal sees the beginning of a series of impressive palaces, their opulent façades facing out on to the water for all to see.

Many remarkable buildings line this section of the Grand Canal, but perhaps one of the most breathtaking is Ca' Vendramin Calergi; its opulence and ostentatious design became a model on which other Venetian palazzos were designed.

Palazzo Labia, *frescoed with Tiepolo's Story of Cleopatra, is intermittently open to the public* (p169).

Ca' dei Cuori *(House of Hearts) was named after the hearts in the family coat of arms.*

San Geremia *houses the relics of St Lucy, formerly preserved in Santa Lucia, where the station now stands.*

→
The Grand Canal from San Geremia to San Stae

Palazzo Giovanelli *was acquired by the Giovanellis in 1755. They were admitted into the Great Council in 1668 for a fee of 100,000 ducats.*

Palazzo Donà Balbi

CA' VENDRAMIN CALERGI

This early Renaissance palace, designed by Mauro Coducci, now houses the Casino di Venezi, Venice's largest casino. The opulent building was once home to numerous doges and prominent people through history. The Wagner Museum is also housed in this building, and it celebrates the life and works of the famous composer who died here in 1883.

Canal-front palazzos and the church of San Geremia at sunrise ↑

170

The number of buildings that line the canal - many of them grand palazzos.

San Marcuola, dedicated to St Ermagora and St Fortunatus, was built in 1728–36 by Giorgio Massari, but the façade was never completed.

Ca' Vendramin Calergi

Palazzo Marcello, was the birthplace of composer Benedetto Marcello in 1686.

Fondaco dei Turchi was once a splendid Veneto-Byzantine building. It now houses Museo di Storia Naturale (p112).

Palazzo Tron

Palazzo Belloni Battagia was built by Longhena in the mid-17th century for the wealthy Belloni family, who bought their way into Venetian aristocracy.

Deposito del Megio, a crenellated building with a reconstructed Lion of St Mark, was a granary in the 15th century.

San Stae is striking for its Baroque façade, graced by marble statues. It was funded by a legacy left by Doge Alvise Mocenigo in 1709 (p113).

0 metres 50
0 yards 50

N ↑

THE GRAND CANAL
PALAZZO BARBARIGO TO THE MARKETS

Here the canal is flanked on both sides by stately palaces, built over a period of five centuries. Look out for the spectacular Ca' d'Oro, whose Gothic façade once glittered with gold.

As you cruise down this section of Venice's main waterway, the opulence of the canalside palazzos continues. With its stalls of fresh produce and local delicacies, the Rialto Market (p107) is a perfect stopping point for hungry travellers to disembark and sample some of the finest local flavours before continuing their exploration of the canal.

Palazzo Barbarigo
retains its 16th-century frescoed façade.

Ca' Foscarini, *a Gothic building of the 15th century, belonged to the Foscari family before it became the residence of the Duke of Mantua in 1520.*

Ca' Pesaro, *a huge and stately Baroque palace designed by Longhena, houses the Galleria Internazionale d'Arte Moderna and the Museo d'Arte Orientale (p113).*

Ca' Corner della Regina *is owned by the Fondazione Prada. It houses the Prada contemporary art collection.*

Ornate interior and covered internal courtyard *(inset)* overlooking the Grand Canal of the Ca' d'Oro

Palazzo Barbarigo to the Markets

Locator Map

CANALETTO

Antonio Canale (1697–1768), known more commonly as Canaletto, is best known for his *vedute* or views of Venice, in which he portrayed the daily life of his beloved city. He studied in Rome, but lived in Venice for most of his life. One of his patrons was Joseph Smith (1682–1770) who became the English consul in Venice. Sadly, there are very few of his paintings left on view in the city.

The façade of **Palazzo Gussoni-Grimani** *once had frescoes by Tintoretto. It was home to the English ambassador in 1614–18.*

Palazzo Fontana Rezzonico *was the birthplace of Count Rezzonico (1693), the fifth Venetian pope.*

Ca' d'Oro, *the most famous of Venetian Gothic palaces (p158), houses paintings, frescoes and sculpture from the collection of Baron Giorgio Franchetti.*

Palazzo Sagredo *passed from the Morosini to the Sagredo family in the early 18th century and exemplifies Veneto-Byzantine and Gothic styles.*

Palazzo Foscarini *was the home of Marco Foscarini, a diplomat who rose to the position of doge in 1762.*

0 metres   50   N
0 yards   50

Palazzo Morosini Brandolin

The **Pescheria** *has been the site of a busy fish market for six centuries.*

The Grand Canal from Barbarigo to the Markets ↑

Tribunale Fabbriche Nuove, *Sansovino's market building, is now the seat of the Assize Court.*

THE GRAND CANAL
THE RIALTO QUARTER

As you chug along, the canal meanders back on itself, bringing into view the famous Rialto Bridge, one of the most recognizable in the city. This marks your arrival in the Rialto Quarter.

The area around the Rialto Bridge is the oldest and busiest quarter of the city. Traditionally it was a centre of trade, and crowded quaysides and colourful food markets still border the canal south of the bridge. Gaze upon the action from the top deck as locals and tourists alike jostle for space and bargains.

THE DANDOLO FAMILY

The illustrious Dandolo family produced four doges, 12 procurators of San Marco, a patriarch of Grado and a queen of Serbia. The first of these doges was Enrico Dandolo (d 1205), who, despite being old and blind, was the principal driving force in the Crusade to sack Constantinople in 1204. The other remarkable doge in the family was the humanist and learned historian Andrea Dandolo (d 1354).

Palazzo Papadopoli, is now the luxury Aman Canal Grande Venice Hotel, but its splendid hall of mirrors has been preserved.

Palazzo Barzizza, rebuilt in the 17th century, still preserves its early 13th-century façade.

Palazzo Grimani was built in 1556 by Michele Sanmicheli for the Procurator, Girolamo Grimani. It is now the city's Court of Appeal.

Locator Map

↑ The iconic Rialto Bridge linking the two sides of the Rialto

Fondaco dei Tedeschi, *originally used as a warehouse and lodgings for German traders, has been refurbished as a luxury department store.*

Palazzo Camerlenghi, *built in 1528, was once the offices of the city treasurers (camerlenghi). The ground floor was the state prison.*

The Rialto Bridge (p107), *was built to span the Grand Canal in the city's commercial quarter.*

0 metres	50	N
0 yards	50	↑

Riva del Ferro *is the quayside where German barges off loaded iron (ferro).*

Palazzo Manin-Dolfin *was built by Sansovino, but only his Classical stone façade survives. The interior was completely transformed for Ludovico Manin, last doge of Venice.*

Palazzo Bembo, *a 15th-century Gothic palace, was the birthplace of the Renaissance cardinal and scholar Pietro Bembo, who wrote one of the earliest Italian grammars.*

Casetta Dandolo *was the birthplace of Doge Enrico Dandolo (ruled 1192–1205).*

Palazzo Farsetti and **Palazzo Loredan** *are both occupied by the City Council. Palazzo Farsetti became an academy for young artists, one of whom was Canova.*

Palazzo Farsetti

↑ The Grand Canal cuts through the bustling Rialto Quarter

THE GRAND CANAL
LA VOLTA DEL CANALE

This section of the tour encompasses yet more grand palazzos, some of which now form part of the Ca' Foscari University, founded in 1868.

The point where the canal doubles back sharply on itself is known as La Volta – the bend. This splendid curve was long ago established as the finishing stretch for the highly anticipated Regata Storica, which still takes place on the first Sunday in September every year.

Did You Know?

The Grand Canal follows the route of an ancient river, probably a branch of the Brenta.

0 metres 50
0 yards 50
N

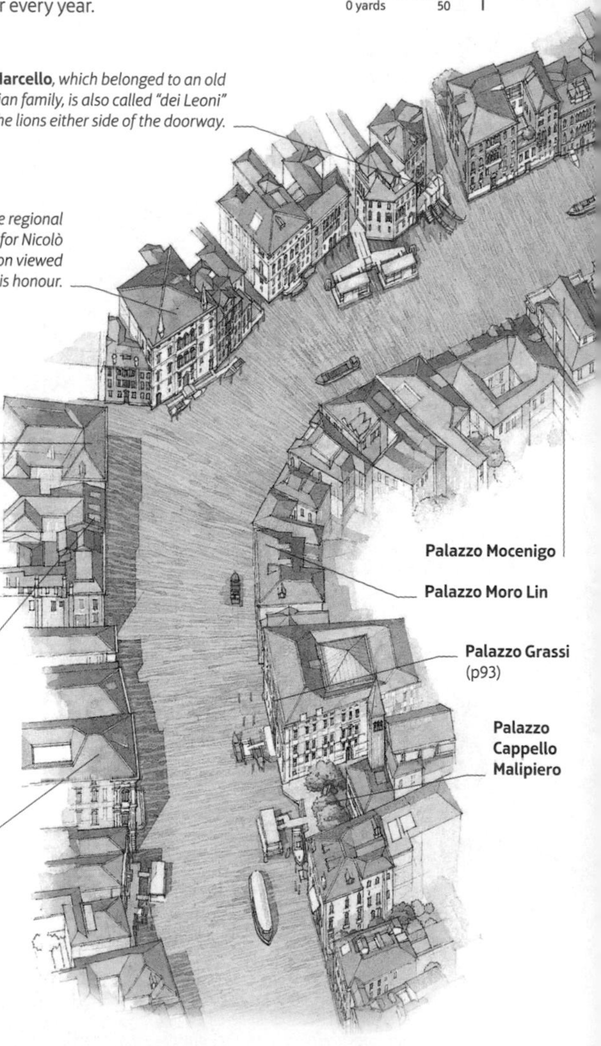

Palazzo Marcello, *which belonged to an old Venetian family, is also called "dei Leoni" because of the lions either side of the doorway.*

Palazzo Balbi, *seat of the regional government, was built for Nicolò Balbi. From here, Napoleon viewed the 1807 regatta, held in his honour.*

Ca' Foscari *was built for Doge Francesco Foscari in 1437. It is now part of the University of Venice.*

Palazzo Giustinian *was the residence of Wagner in 1858–9, when he was composing the second act of* Tristan and Isolde.

Ca' Rezzonico, *now the museum of 18th-century Venice (p130), became the home of the poet Robert Browning and his son, Pen, in 1888.*

Palazzo Mocenigo

Palazzo Moro Lin

Palazzo Grassi (p93)

Palazzo Cappello Malipiero

Palazzo Barbarigo della Terrazza, *built in the 1560s, was known for its roof terrace. It now houses the German Institute.*

Palazzo Cappello-Layard *was the home of English archaeologist Sir Austen Henry Layard.*

La Volta del Canale

Locator Map

←
La Volta del Canale as it turns a sharp bend

Palazzo Corner Spinelli, *Mauro Coducci's outstanding Renaissance palace, became a prototype for other mansions in Venice.*

Palazzo Garzoni *is now part of the university. The traghetto linking Calle Garzoni to San Tomà is one of the oldest in Venice.*

Palazzo Balbi, Ca' Foscari University and the ballroom at Ca' Rezzonico *(inset)* ↓

THE GRAND CANAL
CA' REZZONICO TO THE GUGGENHEIM

The southern stretch of the canal widens somewhat, and as buildings become increasingly spaced out, this epic parade of palaces is interspersed with open spaces and leafy gardens.

This section of the Grand Canal takes in some of the most prestigious art galleries in the world. Hop off at Accademia to see works by Venetian masters such as Titian, Bellini and Giorgione at the Accademia galleries, or visit the marvellously modern Peggy Guggenheim collection just downstream. Here you will find works by more than 200 contemporary artists representing powerful avant-garde movements such as Cubism, Futurism and Surrealism. Then hop back on board to head to Venice's crown jewel, Piazza San Marco.

Palazzo Franchetti Cavalli *belonged to Archduke Frederick of Austria, who died here in 1836.*

Palazzo Falier *was said to have been home to Doge Marin Falier, who was beheaded for treason in 1355.*

The Accademia *galleries, within the former church, monastery and Scuola della Carità, house the world's greatest collection of Venetian paintings (p140).*

The wooden **Accademia Bridge** *was built in 1932 as a temporary structure to replace a 19th-century iron bridge. By popular demand it has been retained.*

Ca'Rezzonico to the Guggenheim

Locator Map

Palazzo Contarini del Zaffo, *a magnificent Renaissance palace of the late 1400s, was built for a branch of the ubiquitous Contarini family. It is now owned by the Polignac family.*

Looking down the canal
from the wooden Accademia
Bridge *(inset)*

Palazzo Darbaro
*comprises two palaces,
one of which was bought
by the Curtis family in
1885. Monet and
Whistler painted here
and Henry James wrote
The Aspern Papers here.*

Casetta delle Rose
*was the home of
Italian poet Gabriele
d'Annunzio during
World War I.*

Ca' Grande, *a huge Classical
palace, was designed in 1545 by
Sansovino for Giacomo Cornaro,
nephew of the Queen of Cyprus.
The family was one of the
richest in Venice.*

0 metres		50	N
0 yards		50	↑

Ca' Dario, *built in
1487, is a charming
but strangely
ill-fated palace.*

↑ Ca'Rezzonico to the
Peggy Guggenheim
Collection

Peggy Guggenheim *established her
collection of modern art in Venice in 1951
(p144). She chose as her venue the
unfinished Palazzo Venier dei Leoni.*

↑ The Grand Canal teems with motorboats in the San Marco basin

The Palazzo Gritti-Pisani, *where Ruskin stayed in 1851, is better known today as the five-star Hotel Gritti Palace.*

Palazzo Contarini Fasan *is known as the House of Desdemona from Shakespeare's Othello.*

Palazzo Salviati, *the former headquarters of the Salviati glass company.*

The deconsecrated Gothic brick church of **Abbazia San Gregorio.**

Santa Maria della Salute, *a Baroque church of monumental proportions (p145), is supported by over a million timber piles.*

To La Salute and San Marco

Locator Map

THE GRAND CANAL
TO LA SALUTE
AND SAN MARCO

The view along the final stretch of the canal is one of the finest and most familiar in Venice. At the mouth rises the magnificent church of La Salute with the busy San Marco Basin beyond.

Time your vaporetto trip to arrive at the church of Santa Maria della Salute at sunset to see this iconic area of the city at its most spectacular. Disembark at Salute and stroll along Fondamenta Salute to the Punta della Dogana. The view from here, taking in the Palazzo Ducale, the towering Campanile of San Marco and the Zecca, is easily one of the most memorable in Venice.

Palazzo Giustinian *is the headquarters of the Venice Biennale*

← Santa Maria del Gilgio to La Salute and San Marco

Giardinetti Reali, *the Royal Gardens, were created by Napoleon to improve his view from the Procuratie Nuove.*

0 metres 50
0 yards 50

N ↑

The Punta della Dogana *(p146)*

→ Giardinetti Reali, a tranquil green space just off Piazza San Marco

EXPERIENCE

Cycling in Piazza delle Erbe, Padua

Caffè Florian, Piazza San Marco

SAN MARCO

Home of the political and judicial nerve centres of Venice, the *sestiere* of San Marco has been the heart of Venetian life since the early days of the Republic. It was here, in around the 9th century, that early settlers, migrating to the inner lagoon from nearby coastal towns, made their homes and built their most important places of worship. It was also here that the first Chapel of the Doge was constructed, not far from the present site of the basilica. It was dedicated to San Theodore, the first patron saint of Venice. However, he was later ousted by San Marco, whose relics were plundered from Alexandria and brought to Venice in 828 in what was by all accounts a bold move in Venice's pursuit of freedom from Byzantium.

The greatest showpiece of the Serenissima was the Piazza San Marco, conceived as a vista for the Palazzo Ducale, home to the rulers of the longest enduring republic in Europe, and the Basilica di San Marco, the most ostentatious church in the Christian world. The square, described by Napoleon as "the most elegant drawing room in Europe", was the only one deemed fit to be called a piazza, the others were merely denoted *campi*, or fields.

SAN MARCO

Must Sees

1. Piazza San Marco
2. Basilica di San Marco
3. Palazzo Ducale
4. Campanile

Experience More

5. Torre dell'Orologio
6. Biblioteca Nazionale Marciana
7. Museo Correr
8. Museo Archeologico
9. Harry's Bar
10. Columns of San Marco and San Teodoro
11. San Moisè
12. Palazzo Contarini del Bovolo
13. Ridotto
14. Santa Maria Zobenigo
15. Campo San Bartolomeo
16. La Fenice
17. Campo Santo Stefano
18. Palazzo Grassi
19. San Salvatore
20. Museo Fortuny
21. San Giorgio Maggiore
22. Stanze del Vetro
23. San Zulian
24. Mercerie

Eat

1. Bar All'Angolo
2. Le Café
3. Acqua Pazza
4. Al Bacareto
5. Bacaro Da Fiore
6. Trattoria Vini da Arturo

Drink

7. Caffè Florian
8. Gran Caffè Lavena
9. Museo Correr Coffee Shop

Stay

10. Hotel Novecento
11. Hotel Santo Stefano
12. Hotel Bauer il Palazzo

Shop

13. Bevilacqua
14. Chiarastella Cattana
15. Rubelli

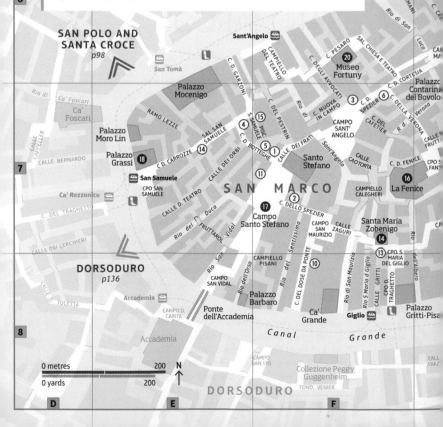

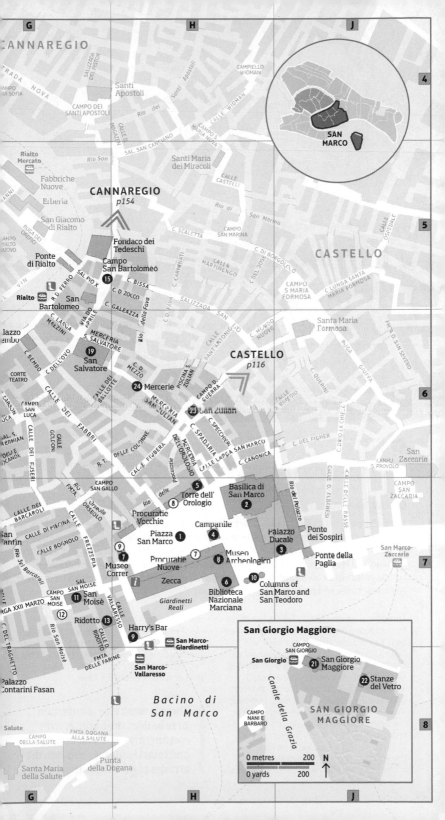

CANNAREGIO

G

Santi
Apostoli

CAMPIELLO
WIDMAN

4

SAN
MARCO

Rialto
Mercato

Fabbriche
Nuove

Erberia

San Giacomo
di Rialto

CANNAREGIO
p154

Santi Maria
dei Miracoli

CASTELLO

5

Fondaco dei
Tedeschi

Ponte
di Rialto

Rialto

San
Bartolomeo

Campo
San Bartolomeo
15

Santa Maria
Formosa

Palazzo
embo

MERCERIA
S. SALVATORE

San
Salvatore
19

CASTELLO
p116

CORTE
TEATRO

24 Mercerie

Santa Maria
Formosa

CAMPO
SAN
LUCA

San Zulian
23

San
Zaccaria

San
antin

CAMPO
SAN GALLO

Torre dell'
Orologio
5
8

Basilica di
San Marco
2

Procuratie
Vecchie

Piazza
San Marco
1

Campanile
4

Palazzo
Ducale
3

Ponte
dei Sospiri

Museo
Correr
9
7

Procuratie
Nuove
7

Museo
Archeologico
8

Ponte della
Paglia

San Marco-
Zaccaria

Zecca

Biblioteca
Nazionale
Marciana
6

10
Columns of
San Marco and
San Teodoro

7

Museo
Correr

GA XXII MARZO

CAMPO
SAN
MOISÈ

11 San Moisè

Ridotto **13**

12

Harry's Bar
9

San Marco-
Giardinetti

Giardinetti
Reali

San Marco-
Vallaresso

San Giorgio Maggiore

CAMPO
SAN GIORGIO

Palazzo
Contarini Fasan

San Giorgio

San Giorgio
Maggiore
21

Stanze
del Vetro
22

Salute

CAMPO
DELLA SALUTE

Bacino di
San Marco

CAMPO
NANI E
BARBARO

SAN GIORGIO
MAGGIORE

8

Santa Maria
della Salute

Punta
della Dogana

0 metres   200
0 yards   200

N

G   H   J

Did You Know?

Piazza San Marco is the only square in Venice which is called a Piazza.

PIAZZA SAN MARCO

◻H7 🚢San Marco

Long the political and religious heart of Venice, Piazza San Marco was once just a monastery garden crossed by a stream. The glittering Basilica di San Marco and Palazzo Ducale command the east side of the square, while the stately Procuratie Vecchie and Nuove that mark its borders have, for centuries, been the backdrop for magnificent processions. Today the piazza continues to bustle, with a museum complex, cafés and costumed Carnival crowds.

Throughout its long history Piazza San Marco has witnessed pageants, processions, political activities and countless Carnival festivities. Tourists flock here in their thousands to see the Piazza's eastern end, which is dominated by two of the city's most impressive and important sights – the Basilica di San Marco (p78) and the Palazzo Ducale (p82). However, there is much else to entertain here besides the basilica, with elegant cafés, open-air orchestras and smart boutiques beneath the arcades of the Procuratie. So close to the waters of the lagoon, the Piazza is one of the first points in the city to suffer at *acqua*

alta (high tide). Tourists and Venetians alike can then be seen picking their way across the duckboards that crisscross the flooded square. The best time to appreciate the beauty of the Piazza is in the early hours, when only the city sweepers and pigeons are here.

> **There is much else to entertain here besides the basilica, with elegant cafés, open-air orchestras and smart boutiques beneath the arcades of the Procuratie.**

↑ The grand arches of the Procuratie surround Piazza San Marco

Timeline

AD 814
Foundations of Doge's Palace laid.

1720
▲ Caffè Florian is thought to be the oldest café in Europe. It was opened on 29 December, by Floriano Francesconi as "Alla Venezia Trionfante" (to the Triumphant Venice).

1810
Napoleon demolishes San Geminiano church to make way for Ala Napoleonica.

1902
▼ Campanile crumbles to the ground.

1966
Record floods hit the Piazza, with water levels 1.94 m (6.4 ft) above sea level.

1989
▼ Pink Floyd concert, on a floating stage, attracts over 100,000 people.

2 🤿 🐾 🛍

BASILICA DI SAN MARCO

📍H7 🏛Piazza San Marco 🚏San Marco 🕐9:30am–5pm Mon–Sat, 2–5pm Sun (Nov–Easter: to 4pm Sun) 🌐basilicasanmarco.it

Dark, mysterious and enriched with the spoils of conquest, Venice's famous basilica blends the architectural and decorative styles of East and West to create one of Europe's greatest buildings. Inside, this Byzantine extravaganza is embellished with golden mosaics, icons and ornate marble carvings.

Exterior of San Marco

Built on a Greek cross plan and crowned with five huge domes, San Marco owes its almost Oriental splendour to countless treasures from the Republic's overseas empire. Among these are copies of the famous bronze horses brought from Constantinople in 1204, and a wealth of columns, bas-reliefs and coloured marbles studded across the main façade. Mosaics from different epochs adorn the five doorways, while the main portal is framed by some of Italy's loveliest Romanesque carving (1240–65). Initially built in the 9th century, this is the third church to stand on the site.

↑ Romanesque carvings surrounding the arches of the main portal

> **San Marco owes its almost Oriental splendour to countless treasures from the Republic's overseas empire.**

← Façade and campanile of the basilica, seen from Piazza San Marco

Timeline

828–978

△ A church is built to house relics of St Mark, stolen from Alexandria. It burns down in 976 and is rebuilt in 978.

978–1117

△ The church is replaced by a grand basilica, "the House of St Mark", reflecting Venice's growing power.

1117–c1300

△ 4,240 sq m (45,622 sq ft) of gleaming golden mosaics are added to the domes, walls and floors of the Basilica.

1807

△ The doge's private chapel until 1807, San Marco succeeds San Pietro di Castello as the cathedral of Venice.

↑ Ornate coloured marble panels on the exterior of the basilica

Inside the Basilica

San Marco's magnificent interior is clad with dazzling mosaics, which begin in the narthex, or atrium, of the basilica, and culminate in the glittering panels of the Pentecost and Ascension domes. The Genesis Cupola in the atrium has a stunning scene of the Creation of the World described in concentric circles. The *pavimento*, or floor, is also patterned with mosaics in marble and glass. Steps from the atrium lead to the Museo Marciano, home to the basilica's famous horses. Other treasures include the jewel-encrusted Pala d'Oro, the Nicopeia icon and the precious hoards of silver, gold and glassware in the Treasury.

Statues of St Mark and angels, which crown the central arch, are additions from the early 15th century.

The Pentecost Dome was probably the first dome to be decorated with mosaics.

The four horses of St Mark are replicas of the gilded bronze originals now protected inside the basilica's museum.

> San Marco's magnificent interior is clad with dazzling mosaics, which culminate in the glittering panels of the Pentecost and Ascension domes.

→ Stunning mosaic of Christ in Glory in the vast Ascension Dome

The Ascension Dome features a magnificent 13th-century mosaic of Christ surrounded by angels, the 12 Apostles and the Virgin Mary.

The alabaster columns of the altar canopy, or baldacchino, are adorned with New Testament scenes.

St Mark's body, believed lost in the fire of AD 976, reappeared when the new church was consecrated in 1094. The remains are housed in the altar.

The mosaic pavement shows beautiful pictures of birds and beasts.

The Treasury is a repository of precious artifacts from both Italy and Constantinople.

PALA D'ORO

Beyond the Cappella di San Clemente lies the entrance to San Marco's most valuable treasure; the Pala d'Oro. This bejewelled altarpiece consists of 250 enamel paintings on gold, enclosed within a gilded silver frame. Napoleon stole some of the precious stones in 1797, but the screen still gleams with rubies, pearls and sapphires.

Mosaics

The earliest of the basilica's gleaming mosaics date from the 12th century, and were the work of mosaicists from the East. Their delicate techniques were soon adopted by Venetian craftsmen who gradually took over the basilica's decoration, combining Byzantine inspiration with Western influences. During the 16th century, many works by Tintoretto, Titian, Veronese and other leading artists were reproduced in mosaic.

Museo Marciano

Look out for signposts to the Loggia dei Cavalli which lead you up to the museum. Here, the gallery offers a splendid view into the basilica. The star exhibits are gilded bronze horses, stolen from the top of the Hippodrome (ancient racecourse) in Constantinople in 1204.

←

Gilded bronze horses housed in the Museo Marciano

③ 🏃 Ⓜ️ 💻 🏛️

PALAZZO DUCALE

📍J7 🏛️Piazza San Marco 1 🚤San Marco ⏰8:30am–5:30pm daily (Apr–Oct: to 7pm); last adm: 1 hour before closing 🚫1 Jan, 25 Dec 🌐palazzoducalevisitmuve.it

A magnificent combination of Byzantine, Gothic and Renaissance architecture, the Palazzo Ducale (Doge's Palace) was the official residence of the 120 doges who ruled Venice from 697 to 1797. Artists such as Titian, Tintoretto and Bellini vied with each other to embellish the palace with painting and sculpture, not to mention architects Antonio Rizzo and Pietro Lombardo, the latter responsible for the ornate western façade.

The Palazzo Ducale was founded in the 9th century, when a fortress-like structure stood on this spot. The present palace owes its external appearance to the building work of the 14th and early 15th centuries, despite a string of fires in the 1500s. The designers broke with tradition by perching the bulk of the pink Verona marble palace on lace-like Istrian stone arcades, with a portico supported by columns below. The result is a light and airy masterpiece of Gothic architecture.

Sala del Senato

Sala delle Quattro Porte

Sala del Collegio

Anticollegio

The walls of the Sala dello Scudo, once part of the doge's private apartments, are covered with maps of the world. In the centre are two giant 18th-century globes.

The Porta della Carta was the main entrance to the palace.

New doges were crowned on the Giant's Staircase with the glittering zogia or dogal cap.

💬 INSIDER TIP
Avoid Queues

Skip the huge queue for the Palazzo Ducale by buying your ticket online in advance. Failing that, head to the Correr Museum where you can buy a combined ticket without the wait.

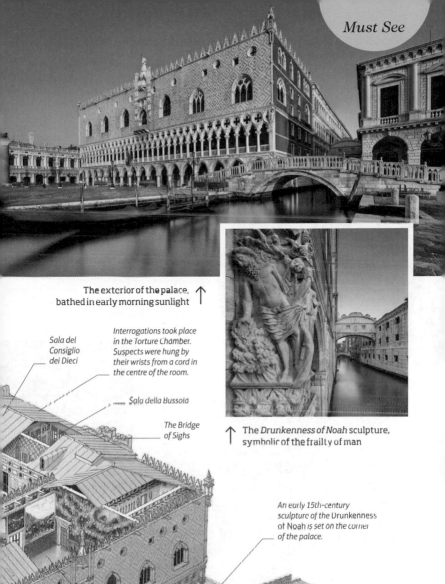

The exterior of the palace,
bathed in early morning sunlight ↑

**Sala del
Consiglio
dei Dieci**

Interrogations took place
in the Torture Chamber.
Suspects were hung by
their wrists from a cord in
the centre of the room.

Sala della Bussola

The Bridge
of Sighs

↑ The *Drunkenness of Noah* sculpture,
symbolic of the frailty of man

An early 15th-century
sculpture of the Drunkenness
of Noah is set on the corner
of the palace.

The Ponte della Paglia,
built of Istrian stone, has
a pretty balustrade of
columns and sculpted
pine cones.

Tintoretto's huge
Paradise (1590) fills the
end wall of the Sala del
Maggior Consiglio.

The Loggia commands
fine views of the lagoon.

←

The grand Palazzo
Ducale, seen from
Piazza San Marco

Exploring the Palazzo Ducale

A tour of the Palazzo Ducale takes visitors through a succession of richly decorated chambers and halls, arranged over four floors, culminating with the Bridge of Sighs, which links the palace to the prisons. The Secret Itineraries tour gives access to parts of the palace normally out of bounds, including the prison cell from which Casanova escaped.

State Apartments and Council Chambers

The doge's private State Apartments on the second floor were built after the fire of 1483. Looted under the orders of Napoleon, they are bare of furnishings, but the lavish ceilings and colossal carved chimneypieces in some of the rooms give an idea of the doges' lifestyle. The Sala dello Scudo, or map room, contains maps and charts, while the picture gallery features some incongruous wooden demoniac panels by Hieronymous Bosch.

The Scala d'Oro ("golden staircase") leads to the third floor and its Council Chambers. In the Sala del Consiglio dei Dieci, the awesomely powerful Council of Ten, set up in 1310, would meet to investigate and prosecute crimes concerning the security of the state. Napoleon pilfered some of the Veroneses from the ceiling

←

Veronese's *Rape of Europa* in the Anticollegio chamber

→

The magnificent Sala del Maggior Consiglio, featuring Tintoretto's *Paradise*

WHO COULD JOIN THE GREAT COUNCIL?

By the mid-16th century Venice's influential Great Council had around 2,000 members. Any Venetian of high birth over the age of 25 was automatically entitled to a seat - with the exception of those married to someon of non-noble birth. From 1646, those from merchant or professional classes with 100,000 ducats to spare could buy their way in.

but two of the finest found their way back here in 1920: *Age and Youth* and *Juno Offering the Ducal Crown to Venice* (both 1553–4).

The magnificent Anticollegio chamber was the waiting room for those meeting with the Council. The end walls are decorated with mythological scenes by Tintoretto: *Vulcan's Forge*, *Mercury and the Graces*, *Bacchus and Ariadne* and *Minerva Dismissing Mars*, all

↑ Dank corridor leading to cells in the palace prisons

painted in 1578. Veronese's masterly *Rape of Europa* (1580), opposite the window, is one of the most eye-catching works in the palace.

In the Sala della Bussola were lions' heads, where citizens could post anonymous bills denouncing others for their crimes, real or imaginary. The wooden door in this room leads to the rooms of the Heads of the Ten, the State Inquisitors' Room and thence to the torture chamber and prisons.

The star attraction of the palace is the monumental Sala del Maggior Consiglio. It was here that the Great Council convened to vote on constitutional questions, to pass laws and elect the top officials of the Serene Republic. Tintoretto's huge *Paradise* (1587–90) occupies the eastern wall. Measuring 7.45 by 24.65 m (25 by 81 ft), it is one of the largest oil paintings in the world. A frieze along the walls illustrates 76 doges by Tintoretto's pupils. The portrait covered by a curtain is of Marin Falier, beheaded for treason in 1355.

Prisons

The Bridge of Sighs links the palace to what were known as the New Prisons, built between 1556 and 1595. Situated at the top of the palace, just below the leaded roof, are the *piombi* cells (*piombo* means lead). These cells are hardly inviting but prisoners here were far more comfortable than the criminals left to fester in the *pozzi* – the dark dank dungeons at ground level. The windowless cells of these ancient prisons are still covered with the graffiti of the convicts.

Did You Know?

Notorious womanizer Casanova escaped from the palace prisons through a hole in the roof of his cell.

→

The Campanile, illuminated in evening sunlight

4 ⚐

CAMPANILE

⚐ H7 ⌂ Piazza San Marco 🚊 San Marco 🕐 Apr: 9:30am–5pm (to 4:45pm Sat & Sun);
May–Aug: 8:30am–8:45pm; Sep: 8:30am–7:45pm; Oct–Mar: 9:30am–4:45pm daily
🔒 In bad weather 🌐 basilicasanmarco.it

From the top of San Marco's campanile, towering high above the Piazza, visitors can enjoy sublime views across the city, the lagoon and, visibility permitting, the peaks of the Italian Alpine range on the horizon.

The first tower, completed in 1173, was built as a lighthouse to assist navigators in the lagoon. In the Middle Ages, it took on a less benevolent role as the support for a torture cage where offenders were imprisoned and in some cases left to die. The tower's present appearance dates from the early 16th century, when it was restored after an earthquake. The tower survived the vicissitudes of time until 14 July 1902, when its foundations gave way and it collapsed. The only casualties were the Loggetta at the foot of the tower and the custodian's cat. The following year, with the help of many donations, the foundation stone was laid for a campanile "dov'era e com'era" (where it was and how it was). The new tower was opened on 25 April (St Mark's Day) 1912. Due to small structural shifts, work has begun in order to reinforce the foundations. There is no known end date for the work

---

THE BELLS OF THE CAMPANILE

Booming through the city, the five bells in the Campanile have been employed to mark Venice's city rhythms for centuries. The Maleficio bell was sounded to announce an execution, the Nona rang at midday, the Trottiera spurred on the nobles' horses for assemblies in the Palazzo Ducale, and the Mezza Terza was used to indicate that the Senate was in session. The Marangona bell is still sounded to mark midnight.

EXPERIENCE MORE

5

Torre dell'Orologio

⬛H7 ⬛Piazza San Marco ⬛San Marco ⬛For guided tours only ⬛1 Jan, 25 Dec ⬛visitmuve.it

This richly decorated Renaissance clock tower stands on the north side of the Piazza, over the archway leading to the Mercerie (p95). Built in the late 15th century, its central section is thought to have been designed by Mauro Coducci. Displaying the phases of the moon and the zodiac, the gilt and blue enamel clock was designed with seafarers in mind. A story was spread by scandalmongers that the two inventors of the complex clock mechanism subsequently had their eyes gouged out to prevent them from ever creating a replica.

During Ascension week and Epiphany, the clock draws large crowds, who watch the figures of the *Magi* emerge from side doors to pay their respects to the Virgin and Child, whose figures are set above the clock. At the very top, two bronze *Mori* (Moors) strike the bell on the hour.

Guided tours must be booked in advance. English-language tours depart from the Museo Correr ticket office at 11am and noon Mon–Wed, and at 2pm and 3pm Thu–Sun.

6

Biblioteca Nazionale Marciana

⬛H7 ⬛Piazzetta (entrance from Museo Correr) ⬛041 240 72 11 ⬛San Marco ⬛8:20am-7pm Mon-Fri, 8:20am-1:30pm Sat, 24 & 31 Dec

Praised by Andrea Palladio as the finest building since antiquity, the library was designed by the architect Jacopo Sansovino. During construction the vaulting collapsed; Sansovino was blamed and imprisoned. Freed only after an appeal, he had to reconstruct the building at his own expense.

At the top of the great stairway is a rare example of Jacopo de' Barbari's bird's-eye view map of Venice dating to 1500 (p88). The salon features two fine ceiling paintings by Paolo Veronese.

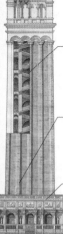

The spire, 98.5 m (323 ft) high, is topped with a golden weathervane.

The five bells in the tower each had their role during the Republic.

An internal lift, installed in 1962, provides easy access to the top of the tower.

The Loggetta was built in the 16th century by Jacopo Sansovino.

Allegorical reliefs from Verona were carefully rebuilt after 1902.

↑ The towering Campanile dominates the Venetian skyline

↑ Manuscripts displayed beneath the gilded ceiling in the Biblioteca Nazionale Marciana

7

Museo Correr

H7 ☐Procuratie Nuove; entrance Ala Napoleonica ☐San Marco ☐Apr-Oct: 10am-7pm daily; Nov-Mar: 10:20am-5pm daily ☐visitmuve.it

With the 19th-century Royal Palace serving as backdrop, a collection of marble statues by Italian Neo-Classical sculptor Antonio Canova (1757–1822) is the first exhibit at the Museo Correr. This is followed by the bathroom and boudoir of Sissi, the Empress Elizabeth, along with other sumptuous rooms laid out in the 1830s and 1850s that make up the restored Imperial Apartments. The next section, titled Venetian Culture, is found in the older, but confusingly named, Procuratie Nuove. This collection captures the history of the Venetian Republic, from daily life to its peculiar public institutions, through maps, armour and a host of doge-related exhibits.

On the second floor is the Wunderkammer (Collection of Wonders), which draws from the legacy of the wealthy abbot and art collector Teodoro Correr, founder of the museum. The collection includes coins, a narwhal tooth and the famous

GREAT VIEW
Piazza Perfetto

For stunning vistas of St Mark's Square, the first-floor windows of the Museo Correr offer a panoramic view and directly face the basilica; in late afternoon, the sun bounces off the gold mosaics of its façade.

Map of Venice by Italian painter and printmaker Jacopo de Barbari. This spectacular woodcut, completed in 1500, depicts a bird's-eye view of Venice, intricately carved from six wooden blocks to create a mural-size print with every building, canal and *campo* accounted for. The Pinacoteca (picture gallery) is also located on this floor. Images are displayed chronologically so that the evolution of Venetian painting is evident. The most famous works in the gallery are the Carpaccios: *A Portrait of a Young Man in a Red Hat* (c 1490) and *Two Venetian Ladies* (c 1507).

8

Museo Archeologico

H7 ☐Piazzetta; entrance from Museo Correr ☐041 296 76 63 ☐San Marco ☐10am-7pm daily (Nov-Mar: to 5pm)

Housed in rooms in both the Biblioteca Nazionale Marciana and the Procuratie Nuove, the museum provides a quiet retreat from the bustle of San Marco. The collection owes its existence to the generosity of Domenico Grimani, son of Doge Antonio Grimani, who bequeathed all

← Daedalus ties wings to his son Icarus in this Canova sculpture, Museo Correr

of his Greek, Roman and earlier sculpture, together with his library, to the state in 1523.

9

Harry's Bar

H7 ☐Calle Vallaresso 1323 ☐San Marco

Celebrated for cocktails, *carpaccio* and its American clientele, Harry's Bar is famous throughout Venice. Founded in 1931 by the late Giuseppe Cipriani, it was financed by a Bostonian called Harry who thought Venice had a dearth of decent bars. They chose a storeroom at the Grand Canal end of the Calle Vallaresso as their location, conveniently close to Piazza San Marco. Since then, the bar has seen a steady stream of American visitors, among them Ernest Hemingway, who used to come here after shooting in the lagoon. The bar became the most popular venue in Venice, patronized by royalty, film stars and heads of state. These days, there are far more American tourists than

↑ The winged lion of St Mark overlooking the Piazza from its column

famous figures, often there to sample the Bellini cocktail, a mix of sparkling prosecco and white peach purée, which Giuseppe Cipriani invented. Aesthetically, the place is unremarkable and there is no terrace for meals alfresco.

---

⑩ Columns of San Marco and San Teodoro

☑ H7 ⚓ Piazzetta 🚤 San Marco

Along with all the bounty from Constantinople came the two huge granite columns which now tower above the Piazzetta. These were said to have been erected in 1172 by the engineer Nicolò Barattieri, architect of the

> **Venetians are a superstitious lot; you'll never catch them walking between the two columns of San Marco and Teodoro.**

very first Rialto Bridge. For his efforts he was granted the right to set up gambling tables between the columns. A more gruesome spectacle on the same spot was the execution of criminals, which took place here until the mid-18th century. Venetians are a superstitious lot; you'll never catch them walking between the two columns.

The western column is crowned by a marble statue of St Theodore, who was the patron saint of Venice before St Mark's relics were smuggled from Alexandria in AD 828. The statue is a modern copy – the original is kept for safety in the Palazzo Ducale (p82).

The second column is surmounted by a huge bronze of the Lion of St Mark. Its origin remains a mystery, though it is thought to be a Chinese chimera with wings added to make it look like a Venetian lion. In September 1990 the 3,000-kg (3-ton) beast made the journey to the British Museum in London for extensive restoration, and was returned with great ceremony and skill to the top of the column.

DRINK

Caffè Florian
The oldest coffeehouse in Europe, and one of the most expensive. Sit at a table or stand at the bar and rub shoulders with the locals.

☑ H7 ⚓ Piazza San Marco 57 🌐 caffeflorian.com

Gran Caffè Lavena
Richard Wagner's old haunt has Florian's glamour but with a smaller bar bill.

☑ H7 ⚓ Piazza San Marco 133/4 🌐 lavena.it

Museo Correr Coffee Shop
Enjoy one of the best views in town with your coffee – you don't need a museum ticket.

☑ H7 ⚓ Procuratie Nuove 🌐 correr.visitmuve.it

San Moisè

⑪

📍G7 🏛Campo San Moisè
📞041 724 10 44 🚉San
Marco 🕐9:30am-12:30pm
Mon-Sat

A church that people love to hate, San Moisè displays a ponderous Baroque façade. Completed in 1668, it is covered in grimy statues, swags and busts. John Ruskin, author of *The Stones of Venice*, described it (in characteristic anti-Baroque outrage) as the clumsiest church in Venice. The interior has a mixed collection of paintings and sculpture from the 17th and 18th centuries. In the nave is the tombstone of John Law, a Scottish financier who founded the Compagnie d'Occident to develop the Mississippi Valley. His shares collapsed in 1770 in the notor-

→

The photogenic spiral staircase at Palazzo Contarini del Bovolo

ious South Sea Bubble, and he fled to Venice, surviving on his winnings at the Ridotto.

⑫

Palazzo Contarini del Bovolo

📍G7 🏛Corte Contarini del Bovolo, 4303 San Marco 🚉Rialto or Sant'Angelo 🕐10am-6pm daily 🌐scala contarinidelbovolo.com

Tucked away in a maze of alleys (follow signs from Campo Manin), this palazzo is best known for the graceful external stairway that leads to the top of its tower. In Venetian dialect *bovolo* means

"snail shell", appropriate to the spiral shape of the stairway. Built in 1499, the tower is open to the public. The ticket for the palazzo also admits you to the Tintoretto room located on the second floor, which houses a collection of art from the 16th and 17th centuries.

⑬

Ridotto

📍7 B3 🏛San Marco, 1332 🚉San Marco 🕐To hotel guests and on request 🌐hotelmonaco.it

In an effort to control the gambling mania that swept Venice in the 1600s, the state

📷 PICTURE PERFECT
Double Vision

The Bovolo staircase offers two great photo ops: capture a graphic, architectural image looking up from below (you'll need to crouch), then a wonderful view of the Basilica di San Marco from the top.

←

The much-maligned Baroque façade of the church of San Moisè

EAT

Bar All'Angolo
Friendly bar selling scrumptuous sandwiches, light meals and salads. Great if you're on the go.

🜨 F7 🏠 Campo Santo Stefano 3465 📞 041 520 92 99 🕒 7am-8pm Mon-Sat

€€€

Le Café
Great coffee, light meals and cakes galore.

🜨 F7 🏠 Campo Santo Stefano 2797 🌐 lecafe venezia.com

€€€

Acqua Pazza
The Amalfi Coast comes to Venice, with delectable coastal dishes and outdoor seating in the square.

🜨 F7 🏠 Campo Sant'Angelo 3808-10 🌐 venice acquapazza.com

€€€

Al Bacareto
A family-run restaurant serving local specialities.

🜨 F7 🏠 Calle delle Botteghe 3447 🌐 bacareto.it

€€€

Bacaro Da Fiore
A wide array of *cichetti* and wines, and restaurant service for a formal meal.

🜨 F7 🏠 Calle delle Botteghe 3461 🌐 dafiore.it

€€€

Trattoria Vini da Arturo
A Venetian staple and one of the few to focus on hearty meat dishes. Small menu, superb wines.

🜨 F6 🏠 Calle degli Assassini 📞 041 520 69 74 🕒 Noon-2.30pm, 7-11pm Mon-Sat

€€€

allowed Marco Dandolo to use a wing of his palace as the first public gaming house in Europe. In 1638 the Ridotto was opened, with the proviso that players came disguised in a mask. In 1774 the Great Council closed the casino's doors on account of the number of Venetians ruined at its tables, the stated aim being "to preserve the piety, sound discipline and moderate behaviour" of the city's people.

In 1947, the old Palazzo Dandolo was converted into a theatre. Now restored, it is part of the Monaco and Grand Canal hotel.

---

14 🜨 🏠

Santa Maria Zobenigo

🜨 F7 🏠 Campo Santa Maria del Giglio 🚏 Santa Maria del Giglio 🕒 3-4:30pm Mon-Sat 🗓 1 Jan, Easter, 15 Aug, 25 Dec 🌐 chorusvenezia.org

Named after the Jubanico family, who are said to have founded it in the 9th century, this church is also referred to as Santa Maria "del Giglio" ("of the lily"). The exuberant Baroque façade, completed in 1681, was financed by the affluent Barbaro family and was designed to glorify their naval and diplomatic

achievements. Instead of the traditional biblical imagery, the centre of the façade is occupied by a statue of Admiral Antonio Barbaro (who died in 1679), surrounded by representations of various heroic virtues and marble relief maps of locations, such as Corfu and Split, where the admiral served the Republic. Other statues are of his brothers, and at the top is the Barbaro coat of arms.

Inside, the furnishings are more conventional, with a tiny museum of church ornaments and statues depicting the Annunciation. Paintings include *The Sacred Family*, attributed to Rubens (if so, it is the only work by the Flemish painter in Venice) and two works by Tintoretto.

15

Campo San Bartolomeo

🜨 G5 🚏 Rialto

Close to the Rialto on its eastern side, the square of San Bartolomeo, named for the apostle Bartholomew, bustles with life, particularly in the early evening, when young Venetians rendezvous here. They meet at the cafés and bars that line the square or by the bronze statue of Carlo Goldoni (1707–93), Venice's prolific and most celebrated playwright. His statue, in a fitting spot for a writer who drew his inspiration from daily social intercourse, was created by Italian sculptor Antonio del Zotto in 1883.

SHOP

Venice's most exclusive neighbourhood, San Marco is home to several sumptuous furnishing stores, some of which have been producing textiles for centuries. Whether you are looking for velvet damask or the finest linen, these stores are sure to have it.

Bevilacqua
📍F7 🏠Campo Santa Maria del Giglio 2520
🌐bevilacquatessuti.com

Chiarastella Cattana
📍E7 🏠Salizada San Samuele 3216 🌐chiarastellacattana.com

Rubelli
📍E7 🏠Piscina Sam Samuele 3393
🌐rubelli.com

La Fenice
📍G7 🏠Campo San Fantin 🚉San Marco
🌐teatrolafenice.it

Theatre houses were enormously popular in the 18th century, and La Fenice, the city's oldest theatre, was no exception. Built in 1792 in Classical style, it was one of several privately owned theatres showing plays and operas to audiences from all strata of society. In December 1836, a fire destroyed the interior but a year later it was resurrected, just like the mythical bird, the phoenix *(fenice)*, which is said to have arisen from its ashes.

Another fire in early 1996 again destroyed the theatre, except for its façade. Now beautifully rebuilt, La Fenice shares the concert and opera season with the Malibran Theatre near Rialto.

Throughout the 19th century the name of La Fenice was linked with great Italian composers. Verdi's *La Traviata* (1853) and Rossini's *Tancredi* (1813) and *Semiramide* (1823)

→
Statue of the Dalmation scholar Nicolò Tommaseo in Campo Santo Stefano

all premiered here. During the Austrian Occupation *(p52)*, red, white and green flowers, symbolizing the Italian flag, were thrown on stage to shouts of "Viva Verdi" – the letters of the composer's name standing for "Vittorio Emanuele Re d'Italia". More recently, the theatre saw premieres of Stravinsky's *The Rake's Progress* (1951) and Britten's *The Turn of the Screw* (1954).

17
Campo Santo Stefano
📍F7 🚉Accademia or Sant'Angelo

Also known as Campo Francesco Morosini after the 17th-century doge who once lived here, this *campo* is one of the most spacious in the city. Bullfights were staged until 1802, when a stand fell and killed some of the spectators. It was also a venue for balls

Contemporary stage set amid restored Rococo opera boxes at La Fenice ↑

and Carnival festivities. Today it is a pleasantly informal square. The central statue is Nicolò Tommaseo (1802–74), a key figure in the 1848 rebellion against the Austrians.

Deconsecrated six times on account of the violence that took place within its walls, the 14th-century church of Santo Stefano today is remarkably serene. It houses notable works of art, including some paintings by Tintoretto.

At the southern end, the austere-looking Palazzo Pisani, overlooking the Campiello Pisani, has been the Conservatory of Music since the 19th century. Music wafts from its open windows all through the year.

18 ⊕

Palazzo Grassi

📍E7 🏛Campo S Samuele, San Marco 3231 🚏San Samuele ⏰10am-7pm Wed- Mon 🌐palazzo grassi.it

Set on the Grand Canal, this landmark gallery dates back to 1740, when a merchant family commissioned Giorgio Massari to design the building. It is now home to the François Pinault collection, housing contemporary masterpieces by Jeff Koons, Damien Hirst and Michelangelo Pistoletto. Its inspirational sister gallery is Punta della Dogana (p146).

19

San Salvatore

📍G6 🏛Campo San Salvatore 🚏Rialto ⏰9am-noon, 3-7:15pm Mon-Sat, 4-7pm Sun 🌐chiesasansalvador.it

The interior of this church is an excellent example of Venetian Renaissance architecture. If the main door is closed visitors can enter by the side entrance, which is squeezed between shops on the Mercerie (p95). The present church was designed by Giorgio Spavento in the early 16th century, and continued by Tullio Lombardo and Jacopo Sansovino. The pictorial highlight is Titian's *Annunciation* (1566) over the third altar on the right.

20 ⊕

Museo Fortuny

📍F6 🏛Palazzo Pesaro degli Orfei, Campo San Beneto 🚏Sant'Angelo ⏰Exhibitions only 🌐fortuny.visitmuve.it

Mariano Fortuny y Madrazo was born in 1871 in Granada and moved to Venice in 1889. In the early 20th century he purchased the Palazzo Pesaro, a late Gothic palazzo that was owned by the influential Pesaro family.The large rooms make a splendid setting for the precious Fortuny fabrics. Woven with gold and silver threads, created using Renaissance techniques and ancient dyes. The collection also includes paintings by Fortuny, decorative panels and a few of the finely pleated silk dresses considered a milestone in early 20th-century women's fashion. Today, the rooms are open during visiting design and photo exhibitions.

FORTUNY FACTORY

Mariano Fortuny was an entrepreneurial grafter and Renaissance man, interested in science as much as art. He opened the Fortuny factory on Giudecca island in 1921. It was here that his workers created Fortuny's trademark fabrics. Still in operation today, the factory is shrouded in secrecy and out of bounds, although it is possible to visit the showroom, strictly by appointment only.

STAY

Hotel Novecento

Enjoy Oriental-style rooms at this calm Venetian retreat.

📍H5 🏠Calle del Dose 2683-4
🌐novecento.biz

€€€

Hotel Santo Stefano

Elegant rooms in a 15th-century watchtower.

📍F7 🏠Campo Santo Stefano 2957
🌐hotelsantostefano venezia.com

€€€

Hotel Bauer il Palazzo

Lavish palace views over the Grand Canal from the rooftop.

📍G7 🏠Campo San Moisè 1459
🌐bauervenezia.com

€€€

㉑
San Giorgio Maggiore

📍J8 📞041 522 78 27
🚤San Giorgio 🕐9am-7pm daily (8:30am-6pm Nov-Mar)

Appearing like a stage set across the water from the Piazzetta, the little island of San Giorgio Maggiore has been captured on canvas countless times. The church and monastery, built between 1559 and 1580, are among Andrea Palladio's greatest architectural achievements. The church's temple front and spacious, serene interior, with its perfect proportions and cool beauty, are typically Palladian in that they are modelled on the Classical style of ancient Rome. Within the church, the major works of art are the two Tintorettos on the chancel walls: *The Last Supper* and *Gathering of the Manna* (both 1594). In the Chapel of the Dead is his last work, *The Deposition* (1592-4), finished by his son Domenico. The top of the tall campanile, reached by a lift, affords a superb panorama of the city and lagoon.

Centuries ago, Benedictine monks occupied the original monastery. It later became a centre of learning and a residence for eminent foreign visitors. Following the fall of the Republic in 1797 (*p52*) the monastery was suppressed and its treasures plundered.

In 1829 the island became a free port, and in 1851 the headquarters of the artillery. By this time it had completely changed out of all recognition. The complex regained its role as an active cultural centre when the monastery, embracing Palladio's cloisters, refectory and library, was purchased in 1951 by Count Vittorio Cini. Today it is a thriving Venetian cultural foundation, hosting concerts, international events and fascinating exhibitions.

Did You Know?

San Giorgio Maggiore's original buildings were destroyed in an earthquake in the 13th century.

↑ One of the most timeless views in Venice, across the lagoon to San Giorgio

In the middle of the park on the island is an evocative open-air amphitheatre, the Teatro Verde, constructed of white Vicenza stone.

22 🛍
Stanze del Vetro

📍J8 🏛 Isola di San Giorgio Maggiore 8 🚤 San Giorgio ⏰ 10am–4:30pm Thu–Tue (later in summer) 🌐 lestanzedelvetro.org

Standing behind the Church of San Giorgio Maggiore is the Stanze del Vetro (the Glass Rooms). A joint project between the Cini Foundation and Pentagram Stiftung, the aim is to celebrate and study the art of glass-making from the 19th century until today. The modern exhibition space is housed in part of the erstwhile boarding school that once stood on the island. Temporary exhibitions of major artists run throughout the year, even spilling out into the garden for larger installations. The giftshop has an excellent range of books about glass art, as well as delightful glass souvenirs.

23
San Zulian

📍H6 🏛 Campo San Zulian (Giuliano) 🚤 San Marco ⏰ 9am–7pm daily

On the busy Mercerie, the church of San Zulian (or Giuliano) provides a refuge from the crowded alleys. Its interior features gilded woodwork, 16th- and 17th-century paintings, and sculpture. The central panel of the frescoed ceiling portrays *The Apotheosis of St Julian*, painted in 1585 by Palma il Giovane. The 16th-century church façade was designed by Sansovino and paid for by the rich and immodest physician Tommaso

→ Statue of Thomas Rangone atop the entrance to San Zulian

Rangone. His bronze statue stands out against the white Istrian stone walls.

24
Mercerie

📍H6 🚤 San Marco or Rialto

Divided into the Merceria dell'Orologio, Merceria di San Zulian and Merceria di San Salvatore, this is a principal shopping thoroughfare. Linking Piazza San Marco with the Rialto, it is made from a string of narrow alleys, lined by small shops and boutiques. The 17th-century English author John Evelyn described it as "the most delicious streete in the World for the sweetnesse of it". He wrote of perfumers, apothecary shops and nightingales. Today all this has been replaced with fashions, footwear and glass.

At the southern end, the relief over the first archway on the left portrays the woman who in 1310 accidentally stopped a revolt. She dropped her pestle out of the window, killing the standard-bearer of a rebel army. They retreated, and the woman was given a guarantee that her rent would never be raised.

A SHORT WALK
AROUND LA FENICE

Distance 1.5 km (1 mile) **Time** 25 minutes
Nearest Vaporetto San Marco

West of the huge expanse of the ever-crowded Piazza San Marco there is a labyrinth of alleys to explore. At the centre of this part of the *sestiere* is Campo San Fantin, flanked by the Renaissance church of San Fantin. Nearby is the Ateneo Veneto, formerly a *scuola* whose members had the unenviable role of escorting prisoners to the scaffold. The narrow streets around these sights are home to some wonderful little shops, while the Calle Larga XXII Marzo, further south, boasts some of the biggest names in Italian fashion. The quarter in general has some excellent restaurants but, being San Marco, the prices in the majority of establishments are fairly steep.

*Campo San Fantin has a late Renaissance church, **San Fantin**, with a particularly beautiful apse designed by Jacopo Sansovino.*

La Fenice (p92), *Venice's most famous opera house, is now beautifully restored after it was destroyed by fire for a second time in 1996*

The Rio delle Veste *leads past the rear of the theatre. This is the route taken by those fortunate enough to arrive for their night out by gondola.*

↑ Exterior of La Fenice, Venice's most famous theatre and opera house

*The carvings on **Santa Maria Zobenigo** (p91) feature the Barbaro family, who paid for the church façade. Ground-level reliefs show towns where the family held high-ranking posts.*

The statue of Daniele Manin, leader of the 1848 uprising, stands on **Campo Manin** gazing towards the house where he once lived.

Locator Map
For more detail see p74

Tucked away off the main street, **Palazzo Contarini del Bovolo** *(p90) is tricky to find, but worth seeking out for its fairy-tale external stairway.*

CALLE D LOCANDE

CALLE DEI FUSERI

DI SAN LUCA

RIO FUSERI

C DEI BARCAROLI

EL FRUTTAROL

PISC DI CHIZZERIA

DI PISCINA

CALLE BUGNOLO

FREZZERIA

RIO DEI BARCAROLI

PISC S MOISE

SAL SAN MOISE

CALLE D VESTE

CAMPO SAN MOISE

CALLE LARGA XXII MARZO

0 metres   50   N
0 yards   50   ↑

Did You Know?

La Fenice – meaning "the phoenix" – was named after it was restored from the ashes of a fire in 1836.

Frezzeria, *in medieval times, was the street where citizens went to purchase their arrows (frecce). Its shops now sell exotic clothes.*

The exuberant Baroque façade of **San Moisè** *(p90) was funded by a legacy from the patrician Vincenzo Fini, whose bust features above a side door.*

Calle Larga XXII Marzo *was named after 22 March 1848, the day of Manin's rebellion. Today the street is best known for its fashionable designer boutiques.*

→
The view from the arcade at the top of Palazzo Contarini del Bovolo

SAN POLO AND SANTA CROCE

The *sestieri* of San Polo and Santa Croce, bordered by the upper sweep of the Grand Canal, were both named after churches that stood within their boundaries – San Polo, originally constructed in the 9th century and heavily remodelled in the centuries to follow, and Santa Croce, established by refugees fleeing the Lombards in the 6th century, only to be demolished by Napoleon in 1808.

The first inhabitants are said to have settled on the cluster of small islands called Rivus Altus (high bank) or Rialto. When markets were established in the 11th century, the quarter became the commercial hub of Venice, giving the area its reputation as the bazaar of Europe. Almost anything could be traded here, from gold and jewellery to spices, dyes and unusual delicacies from far-flung lands. In 1514 a fire raged through the Rialto, destroying everything except the church. Rebuilding started straight away, restoring the market and surrounding area to its former glory.

San Polo continues to be one of the liveliest *sestieri* of the city, with its market stalls, busy shops and local bars. The bustle of the market gives way to a maze of narrow alleys opening on to squares. Santa Croce for the most part is an area of narrow, tightly packed streets and squares where you will see the humbler side of Venetian life.

B

- **0 metres** 200
- **0 yards** 200

N ↑

CALLE PRIULI
DEI CAVALLETTI

CALLE LUNGA CHIOVERETTE

Stazione Ferrovie
dello Stato
Santa Lucia

Ferrovia 🚃

FONDAMENTA

SAN SIMEON PICCOLO

CALLE TRAGHETTO DI SANTA LUCIA

C. BERGAMASCHI

Ponte della
Costituzione

FMTA CROCE

FONDAMENTA DEI MONASTERO

Giardino
Papadopoli

FONDAMENTA COSSETTI

PIAZZALE
ROMA

FONDAMENTA PAPADOPOLI

⑦

CORTE CASE NUOVE

CAMPO DELLA LANA

CORTE
DEGLI AMAI

CAMPO DEI
TOLENTINI

⑤ ⑫

San Nicolò
da Tolentino

FONDAMENTA
MINOTTO

FONDAMENTA CONDULMER

Rio del Malcanton

FMTA DEL GAFFARO

SAL. SAN. PANTALON

FMTA
DEI

FMTA DELLE SACCHERE

RIO
Nuovo

C.D. MISERICORDIA

FMTA RIO NUOVO

FONDAMENTA

FMTA PECAN

FMTA CZIZZIOLA

Rio della Cazziola

C. DELLA SBIACCA

CORTE
GALLO

CALLE E CORTE BASEGO

FONDAMENTA
DEL RIO NUOVO

Rio Nuovo

FONDAMENTA
DELLE PROCURATIE

FMTA DEI CERERI

Rio Briati

CALLE RAGUSEI

CALLE
LARGA RAGUSEI

CALLE NUOVA

C

Ponte
degli Scalzi

San Simeone
Piccolo

FMTA
TOLENTINI

CORTE
DEGLI AMAI

CALLE TALIER

CALLE delle Muneghette

CPLO.
DIETRO
CASTELFORTE

②

CALLE
VINANTI

CPLO
MOSCA

CALLE DEI PRETI CROSERA

San
Pantalon

Rio di Ca' Foscari

▽▽
DORSODURO
p136

CAMPO
SANTA
MARGHERITA

Casa dei Varoteri

DORSODURO

CAMPO S.
BARNABA

CALLE LUNGA SAN BARNABA

Rio Malpaga

D

CPLO FLANGINI

San
Geremia

Canal Grande

🚊 Riva di Bíasio

RIVA DI BIASIO

CALLE ZEN

RIO TERRA

Palazzo
Donà Balbi

SAL. D. CHIESA

CALLE PISANI

San Simeone
Grande

CPO.
S. SIMEON
GRANDE

C. LARGA DEI BARI

LISTA VECCHIA DEI BARI

⑥

C. ORSETTI

Rio Marin

FMTA RIO MARIN

FONDAMENTA GRADENIGO

CAMPO
NAZARIO
SAURO

RG BELLA

C. D. SAVIO

SALIZZADA ZUSTO

RM CAZZA

CALLE
RUGA VECCHIA

San 2
Dege

⑩

CAMPO S
ZAN DEGO

C. BEMBO

Rio di San Zan

Degolà

④

CAMP
S. GIACO
DELL'O

⑪

San Giacomo
dell'Orio

SANTA CROCE

CAMPO DEI
TEDESCHI

CAMPO
DELLE STROPE

CORTE CANAL

CALLE VISCIGA

FMTA RIO MARIN

O. GARZOTTI

Rio San Giacomo dell'Orio

C. DELLE
OCHE

C. TINTOR

⑧

CALLE LARGA CONTARINA

Rio di San Zuane

C. D. LACCA

FMTA DELLE SACCHERE

CALLE CAMPAZZO

CALLE D. CHIOVERE

C. SAN ZUANE

SOTTOPORTICO LACCA

C. DRIO L'ARCHIVIO

CALLE
DELL'OLIO

Palazzetto
Bru Zane

⑩

CALLE
DELLA VIDA

San Giovanni
Evangelista

⑨

CAMPO
SAN STIN

CALLE DON

Rio di San

C. TINTORETTO

San
Rocco

⑤

Santa Maria
Gloriosa
dei Frari

①

FMTA D. FRARI

Rio dei Frari

CAMPO
D. FRARI

⑫

Scuola
Grande di
San Rocco

②

CAMPO
SAN ROCCO

C. D.
GORII

C. D.
CRISTO

CAMPO
SAN
TOMA

C. CAMPANIEL

Rio della Frescada

LARGA FOSCARI

Palazzo
Balbi

Ca'
Foscari

CALLE SAONERI

RIO TERRA
CANAL

CALLE CAPPELLER

CALLE BERNARDO

Ca'
Rezzonico

San
Samue

Ca' Rezzonico 🚃

C. DEL TRAGHETTO

Rio della Toletta

CALLE D. TOLEDA

SAN POLO AND SANTA CROCE

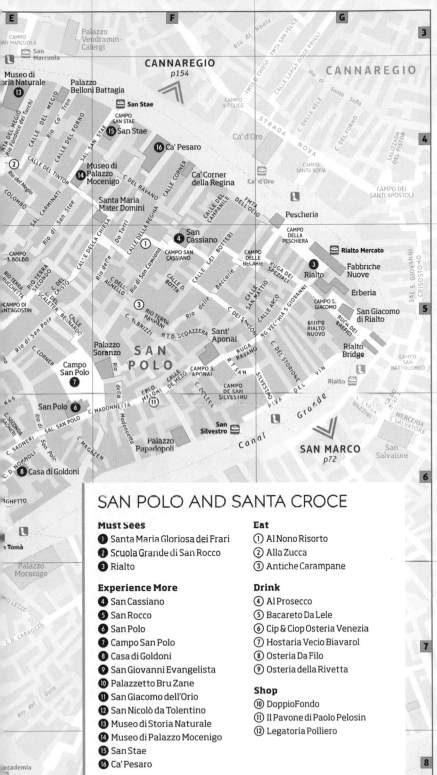

SAN POLO AND SANTA CROCE

Must Sees

1. Santa Maria Gloriosa dei Frari
2. Scuola Grande di San Rocco
3. Rialto

Experience More

4. San Cassiano
5. San Rocco
6. San Polo
7. Campo San Polo
8. Casa di Goldoni
9. San Giovanni Evangelista
10. Palazzetto Bru Zane
11. San Giacomo dell'Orio
12. San Nicolò da Tolentino
13. Museo di Storia Naturale
14. Museo di Palazzo Mocenigo
15. San Stae
16. Ca' Pesaro

Eat

1. Al Nono Risorto
2. Alla Zucca
3. Antiche Carampane

Drink

4. Al Prosecco
5. Bacareto Da Lele
6. Cip & Ciop Osteria Venezia
7. Hostaria Vecio Biavarol
8. Osteria Da Filo
9. Osteria della Rivetta

Shop

10. DoppioFondo
11. Il Pavone di Paolo Pelosin
12. Legatoria Polliero

① ♨

SANTA MARIA GLORIOSA DEI FRARI

📍D6 🏛Campo dei Frari 🚤San Tomà 🕐9am–6pm Mon–Sat, 1–6pm Sun & religious hols
🚫During Mass, 1 Jan, 25 Dec 🌐chorusvenezia.org

More commonly known as the Frari (a corruption of *frati*, meaning "brothers"), this vast Gothic church dwarfs the eastern side of San Polo. The airy interior is striking for the sheer size and quality of its works of art, including masterpieces by Titian and Giovanni Bellini, a statue by Donatello and several grandoise tombs.

The first church on this site was built by Franciscan friars in 1250–1338, but was replaced by a much larger building in the 15th century. The labyrinthine monastery and courtyards adjoining the church have been home to Venice's State Archives since the fall of the Republic. Its 300 rooms are loaded with precious records documenting the history of Venice right back to the 9th century.

Donatello's sculpture of St John the Baptist (1438) appears in the altar of the chapel immediately to the right of the apse.

The Monks' Choir consists of three-tiered stalls (1468), carved with bas-reliefs of saints and Venetian city scenes.

The campanile is 83 m (262 ft) high, the tallest in the city after that of San Marco.

Titian's spectacular work Assumption of the Virgin (1518) draws the eye through the Monks' Choir to the altar, and heavenwards.

Pietro Lombardo and Bartolomeo Bon carved this rood screen (1475) and its decorative marble figures.

The Madonna di Ca' Pesaro (1526) shows Titian's mastery of light and colour.

Canova's pyramidal tomb is based on a design he planned, but never constructed, as a monument for Titian.

The Gothic church of Santa Maria Gloriosa dei Frari →

① The entrance to Santa Maria Gloriosa dei Frari faces the Rio dei Frari canal.

② Titian's famous *Assumption of the Virgin* dominates the apse.

③ The sacristy's altarpiece, *Madonna and Child* (1488), by Bellini, is one of Venice's most beautiful Renaissance paintings.

④ The church's former monastery houses Venice's State Archives.

Courtyard and former monastery

2

SCUOLA GRANDE DI SAN ROCCO

Q D6 **A** Campo San Rocco **🚉** San Tomà **🕐** 9:30am–5:30pm daily
🗓 1 Jan, 25 Dec **w** scuolagrandesanrocco.it

Blinding in the morning sun, the early Renaissance façade of this historic building, home to masterpieces by Jacopo Tintoretto, is a marvel of intertwined sculpted stone wreaths and crouching elephants dwarfed by stately columns.

Founded in honour of St Roch (San Rocco), the Scuola was set up as a charitable institution for the sick. Construction began in 1515 under Bartolomeo Bon and was completed in 1549 by Scarpagnino, financed by donations from Venetians who believed St Roch, the patron saint of contagious disease, would save them from the plague. In 1564 Tintoretto was commissioned to decorate the walls and ceilings of the Scuola. His paintings have no labels, but a useful plan is available (in multiple languages) for free at the entrance. To see the paintings in chronological order, start in the Sala dell'Albergo, followed by the Upper Hall and finally the Ground-Floor Hall.

23

The number of years it took Tintoretto to complete the Scuola's paintings

NOT JUST TINTORETTO

With the overwhelming number of paintings by Tintoretto, it's easy to forget the Scuola holds other artistic treasures, such as Titian's dreamlike *Annunciation* (c 1535). Two masterpieces by Tiepolo hang on the stairs leading to the Treasury. One of the Scuola's greatest pieces is Giorgione's *Christ Carrying the Cross* (below). Once considered miraculous by Venetians, who prayed for cures in front of it, it is a truly moving and magnificent work.

Highlights

Sala dell'Albergo

▷ A competition was held in 1564 to select an artist to paint the central ceiling panel of the Sala dell'Albergo in the Scuola. To the fury of his rivals, Tintoretto installed his painting prior to judging. He won the commission and was later made a member of the Scuola. Over the next 23 years, Tintoretto decorated the entire building. The winning painting, *St Roch in Glory*, can be seen on the ceiling of the Sala dell'Albergo. The most moving work in the cycle is *The Crucifixion* (1565), of which Henry James wrote: "Surely no single picture contains more of human life."

Upper Hall

▽ Scarpagnino's great staircase (1544-6) leads to the Upper Hall, where the ceiling paintings portray scenes from the Old Testament. The three large central square paintings represent *Moses Striking Water from the Rock*, *The Miracle of the Bronze Serpent* and *The Gathering of the Manna*, all alluding to the Scuola's charitable aims. The vast wall paintings in the hall feature episodes from the New Testament, including *The Temptation of Christ* and *Adoration of the Shepherds*.

Ground-Floor Hall

▽ This final cycle, executed in 1582-7, consists of eight paintings illustrating the life of Mary. The series starts with an *Annunciation*, and ends with an *Assumption*, which was restored some years ago. The tranquil scenes of *St Mary of Egypt*, *St Mary Magdalene* and *The Flight into Egypt*, are remarkable for their serenity. In all three paintings, the landscapes, rendered with rapid strokes, play a major role.

← The ornate façade of the Scuola Grande di San Rocco on Campo San Rocco

③
RIALTO

📍 G5 🚃 Rialto

The commercial hub of Venice, the Rialto takes its name from *rivo alto* (high bank) and was one of the first areas of Venice to be inhabited. A financial and then a market district, it remains one of the city's busiest and most bustling areas. Locals and visitors alike jostle among the colourful stalls of the Erberia (fruit and vegetable market) and Pescheria (fish market), while crowds gather on the famous Rialto Bridge, browsing for souvenirs or taking a break to watch the swirl of activity on the Grand Canal below.

→
Gondola boats bobbing on the Grand Canal, with the Rialto Bridge in the background

0 metres   100   N
0 yards   100   ↑

Fondaco dei Tedeschi, originally a warehouse and lodgings for German traders, is now a luxury department store.

↑ The Grand Canal through the Rialto district

Palazzo Camerlenghi, built in 1528, was once the offices of the city treasurers (camerlenghi). The ground floor was the state prison.

Riva del Vin is one of the few spots to sit and relax on the banks of the Grand Canal.

Palazzo Barzizza, rebuilt in the 17th century, still preserves its early 13th-century façade.

Riva del Ferro is where barges unloaded iron (ferro).

Did You Know?

An early wooden Rialto bridge collapsed under the weight of a wedding party in 1444.

① San Giacomo di Rialto

◩ Campo San Giacomo, San Polo ⏰ 9.30am-noon & 4-5pm Mon-Sat, 11am-noon Sun ⏳ During Mass 🌐 chorusvenezia.org

The first church to be built on this site was allegedly founded in the 5th century, making it the oldest church in Venice. The present building dates from between the 11th and 12th centuries, while major restoration work took place in 1601. The original Gothic portico and huge 15th-century 24-hour clock on its façade are the church's most striking features.

The crouching stone figure on the far side of the square is the so-called Gobbo (hunchback) of the Rialto. In the 16th century this was a welcome sight for minor offenders who were forced to run the gauntlet from Piazza San Marco to this square at the Rialto.

② Rialto Market

◩ San Polo ⏰ Fruit and vegetable market: dawn-12:30pm Mon-Sat; Fish market: dawn-12:30pm Tue-Sat.

Venetians have come to the Erberia fruit and vegetable market to buy fresh produce for hundreds of years. Heavily laden barges arrive at dawn and offload their crates on to the quayside by the Grand Canal. Local produce includes red *radicchio* from Treviso, and succulent asparagus and baby artichokes from the islands of Sant'Erasmo and Le Vignole. In the adjoining Pescheria fish market are sole, sardines, skate, squid, crabs, clams and other species of seafood and fish for sale.

③ Rialto Bridge

Very few visitors leave Venice without crossing the iconic Rialto Bridge. The oldest of the four crossings over the Grand Canal, it is a wonderful place to watch the constant activity of boats on the water below. Stone bridges were built in Venice as early as the 12th century, but it was not until 1588, after the collapse, decay or sabotage of earlier wooden structures, that a competition was held for the design of a new Rialto bridge to be built in stone. Andrea Palladio, Jacopo Sansovino and Michelangelo were the eminent contenders, but after months of deliberation it was the aptly named Antonio da Ponte who won the commission. Work was completed on the 48-m (157-ft) bridge in 1591. Until 1854, when the Accademia Bridge was constructed, the Rialto Bridge remained the only means of crossing the Grand Canal on foot.

> INSIDER TIP:
> **Rialto Market**
>
> To see the market in full bustling swing, visitors must arrive early in the morning – by noon the vendors are already starting to pack up.

EXPERIENCE MORE

 San Cassiano

📍F5 📌Campo San Cassiano, San Polo ☎041 721 408 🚢San Stae ⏰9am-noon, 3-7pm daily

The medieval church of San Cassiano is a bizarre mix of architectural styles. Of the original church, only the campanile survives. Jacopo Tintoretto's immensely powerful *Crucifixion* (1568), is displayed in the sacristy.

The *campo* in which the church stands was notorious for prostitutes in the 1500s, but is now a peaceful square.

 San Rocco

📍D6 📌Campo San Rocco, San Polo 🚢San Tomà ⏰9:30am-5:30pm daily 🔒1 Jan, 25 Dec 🌐scuola grandesanrocco.it

Sharing the little square with the celebrated Scuola Grande di San Rocco (p104) is the

---

📷 PICTURE PERFECT
Venice's Cutest Campiello?

Immediately behind the Scuola di San Rocco is a picturesque corner much used by film crews. Best at sunset when the light is fading, this spacious canal side has it all: bridges, water, great architecture and virtually no passers by.

---

church of the same name. Designed by Bartolomeo Bon in 1489 and largely rebuilt in 1725, the exterior is a unique blend of various architectural styles. The ornate façade was added in 1765–71.

Inside, the main interest lies in Tintoretto's paintings in the chancel, which depict scenes from the life of St Roch, a 14th-century pilgrim said to have ministered to the sick on his journey to Rome, and hence patron saint of contagious diseases. Of these the most notable is *St Roch Curing the Plague Victims* (1549).

---

⑥

San Polo

📍E6 📌Campo San Polo 🚢San Silvestro ⏰10:30am-4:30pm Mon-Sat 🔒1 Jan, Easter, 15 Aug, 25 Dec 🌐chorusvenezia.org

Founded in the 9th century, rebuilt in the 15th and revamped in the early 19th in Neo-Classical style, the church of San Polo lacks any sense of homogeneity. Yet it is worth visiting for individual features such as the lovely Gothic portal and the Romanesque lions at the foot of the 14th-century campanile – one holds a serpent between its paws, the other a human head.

Inside, follow the signs for the *Via Crucis del Tiepolo* – 14 canvases of the Stations of the Cross by Giandomenico Tiepolo. The church also has paintings by Veronese, Palma il Giovane (the Younger) and a dark and dramatic *Last Supper* by Tintoretto.

---

⑦ 🛍️

Campo San Polo

📍E5, E6 🚢San Silvestro

The spacious square of San Polo, a popular venue for Carnival festivities today, has

↑ The bell tower of San Cassiano overlooking the canal of the same name

↑ Campo San Polo is Venice's second-largest square, after San Marco; flea market stall *(inset)*

long been host to spectacular events. As far back as the 15th century it was the venue for festivities, masquerades, balls, ceremonies and bullbaiting.

The most dramatic event was the assassination of Lorenzino de' Medici in 1548. He had taken refuge in Venice after brutally killing his cousin Alessandro, Duke of Florence. Lorenzino was stabbed in the square by two assassins who were in the service of Cosimo de' Medici, and both were handsomely rewarded by the Florentine duke.

On the eastern side of the square is the beautiful Gothic Palazzo Soranzo. This was originally two palaces – the one on the left is the older.

Palazzo Corner Mocenigo, which is situated in the northwest corner (No. 2128), was once the residence of the eccentric English writer Frederick Rolfe (1860–1913), alias Baron Corvo. He was thrown out of his lodgings when his English hostess read his manuscript of *The Desire and Pursuit of the Whole* – a cruel satirization of English society in Venice.

---

8 🎨 🏛

Casa di Goldoni

📍 E6 🏠 Palazzo Centani, Rio Terà' dei Nomboli, San Polo 2794 🚤 San Tomà ⏰ Noon–5pm Thu–Tue 🚫 1 Jan, 1 May, 25 Dec 🌐 carlogoldoni.visitmuve.it

Carlo Goldoni, one of the city's favourite sons, wrote over 250 comedies, many based on *commedia dell'arte* figures. Goldoni was born in the beautiful Gothic Palazzo Centani (or Zantani) in 1707. The house was left to the city in 1931 and is now a centre for theatrical studies and has a collection of theatrical memorabilia. The enchanting courtyard has a 15th-century open stairway and a superb wellhead, which features carved lions and a coat of arms bearing a hedgehog.

DRINK

Al Prosecco

Superb range of wines and top-notch meals in a pretty square.

📍 E5 🏠 Campo San Giacomo dell'Orio 1503 🕐 Sun 🌐 alprosecco.com

---

Bacareto Da Lele

Students flock here for reasonably-priced beers and wine by the glass.

📍 C5 🏠 Campo dei Tolentini 🕐 Until 2pm Sat

Cip & Ciop Osteria Venezia

This *osteria* has a southern look, but the *cichetti* are very much Venetian. Great wines and craft beer.

📍 D4 🏠 Calle Larga dei Bari 1162 🕐 9am-9pm Wed-Mon

Hostaria Vecio Biavarol

This champion of the "slow food" movement serves cold cuts, cheese and quality wines.

📍 C5 🏠 Fondamenta dei Tolentini 225 🕐 11am-2:30pm, 5:30-9:30pm daily

---

Osteria Da Filo

Another busy student hangout, with live music on Wednesdays.

📍 E4 🏠 Calle dell Tintor 1539 🕐 4-11pm daily

Osteria della Rivetta

This convivial *osteria* is a favourite with locals thanks to its plentiful bar snacks.

📍 C5 🏠 Calle Sechera 637/A 🕐 9:30am-9:30pm Mon-Sat

One of Venice's five *scuole grandi,* San Giovanni Evangelista ↑

San Giovanni Evangelista

📍 D5 🏠 Campiello de la Scuola, San Polo 🚢 San Tomà 🕐 9:30am-1pm & 2-5:15pm if no events are being held (check website) 🌐 scuolasangiovanni.it

A confraternity of flagellants founded the Scuola of St John the Evangelist in 1261. Today, the complex comprises a church, *scuola*, a bookshop and court-yard. Separating the square from the street is Pietro Lombardo's elegant white and grey screen and portal (1480), and in the arch crowning the portal a carved eagle representing St John the Evangelist takes pride of place.

The main hall of the Scuola is reached via a splendid 15th-century double stairway by Mauro Coducci (1498). Large, dark canvases decorate the ceiling and walls of the 18th-century hall. The Scuola's greatest art treasure, the cycle of paintings depicting *The*

> 💬 INSIDER TIP
> ### Green Retreat
>
> Book yourself a peace-ful morning visit to the famed garden of Palazzo Soranzo Cappello, home to the Venice Super-intendency of Fine Arts and Landscape *(www. soprintendenza.pdve. beniculturali).*

Stories of the Cross, is now on display in the Accademia gallery *(p140).* It formerly embellished the oratory (located just off the main hall) where the Reliquary of the True Cross is still carefully preserved.

Palazzetto Bru Zane

📍 D5 🏠 Calle dell'Olio, San Polo 2368 🚢 San Tomà 🌐 bru-zane.com

Years of extensive restoration works have returned this 17th-century palazzetto to its

⑪ San Giacomo dell'Orio

📍E4 🏛Campo San Giacomo dell'Orio, Santa Croce 🚉Riva di Biasio or San Stae ⏱10:30am-4:30pm Mon-Sat 🚫1 Jan, Easter, 15 Aug, 25 Dec 🌐chorusvenezia.org

This church is a focal point of a quiet quarter of Santa Croce. The name *dell'Orio* may derive from a laurel tree *(alloro)* that once stood near the church.

Founded in the 9th century, rebuilt in 1225 and repeatedly modified, it exhibits a rare mix of architectural styles. The basilica ground plan, campanile and Byzantine columns survive from the 13th century. The ship's keel roof and the columns are from the Gothic period and the apses are Renaissance. The sacristy ceiling was decorated by Veronese and there are some gripping altar paintings. The main altarpiece, *Virgin Mary and Child with Apostles and Saints*, was painted in 1546 by Lorenzo Lotto, an artist who was born in Venice but travelled widely in search of commissions; as a result, few of his works are found in Venice.

⑫ San Nicolò da Tolentino

📍C5 🏛Campo dei Tolentini, Santa Croce 🚉Piazzale Roma ☎041 522 21 60 ⏱8:30am-noon, 4:40-6:30pm daily 🚫During Mass

Close to Piazzale Roma is this imposing 17th-century church with a huge Classical portico. The interior, magnificently decorated with 17th-century paintings, is the resting place of Francesco Morosini (d 1678), Venetian patriarch and doge.

A cannonball embedded in the façade is a memento of an Austrian bombardment during the siege of 1849.

former glory, and the unique acoustics of the Bru Zane's 100-seat auditorium attract world-famous musicians from around the globe once again. Previously home to the Habsburgs, one of the most prominent dynasties of Europe from the 15th to the 20th century, and still bearing their crest on the doorbell, Bru Zane was bought by the Swiss Fondation Bru and now houses the prestigious Centre de Musique Romantique Française. Although the name suggests a particular focus on French romantic music, there are regular forays into many other genres and eras.

The palace also has a delightful leafy courtyard with plenty open-air seating that can be enjoyed whether you are coming for the music or not. Free guided tours of the palace are held every Thursday at 3:30pm.

→ Corinthian capitals on the Classical façade of San Nicolo de Tolentino

⑬ 🚶

Museo di Storia Naturale

📍E4 🏛Canal Grande, Santa Croce 1730 🚏San Stae 🕐Jun–Oct: 10am–6pm Tue–Sun; Nov–May: 9am–5pm Tue–Fri, 10:30am–5pm Sat & Sun 🌐msn.visitmuve.it

The Museo di Storia Naturale (Natural History Museum) has occuied the Fondaco dei Turchi since 1923. There is a collection of stuffed animals, crustacea and dinosaur fossils and a section on lagoon life. Prize exhibits include a skeleton of an *Ouranosaurus nigeriensis*, 7 m (23 ft) long and 3.6 m (12 ft) tall, and a fossil of a *Sarcosuchus imperator* – an ancestor of the crocodile. The building itself has a chequered history. In the 13th century it was one of the largest palazzos on the Grand Canal. In 1381 it was bought by the state for the Dukes of Ferrara and its lavish rooms were used for banquets and state functions. In 1621 the Turks set it up as a warehouse *(fondaco)*, but when commerce with the Orient declined, the structure fell into disrepair until, roused by Ruskin's passionate interest, the Austrians began restoration work in the 1850s.

⑭ 🚶 🛍

Museo di Palazzo Mocenigo

📍E4 🏛Salizzada San Stae, Santa Croce 1992 🚏San Stae 🕐10:30am–5pm Tue–Sun (Nov–Mar: to 4:30pm) 🚫1 Jan, 1 May, 25 Dec 🌐mocenigo.visitmuve.it

One of the oldest Venetian families, the Mocenigos produced seven doges. There were various branches of the family, one of which resided in this 17th-century mansion. Count Alvise Nicolò Mocenigo, the last of this particular branch, died in 1954, bequeathing the palace to the Comune di Venezia (city authorities).

The entrance façade is unremarkable, but the interior is elegantly furnished and gives you a rare opportunity of seeing inside a palazzo preserved more or less as it was in the 18th century. The frescoed ceilings and other works of art are celebrations of the family's achievements. The illustrious Mocenigos are portrayed in a frieze around the *portego* on the first floor.

The Museo del Tessuto e del Costume inside the house contains antique fabrics and exquisitely made costumes. It also has five fascinating rooms dedicated to the history of perfumes and

Butterflies *(inset)* on display at the Museo di Storia Naturale ↓

←

Rodin's third plaster version of *The Burghers of Calais* in Ca' Pesaro

EAT

Al Nono Risorto
Traditional dishes at decent prices. Check out the wisteria-clad courtyard.

F5 Sottoportico di Siora Bettina, Santa Croce 2338 nono risortovenezia.com

€€€

Alla Zucca
Though the menu is pretty meaty, this fabulous neighbourhood restaurant was one of the first to be vegetarian-friendly.

E4 Ponte del Megio, Santa Croce 1762 lazucca.it

€€€

Antiche Carampane
Difficult to find, but worth it, this Venetian stalwart serves up fish dishes with style.

F5 Rio Terà delle Carampane, San Polo 1911 antiche carampane.it

€€€

perfume-making, with videos, sensorial experiences and a wonderful collection of perfume bottles.

 15

San Stae

F4 Campo San Stae, Santa Croce San Stae 1:45–4:30pm Mon-Sat 1 Jan, 25 Dec chorus venezia.org

Restored in 1977–8 by the Pro Venezia Foundation, San Stae (or Sant'Eustachio) has a spick-and-span sculpted

façade. It was built in 1709 by Domenico Rossi, and works by Piazzetta, Tiepolo and other celebrated 18th-century artists adorn the chancel. Near the second altar on the left is a bust of Antonio Foscarini, executed for treason in 1622 but then pardoned the following year.

 16

Ca' Pesaro

F4 Canal Grande, Santa Croce 2076 San Stae 10:30am–6pm Tue-Sun (Nov-Mar: to 4:30pm); last entry 30 mins earlier 1 Jan, 1 May, 25 Dec capesaro.visitmuve.it

It took 58 years to complete this magnificent Baroque palace. Built for the Pesaro family, it was the masterpiece of Baldassare Longhena, who worked on it until his death in 1682. Antonio Gaspari then took over Longhena's design, eventually completing the structure in 1710.

In the 19th century the Duchess of Bevilacqua La Masa bequeathed the palace to the city for exhibiting the works of unestablished Venetian artists. The Galleria Internazionale d'Arte Moderna was founded in 1897. Today this features a permanent exhibition of artists such as Bonnard, Matisse, Miró, Klee, Klimt and Kandinsky, in addition to works by celebrated Italian artists of the 19th and 20th centuries.

The building also contains the Museo d'Arte Orientale, which has an idiosyncratic collection of Chinese and Japanese artifacts collected by the Count of Bardi during his 19th-century travels.

A SHORT WALK
SAN POLO

Distance 2 km (1.5 miles) **Time** 35 minutes minutes **Nearest Vaporetto** San Stae

The Rialto Bridge and markets dominate this area of Venice, and are a huge draw for locals and visitors alike. Traditionally the city's commercial quarter, it was here that bankers, brokers and merchants once conducted their affairs. Today, the streets are no longer lined with stalls selling spices and fine fabrics, but the food markets and pasta shops are an enticing sight. The old-fashioned standing-only bars called *bacari* are filled with locals, especially at aperitivo time. In sharp contrast is the crowded Riva del Vin to the south, where tourists tend to congregate.

Inside **San Cassiano** (p108) *church is a carved altar (1696) and* Crucifixion *by Tintoretto (1568).*

START

The crooked **Ponte Storto** *leads under a portico to Calle Stretta, a narrow alley that is only 1m (3 ft) wide in places.*

↑ Campo San Cassiano, a world away from the busy Riva del Vin

Sant'Aponal, *founded in the 11th century, rebuilt in the 15th, is now deconsecrated.*

Riva del Vin *is one of the few accessible quaysides along the Grand Canal.*

SAN SILVESTRO

0 metres   75 N
0 yards   75 ↑

Did You Know?

The aptly named Riva del Vin was where wine was shipped in and out of the city in the 19th century.

Locator Map
For more detail see p100

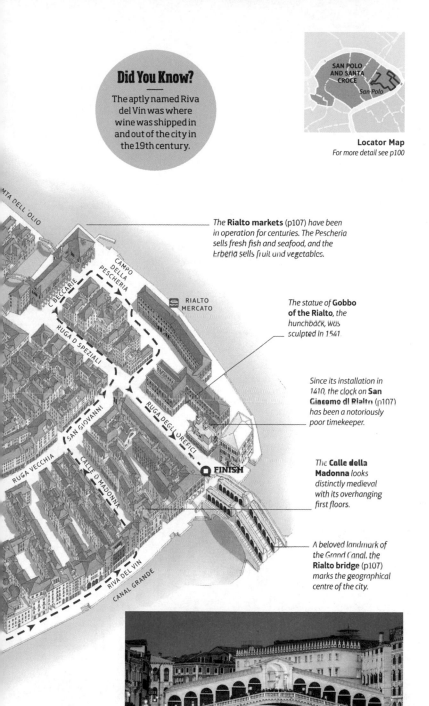

The **Rialto markets** (p107) have been in operation for centuries. The Pescheria sells fresh fish and seafood, and the Erberia sells fruit and vegetables.

The statue of **Gobbo of the Rialto**, the hunchback, was sculpted in 1541.

Since its installation in 1410, the clock on **San Giacomo di Rialto** (p107) has been a notoriously poor timekeeper.

The **Calle della Madonna** looks distinctly medieval with its overhanging first floors.

A beloved landmark of the Grand Canal, the **Rialto bridge** (p107) marks the geographical centre of the city.

→ A gondola passes under the Rialto Bridge at dusk

CASTELLO

The largest of Venice's *sestieri*, Castello stretches from San Marco and Cannaregio in the west to the modern blocks of Sant'Elena in the east. The area takes its name from the 8th-century fortress that once stood on what is now San Pietro, the island that was once the religious focus of the city. The church here was the episcopal see from the 9th century and the city's cathedral from 1451 to 1807.

The industrial hub of Castello was the Arsenale, where the greatest shipyard in the world produced Venice's indomitable fleet of warships. It was once the heart of the Serenissima Republic's maritime wealth, but following the Fall of the Republic in 1797, Napoleon destroyed the docks and stripped the *Bucintoro* (the ceremonial ship of the doge), its cannons and bronzes melted down to contribute to victory monuments celebrating the French Revolution. Castello's most popular and solidly commercial area is the Riva degli Schiavoni promenade. Behind the waterfront it is comparatively quiet, characterised by narrow alleys, elegantly faded palazzos and fine churches, including the great Santi Giovanni e Paolo.

CANNAREGIO p154

Ospedale

Canale delle Fondamente Nuove

San Lazzaro ai dei Mendicanti

Santi Maria dei Miracoli

Ospedale Civile

Scuola Grande di San Marco **13** Santi Giovanni e Paolo **1**

Statue of Colleoni **11** **15** Ospedaletto

San Francesco della Vigna **14**

5 BARBARIA DELLE TOLE

Rio di San Marina

CAMPO SAN MARINA

Rio di San Giovanni Laterano

CASTELLO

Campo Santa Maria Formosa **12**

12 **11**

San Lorenzo **17**

Santa Maria Formosa

Palazzo Grimani **10**

BORGOLOCO SAN LORENZO

Santa Maria della Fava

8

Fondazione Querini Stampalia **9**

Scuola di San Giorgio degli Schiavoni **16**

Museo Guidi

4

1

San Giorgio dei Greci **3**

SAN MARCO p72

Museo Diocesano d'Arte Sacra **6**

3

San Zaccaria **5**

Basilica di San Marco

CAMPO S. PROVOLO

CAMPO SAN ZACCARIA

San Giovanni in Bragora **18**

9

PIAZZA SAN MARCO

Palazzo Ducale

Bridge of Sighs **8**

2 Hotel Danieli

10 La Pietà **4** **7**

RIVA DEGLI SCHIAVONI

7 Zecca

8 Ponte della Paglia

7 Riva degli Schiavoni

San Marco-Zaccaria

Arsenale

San Marco-Giardinetti

San Marco-Vallaresso

Bacino di San Marco

Canale di

8

CASTELLO

San Giorgio

CAMPO SAN GIORGIO

San Giorgio Maggiore

SAN GIORGIO MAGGIORE

9

| 0 metres | 250 |
| 0 yards | 250 |

N

H   J   K

CASTELLO

Must See

1. Santi Giovanni e Paolo

Experience More

2. Hotel Danieli
3. San Giorgio dei Greci
4. La Pietà
5. San Zaccaria
6. Museo Diocesano d'Arte Sacra
7. Riva degli Schiavoni
8. Ponte della Paglia and Bridge of Sighs
9. Fondazione Querini Stampalia
10. Palazzo Grimani
11. Statue of Colleoni
12. Campo Santa Maria Formosa
13. Scuola Grande di San Marco
14. San Francesco della Vigna
15. Ospedaletto
16. Scuola di San Giorgio degli Schiavoni
17. San Lorenzo
18. San Giovanni in Bragora
19. Via Giuseppe Garibaldi
20. San Pietro di Castello
21. Arsenale
22. Museo Storico Navale

Eat

1. Da Remigio
2. Al Covo
3. Alla Rivetta
4. Aciugheta
5. Bacarando Ai Corazzieri
6. Trattoria Giorgione
7. MET

Stay

8. Aqua Palace
9. Hotel Metropole
10. Londra Palace

Shop

11. Libreria Acqua Alta
12. Papier Maché

SANTI GIOVANNI E PAOLO

📍J5 🏠 Campo Santi Giovanni e Paolo (also signposted San Zanipolo)
🚤 Fondamente Nuove, Ospedale Civile 🕐 9am–6pm Mon–Sat, noon–6pm Sun
📅 1 Jan, 25 Dec 🌐 basilicasantigiovanniepaolo.it

Known colloquially as San Zanipolo, the vast and austere Santi Giovanni e Paolo vies with the Frari for the top spot as Venice's greatest Gothic church. Located in the Castello area, it is slightly off the tourist track, meaning it is often very quiet.

Known as the Pantheon of Venice, this striking church, built by the Dominicans in the 14th century, houses monuments to more than 25 doges. Among these are several fine works of art, executed by the Lombardi family and other leading sculptors. On arrival, visitors enter through a doorway decorated with Byzantine reliefs and carvings by celebrated Italian sculptor Bartolomeo Bon. The doorway itself is thought to be one of Venice's earliest Renaissance architectural works. The commanding bronze statue at the opposite end of the church is a monument to Doge Sebastiano Venier, who was Commander of the Fleet at Lepanto. A mere few steps away lies the tomb of Andrea Vendramin, created by Pietro Lombardo in 1476–8, in the form of a Roman triumphal arch.

Further up on the right is the grand Cappella di San Domenico, containing St Catherine of Siena's foot in a precious reliquary. The chapel's ceiling was frescoed by Giovanni Battista Piazzetta; his *Glory of St Dominic*, painted in 1727, displays a mastery of colour, perspective and foreshortening that is said to have had a profound influence on the young Tiepolo.

LOST FOREVER

Like many buildings in Venice, this basilica has suffered its share of fires, none more devastating than the one of 15 August 1867 in the rosary chapel, built in 1582 to commemorate the Venetian Republic's victory in Lepanto. Not only was the chapel entirely gutted, masterpieces by Titian, Tintoretto and Giovanni Bellini placed there for safekeeping were all lost. The fire is believed to have been started by anti-Catholic arsonists, and restoration work on the chapel was not completed until 1959.

↑ The serene interior is packed with works by Venetian masters

↑ Brick façade of Santi Giovanni e Paolo on its quiet *campo*

Highlights

Giovanni Bellini

△ Giovanni Bellini's magnificent polyptych of *San Vincenzo Ferrerei* (1465) still hangs in its original frame.

Lorenzo Lotto

The right transept contains Lorenzo Lotto's *St Antonine Distributing Alms* (1542), bursting with angels and cherubs.

Alvise Vivarini

The sacristy houses Alvise Vivarini's exquisite *Christ Carrying the Cross* (1474), restored by Save Venice.

Cima da Conegliano

▽ The bright colours of Cima da Conegliano's *Coronation of the Virgin* (1490) remain vibrant and remarkable.

Paolo Veronese

△ Paolo Veronese has not one, but three ceiling panels in the rosary chapel.

EXPERIENCE MORE

② Hotel Danieli

📍J7 🏠Riva degli Schiavoni 4196 🚤San Zaccaria
🌐danielihotelvenice.com

One of the most celebrated hotels in all of Europe, Hotel Danieli's deep-pink façade is a landmark on the Riva degli Schiavoni. Built in the 14th century, it became famous as the venue for the first opera performed in Venice, Monteverdi's *Proserpina Rapita* (1630). The palace – described as "the most noble in Venice" – became a hotel in 1822 and soon gained popularity with the literary and artistic set. Over the years, famous guests have included the likes of Balzac, Proust, Dickens, Cocteau, Ruskin, Debussy and Wagner. In the 1830s Room 10 witnessed an episode in the love affair between the French poet and dramatist Alfred de Musset, and novelist George Sand: when de Musset fell ill after a surfeit of orgies, Sand ran off with her Venetian doctor.

↑ The ornate interior of Hotel Danieli *(inset)*, a favoured haunt of Hollywood royalty

③ San Giorgio dei Greci

📍K6 📞041 523 95 69
🚤San Zaccaria ⏰9am-1:30pm, 2:30-4:30pm Mon, Wed-Sun (Sun am for Mass only)

The most remarkable feature of this 16th-century Greek church is the listing campanile, which looks as if it is about to topple into the Rio dei Greci. Inside is the *matroneo* – the gallery where, in keeping with Greek Orthodox custom, the women sat apart from the men. Note also the iconostasis separating the sanctuary from the nave. The nearby Scuola di San Nicolò dei Greci, redesigned in 1678, is now the **Museo dell'Icone** of the Hellenic Institute.

Museo dell'Icone
☎ 041 522 65 81 ⏰ 9am–5pm daily

La Pietà

📍 K7 🏛 Riva degli Schiavoni 🚉 San Zaccaria ⏰ 10am–6pm Tue–Sun 🌐 pietavenezia.org

The church of La Pietà (or Santa Maria della Visitazione) dates from the 15th century. It was rebuilt in 1745–60 by Giorgio Massari, and the Classical façade was added in 1906. It has an elegant oval interior. The resplendent ceiling fresco, *Triumph of Faith* (1755), was painted by Giambattista Tiepolo.

The church formed part of the Ospedale della Pietà, a convent, music school and foundling home for orphans; a large bas-relief by Marsili above the main entrance represents Charity. The institution was so popular that a warning plaque threatening damnation to parents who passed off their children as orphans was placed on the side wall. From 1703 until 1740, Antonio Vivaldi directed the musical groups and wrote numerous pieces for the Pietà choir, and the church became famous for its performances.

It is now a popular venue for concerts, with an emphasis on Vivaldi. These are held throughout the year, usually on Mondays and Thursdays.

Tours of the church are offered from Tuesday to Friday; they start at noon.

→

The Flamboyant Gothic San Zaccaria dominates the quiet campo

> **San Zaccaria's adjoining Benedictine convent, which had close links with the church, became quite notorious for the riotous behaviour of its nuns.**

San Zaccaria

📍 J6 🏛 Campo San Zaccaria ☎ 041 522 12 57 🚉 San Zaccaria ⏰ 10am–noon, 4–6pm Mon–Sat; 4–6pm Sun & pub hols

Set in a quiet square a stone's throw from the Riva degli Schiavoni, this church blends Flamboyant Gothic and Classical Renaissance styles. Founded in the 9th century, San Zaccaria was completely rebuilt between 1444 and 1515. Antonio Gambello began the façade in Gothic style and, when Gambello died in 1481, Mauro Coducci completed the upper section, adding all the Classical detail.

San Zaccaria's adjoining Benedictine convent, which had close links with the church, became quite notorious for the riotous behaviour of its nuns. The majority them were Venetian nobility, sent to the convent to avoid the expense of a dowry. Every Easter the doge came with his entourage to San Zaccaria – a custom which originated as an expression of gratitude to the nuns, who had relinquished part of their garden so that Piazza San Marco could be enlarged.

The artistic highlight of the interior (illuminate with coins in the meter) is Giovanni Bellini's sumptuously coloured *Madonna and Child with Saints* (1505).

On the right of the church is a door to the Chapel of St Athanasius, which leads to the Chapel of San Tarasio. The chapel is decorated with vault frescoes (1442) by Andrea del Castagno, and Gothic polyptychs painted in 1443–4 by Antonio Vivarini and Giovanni d'Alemagna.

The relics of eight *doges* lie buried in the waterlogged crypt. There is a small charge to visit the chapels and crypt.

6

Museo Diocesano d'Arte Sacra

J7 **Sant'Apollonia, Ponte della Canonica** **San Zaccaria** **10am–7pm daily** **Pub hols** **veneziaupt.org**

An architectural gem in a city that brims with architectural wonders, the cloister of Sant'Apollonia is the only Romanesque building in Venice. Only a few steps from Piazza San Marco, it provides a quiet retreat from the Piazza.

The monastery was once the home of Benedictine monks. In 1976 its cloisters became the home of the Diocesan Museum of Sacred Art, founded to provide a haven for works of art from closed or deconsecrated churches. The collection includes paintings, statues, crucifixes and many pieces of valuable silver. There are two workshops, staffed by volunteers who restore the paintings and statues. The collection is ever-changing, but among the major permanent exhibits are works by Luca Giordano (1634–1705), which came from the Church of Sant'Aponal, an impressive

GREAT VIEW
Gaze Across the Lagoon

It might be a cliché, but nothing can beat the view across the pale blue waters of the Venetian Lagoon to the island of San Giorgio Maggiore from the Riva degli Schiavoni.

late 15th-century crucifix from San Pietro di Castello, and a 16th-century wood and crystal tabernacle.

7

Riva degli Schiavoni

K7 **San Zaccaria**

The sweeping promenade that forms the southern quayside of Castello was named after the traders from Dalmatia (Schiavonia) who used to moor their boats and barges here. For those who arrive in Venice by water, this long curving quayside is a

Crowds swarm along the busy Riva degli Schiavoni at dusk ↓

spectacular introduction to the charms of the city.

Originally formed from silt dredged up from the lagoon, the quay was widened and paved in the 18th century to create an elegant promenade. At its western end, close to Piazza San Marco, it teems during the day with tourists thronging the souvenir stalls and people hurrying to and from the vaporetto stops.

The Riva degli Schiavoni has always been busy with boats. Canaletto's drawings in the 1740s and 1750s show the Riva bustling with gondolas, sailing boats and barges. The gondolas are still here, but it is also chock-a-block with water taxis, vaporettos, excursion boats and tugs. Naval ships and the massive – and controversial – forms of ocean liners can also often be seen. After huge local protest, from 2021, giant cruise ships will be banned from St Mark's Basin.

The modern annexe of the Hotel Danieli (p122) caused a great furore when it was built in 1948. Intruding on a waterfront graced by fine Venetian palaces and mansions, its stark outline is still something of an eyesore. The annexe occupies the spot where Doge Vitale Michiel II was stabbed to death in 1172. Three centuries earlier, in 864, Doge Pietro Tradonico had suffered the same fate in nearby Campo San Zaccaria.

↑ Gondolas glide along the Rio di Palazzo below the Ponte dei Sospiri (Bridge of Sighs)

EAT

Da Remigio
Venetian seafood is on the menu at this charming trattoria; the *risotto di pesce* is a particular highlight.

⊙K6 ⌂Salizzada dei Greci 3416 📞041 523 00 89 🕒12:30-2pm Wed-Mon, 7-10pm Wed-Sun

€€€

Al Covo
Tucked away in a hidden square, a husband and-wife team focus on fish. Save room for one of Diane's desserts.

⊙L7 ⌂Campiello della Pescaria 3968 🕒12:45-2pm, 7:30-10pm Fri-Tue ⌨ristorantealcovo.com

€€€

Alla Rivetta
A popular haunt of gondoliers, the tiny Alla Rivetta serves seasonal fish, including *canoce* (mantis shrimp) and *folpetti* (baby octopus).

⊙J6 ⌂Ponte San Provolo 4625 📞041 528 73 02 🕒Noon-2:30pm, 7-10:30pm Mon-Sat

€€€

8
Ponte della Paglia and Bridge of Sighs

⊙J7 🚤San Zaccaria

The name of the Ponte della Paglia may derive from the boats that once moored here to off-load their cargoes of straw (*paglia*). Originally built in 1360, the existing structure dates from 1847. According to legend, the Bridge of Sighs, built in 1600 to link the Palazzo Ducale (*p82*) with the New Prisons, takes its name from the lamentations of the prisoners as they made their way over to the offices of the feared State Inquisitors, catching what might be their last glimpse of Venice through the stone-grilled windows. Access to the bridge is available to the public via the Palazzo Ducale (*p82*).

9
Fondazione Querini Stampalia

⊙J6 ⌂Campo Santa Maria Formosa 🚤San 🕒10am-6pm Tue-Sun; Library: 10am-9pm Tue-Sat, 10am-7pm Sun ⌨querinistampalia.org

The large Palazzo Querini Stampalia was commissioned in the 16th century by the descendants of the Venetian Querini family. Being great art lovers, they filled their palace with all manner of fine paintings. In 1868 the last member of the dynasty bequeathed the palace and the family art to the foundation that bears his name. The paintings include works by Giovanni Bellini, Giambattista Tiepolo and some vignettes by Pietro and Alessandro Longhi. The library on the first floor is a public facility with over 200,000 books, plus newspapers and magazines: bring photo ID so that the staff can issue you with a reader's card.

Did You Know?

In 1819, an escaped circus elephant sought refuge in Riva degli Schiavoni's Church of Sant'Antonin.

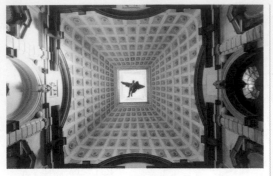

↑ The fabulous ceiling of Palazzo Grimani's Tribuna room, modelled on Rome's Pantheon

🔟 ✏️
Palazzo Grimani

📍F6 🏛️Ramo Grimani, 4858 Castello 🚊San Zaccaria, Ospedale Civile 🕙10am-7pm Tue-Sun 🌐palazzogrimani.org

Palazzo Grimani was once a famous residence-museum. The building housed a fine collection of antiquities collected by the two Grimani brothers, Giovanni, Patriarch of Acquileia, and Vettore, Procurator de Supra for the Venetian Republic, who renovated their grandfather's palace in the mid-16th century. The result is a magnificient work of architecture, which combines Tuscan and Roman elements with the original Venetian ones. The Roman courtyard and staircase are its finest examples.

Many of the Grimani brothers' treasures are now housed in the Museo Archeologico (p88), but even though the rooms are unfurnished, they are a delight: the decoration is rich, with elaborate marble and stucco work, statues, fireplaces and stunning frescoes. Of particular note are the Tribuna and the Sala a Fogliami (Foliage Room). Temporary exhibitions are also held at the palazzo.

1️⃣1️⃣
Statue of Colleoni

📍J5 🏛️Campo Santi Giovanni e Paolo 🚊Ospedale Civile

Bartolomeo Colleoni, the famous *condottiere* or commander of mercenaries, left his fortune to the Republic on condition that his statue was placed in front of San Marco. A prominent statue in the Piazza would have broken with precedent, so the Senate cunningly had Colleoni raised before the Scuola di San Marco instead of the basilica. A touchstone of early Renaissance sculpture, the equestrian statue of the proud warrior is by the Florentine Andrea Verrocchio and, after his death, was cast in bronze by Alessandro Leopardi. The statue has a strong sense of power and movement which arguably ranks it alongside works of Donatello.

MAURO CODUCCI

Little is known about Italian architect Mauro Coducci, who designed both the church of Santa Maria Formosa and the delightful façade of the Scuolo Grande di San Marco. Yet this enigmatic man from Bergamo has left an indelible mark on Venice. In 1469 he started building the church on the island of San Michele (p182), thus creating the first truly Renaissance building in Venice. His other projects include the church of San Zaccaria (p123) and the Ca' Vendramin Calergi palace.

1️⃣2️⃣
Campo Santa Maria Formosa

📍J5, J6 🚊Fondamente Nuove, Rialto

Large, rambling and flanked by handsome palaces, this market square is one of the most characteristic *campi* of Venice. On the southern side is the church of **Santa Maria Formosa**, distinctive for its swelling apses. Built on ancient foundations, the church was designed by Mauro Coducci in 1492,

←

Late 15th-century statue of Bartolomeo Colleoni, Renaissance soldier of fortune

but took over a century to assume its current form. Unusually, it has two main façades – one overlooking the *campo*, the other the canal. Its most notable feature is the stone face at its foot.

Inside, Palma il Vecchio's polyptych *St Barbara and Saints* (c 1523) ranks among great Venetian masterpieces. Palma's portrayal of the dignified figure of St Barbara glorifies Venice's ideal female beauty. St Barbara was the patron saint of soldiers: in wartime they prayed to her for protection; in victory they came for thanksgiving.

Santa Maria Formosa

🕐 10:30am–4:30pm Mon–Sat
📅 1 Jan, Easter, 15 Aug, 25 Dec
🌐 chorusvenezia.org

13

Scuola Grande di San Marco

📍 J5 🏛 Campo Santi Giovanni e Paolo
🚇 Ospedale Civile
🕐 9:30am–5:30pm Tue–Sat
🌐 scuolagrandesanmarco.it

Few hospitals can boast as rich and unusual a façade as that of Venice's Ospedale

↑ The soaring marble façade of the Scuola Grande di San Marco

Civile. It was built originally as the seat of one of the six great confraternities of the city, but this 13th-century building was destroyed by fire in 1485. The Scuola was rebuilt in its current form at the end of the 15th century. The delightful asymmetrical façade, with its arcades, marble panels and trompe l'oeil effects, was the work of Pietro Lombardo working in conjunction with Giovanni Buora. The upper order was finished by Italian architect Mauro Coducci in 1495.

The interior was revamped in the 19th century and, since then, most of the artistic masterpieces the Scuola once contained have been dispersed. The library, boasting a fine carved 16th-century ceiling, is now a Museum of the History of Medicine, displaying antique texts and instruments. The hospital chapel, the Church of San Lazzaro dei Mendicanti, contains an early Tintoretto, *Saint Ursula and the 11,000 Virgins*, together with works by Veronese.

SHOP

Libreria Acqua Alta

Chaos reigns in this whimsical bookshop. Bathtubs and boats are filled with books, a staircase of tomes leads you to a towering view in the courtyard and cats lounge across bookshelves.

📍 J5 🏛 Calle Lunga Santa Maria Formosa 5176/b 📞 041 296 08 41
🕐 9am–8pm daily

Papier Mâché

Merging traditional techniques with contemporary design, this Venetian studio and shop has been producing masks for over 30 years. Hand-painted ceramics and wooden frames are also available here.

📍 J5 🏛 Calle Lunga Santa Maria Formosa 5175/b
🌐 papiermache.it

The tranquil colonnaded cloister of San Francesco della Vigna ↑

⑭
San Francesco della Vigna

📍L5 🏛️Campo di San Francesco della Vigna 📞041 520 61 02 🚉Celestia 🕐9am–noon, 3–5:30pm Tue–Sun

The name "della Vigna" derives from a vineyard that was bequeathed to the Franciscans in 1253. The church which the order built here in the 13th century was rebuilt under Jacopo Sansovino in 1534, with a façade added in 1562–72 by Palladio. The interior has a rich collection of works of art, including sculpture by Alessandro Vittoria, Paolo Veronese's *The Holy Family with Saints* (1562) and Antonio da Negroponte's *Virgin and Child* (c 1450). The *Madonna*

> **Did You Know?**
>
> Usefully meaning both "hello" and "goodbye", the word *"ciao"* originated in Venice.

and Child with Saints (1507) by Giovanni Bellini hangs near the cloister.

---

⑮
Ospedaletto

📍J5 🏛️Calle Barbaria delle Tole, 6691 Castello 📞041 532 29 20 🚉Ospedale Civile 🕐On request

Beyond the south flank of Santi Giovanni e Paolo *(p120)* is the façade of the Ospedaletto or Santa Maria dei Derelitti. The Ospedaletto was set up by the Republic in 1527 as a charitable institution to care for the sick and aged, and to educate orphans and abandoned girls. Such an education consisted largely of the study of music. The girls performed in choirs and orchestras, bringing in funds for the 1776 *Sala della Musica*, which became the main performance venue and has frescoes by Jacopo Guarana.

The church, which formed part of the Ospedaletto, was built by Andrea Palladio in 1575. Its façade was added in 1674 by Baldassare Longhena. The huge, hideous heads on the façade have been

described as anti-Classical abominations, likened to diseased figures and swollen fruit. The interior of the church is decorated with notable 18th-century paintings, including *The Sacrifice of Isaac* (1720) by Giambattista Tiepolo.

---

⑯
Scuola di San Giorgio degli Schiavoni

📍K6 🏛️Calle Furlani, Castello 3959A 📞041 522 88 28 🚉San Zaccaria 🕐2:45–6pm Mon, 9:15am–1pm, 2:45–6pm Tue–Sat, 9:15am–1pm Sun

Within this surprisingly simple *scuola* are some of the finest paintings of Vittore Carpaccio, which were commissioned by the Schiavoni community in Venice in the 15th century.

From the earliest days of the Republic, Venice forged trade links with the nearby coastal region of Schiavonia (Dalmatia) across the Adriatic. By 1420 permanent Venetian rule was established there, and many of the Schiavoni came to live in Venice. By the mid-15th century the Slav

> From the earliest days of the Republic, Venice forged trade links with the nearby coastal region of Schiavonia (Dalmatia) across the Adriatic Sea.

colony in the city had grown considerably and the state gave permission for them to found their own confraternity.

The Scuola was first established in 1451. It is a delightful spot to admire exceptional artworks by Carpaccio, and it has changed very little since it was rebuilt in 1551. The canvasses show scenes from the lives of saints. Outstanding among them are *St George Slaying the Dragon*, *St Jerome Leading the Tamed Lion to the Monastery* and *The Vision of St Jerome*.

⑰ San Lorenzo

📍 K5 ⬭ Campo San Lorenzo 🚤 San Zaccaria 🔒 For restoration

The church of San Lorenzo's only claim to fame is as the alleged burial place of Marco Polo. Unfortunately, there is nothing to show for it because his sarcophagus disappeared

→

Walking on water: an infilled canal now forms Via Giuseppe Garibaldi

during rebuilding in 1592. Bar occasional use during Biennales, the church has lain empty for decades, the foundations of the medieval structure and marble floor having been badly damaged by water seeping in from the adjacent canal. However, the deconsecrated church has now undergone extensive restoration thanks to the Thyssen-Bornemisza Art Contemporary Foundation's Ocean Space project, which focuses on issues surrounding climate change and the ocean. As well as art exhibitions, the San Lorenzo space will house educational and outreach programmes, as well as public workshops and climate-change initiatives.

⑱ San Giovanni in Bragora

📍 K7 ⬭ Campo Bandiera e Moro 📞 041 520 59 06 🚤 Arsenale 🕐 9am-noon, 3-7:15pm Mon-Sat, 3-7pm Sun (Jun-Aug: 4-7pm)

The foundations of this simple church date back to ancient times but the existing building is essentially Gothic (1475–9). The intimate interior has major works of art which demonstrate the transition from Gothic to early Renaissance. Bartolomeo Vivarini's altarpiece, *Madonna and Child with Saints* (1478), is clearly Gothic. In stark contrast with this is Cima da Conegliano's *Baptism of Christ* (1492–5) on the main altar. This large-scale narrative scene, in a realistic landscape, set a precedent for later Renaissance painters.

⑲ Via Giuseppe Garibaldi

📍 M8, M7, N7 🚤 Giardini

This broad, busy street, now a hotspot for restaurants and nightlife, was created by Napoleon in 1808 by filling in a canal. John Cabot and his son Sebastian, the Italian navigators who in 1497 found what they thought to be the coast of China (but in reality was the Labrador coast of Newfoundland), once lived here. Near the end of the street a bronze monument of Garibaldi by Augusto Benvenuti (1885) marks the northern end of the Viale Garibaldi, which leads to the serene public gardens.

20

San Pietro di Castello

P7 ⌂ Calle Seconda de la Fava 70, Castello 🚏 San Pietro di Castello 🕐 10:30am–4:30pm Mon-Sat 🌐 chorusvenezia.org

The old church of San Pietro di Castello and its freestanding, tilting campanile overlook a grassy square. The church, probably founded in the 7th century, became the cathedral of Venice and remained so until 1807, when San Marco took its place. The existing church, built to a Palladian design in the mid-16th century, has several notable features. These include the Lando Chapel, the Vendramin Chapel and the marble throne from an Arabic tombstone, originally said to have been the Seat of St Peter. In the south of the square, is Mauro Coducci's elegant stone campanile, which was built in 1482–8; the cupola was added in 1670. Beside the church, the Palazzo Patriarcale was turned into barracks by Napoleon. The old cloisters are overgrown and strung with washing lines and fishing nets.

21

Arsenale

M7, M6 🚏 Arsenale

Heart of the city's maritime power, the Arsenale was founded in the 12th century and enlarged in the 14th to 16th centuries to become the greatest naval shipyard in the world. The word "arsenal" derives from the Arabic *darsina'a*, house of industry – which indeed it was. At its height in the 16th century, a workforce of 16,000, the *arsenalotti*, was employed to construct, equip and repair the great Venetian galleys. One of the first production lines in Europe, it was like a city within a city, with work-shops, warehouses, factories, foundries and docks. Surrounded by crenellated walls, the site today is largely abandoned. The huge gateway, built in the form of a triumphal arch in 1460 by Antonio Gambello, and the vast site are the only evidence of its former splendour.

The two lions guarding the entrance were pillaged from Piraeus (near Athens) in 1687. A third lion, bald and sitting upright, bears runic inscriptions on his haunches, and is thought to have been carved by Scandinavian mercenaries who fought for the Byzantine emperor.

By the 17th century, when the seeds of Venetian decline were well and truly sown, the *arsenalotti* numbered only 1,000. Following the fall of the Republic, Napoleon destroyed the docks and stripped the famed *Bucintoro* of its cannons and bronzes, which were melted down to make victory monuments to commemorate the French Revolution.

THE ASSEMBLY-LINE SYSTEM

During the Arsenale's heyday, a Venetian galley could be constructed and fully equipped with remarkable speed and efficiency. From the early 16th century, the hulls, which were built in the New Arsenal, were towed past a series of buildings in the Old Arsenal to be equipped in turn with rigging, ammunition and food supplies. By 1570, when Venice was faced with the Turkish threat to take Cyprus, the Arsenale was so fast that it could turn out an entire galley in 24 hours. Henry III of France witnessed the system's efficiency in 1574 when the *arsenalotti* completed a galley in the time it took for him to partake in a state feast.

Exterior wall of the Arsenale complex of ↓ former shipyards

↑ Celebrating the maritime splendour of the past, Venice's Museo Storico Navale

Today the area is under military administration and for the most part closed to the public. The bridge by the arched gateway affords partial views of the shipyard, as do vaporetto 4.1 and 4.2, which follow the perimeter of the Arsenale.

22

Museo Storico Navale

📍L7 🏠Riva San Biagio, Arsenale, Castello 2148 🚤Arsenale 🕐Apr-Oct: 8:45am-1:30pm Mon-Thu, 8:45am-5:30pm Fri & Sat, 10am-5pm Sun 🔒Nov-Mar, pub hols 🌐marina.difesa.it

It was the Austrians who, in 1815, first had the idea of assembling the remnants of the Venetian navy to create a historical naval museum. To a

series of models of vessels produced in the 17th century by the Arsenale they added all the naval paraphernalia they could obtain, including friezes preserved from famous galleys of the past, a variety of maritime firearms and a replica of the doge's ceremonial barge, the *Bucintoro*.

The collection has been housed in an ex-warehouse on the waterfront since 1958, and is now divided into the history of the Venetian navy, the Italian navy from 1860 to today, Adriatic vessels and a Swedish room. The layout and displays are excellent and there are informative explanations in English.

EAT

Aciugheta
Tasty *cichetti* and pizza in a friendly setting.

📍J6 🏠Campo S Filippo e Giacomo 4357 🌐aciugheta.com

€€€

Bacarando Ai Corazzieri
Great service, and tables outdoors in summer.

📍K6 🏠Calle dei Corazzieri 5899 📞041 528 9859 🚫Wed

€€€

Trattoria Giorgione
This lively restaurant serves hearty seafood.

📍M8 🏠Via Garibaldi 1533 🌐ristorante giorgione.it

€€€

MET
Elegant, Michelin-starred restaurant in the Hotel Metropole.

📍K7 🏠Riva degli Schiavoni 4149 🌐met restaurantvenice.com

€€€

A SHORT WALK
CASTELLO

Distance 1 km (0.5 miles) **Time** 10 minutes
Nearest Vaporetto San Zaccaria

A stroll along the Riva degli Schiavoni is an integral part of a visit to Venice. Glorious views of San Giorgio Maggiore compensate for the commercialized aspects of the quayside: souvenir stalls, excursion touts and an abundance of tourists. Associations with literary figures are plentiful. Petrarch lived at No. 4145, Henry James was offered lodgings at No. 4161, and Ruskin stayed at the Hotel Danieli. Inland, the quiet, unassuming streets and squares of Castello provide a contrast to the bustling waterfront.

Palazzo Trevisan-Cappello, used as a showroom for Murano glass, was the home of Bianca Cappello, wife of Francesco de' Medici.

The **Museo Diocesano d'Arte Sacra** (p124) is housed in the cloisters of the ancient Benedictine monastery of Sant'Apollonia.

START

CAMPO SS
FILIPPO E GIACOMO

CALLE DRIO LA CHIESA

SALIZZADA SAN PROV

RIO DEL PALAZZO

CALLE DEGLI ALBANESI

CALLE DELLE RASSE

RIO DEL VIN

Did You Know?

Named by Byron, The Bridge of Sighs is where the condemned would catch their final glimpse of freedom.

Crowds throng the Istrian stone **Ponte della Paglia** (p125) – the "straw bridge" – for the best views of the neighbouring Bridge of Sighs, the covered bridge that links the Palazzo Ducale to the old prisons.

RIVA DEGLI SCHIAVONI

The paved quayside of **Riva degli Schiavoni** (p124) was established over 600 years ago, and widened in 1782.

SAN ZACCARIA PAGLIA

SAN ZACCARIA DANIELI

Joseph da Niel, after whom **Hotel Danieli** (p122) is named, turned Palazzo Dandolo into a hub for 19th-century writers and artists.

0 metres 75
0 yards 75
N ↑

↑ Serene and unassuming Campo Santa Maria Formosa, Castello

Overlooking the quiet Fondamenta Osmarin is a fine Venetian Gothic palace – **Palazzo Priuli**. *The corner window is particularly beautiful, but the early 16th-century façade frescoes have now disappeared.*

Subsidence is the main cause of Venice's tilting bell towers; that of **San Giorgio dei Greci** (p122) *looks particularly perilous.*

Coducci added Renaissance details such as this panel to the Gothic façade of **San Zaccaria** (p123).

In Vivaldi's day, **La Pietà** (p123) *became world famous for the superb quality of its musical performances.*

RIO SAN PROVOLO

FMTA DELL' OSMARIN

CAMPO SAN PROVOLO

CALLE DEI GRECI

CAMPO SAN ZACCARIA

RIO DEI GRECI

CALLE BOSELLO

CALLE DELLA PIETA

RIVA DEGLI SCHIAVONI

FINISH

SAN ZACCARIA JOLANDA

MVE

Pensione Wildner *is where Henry James completed* Portrait of a Lady (1881).

The **Statue of Vittorio Emanuele II**, *the first king of a united Italy, was sculpted by Ettore Ferrari in 1887.*

↑ The Campanile of San Giorgio dei Greci towers over the Rio dei Greci

A LONG WALK
EASTERN CASTELLO

Distance 5 km (3 miles) **Walking time** 1 hour **Terrain** Paved and relatively flat **Nearest Vaporetto** Arsenale

This peaceful stroll takes you from the animated Castello quayside to the quieter eastern limits of the city. The focal point of the tour is the solitary island of San Pietro di Castello, site of the former cathedral of Venice. From here you head south to the island of Sant'Elena with its historic church and Venice's football stadium, and return via the public gardens along the scenic waterfront. There are a handful of simple cafés along the route; most are found on Via Giuseppe Garibaldi. Caffè Paradiso at the entrance to the Giardini Pubblici has excellent views, and the shady parks are a welcome retreat from the bustle of the city.

Locator Map
For more detail see p118

Campo Ruga *is a pretty, residential square, tucked between two quiet canals.*

Rio de le Vergini

Rio de San Gerolamo

SAL. STRETTA

CAMPO RUGA

Pause on the bridge for distant views of the **Arsenale** *(p130).*

Rio della Tana
FMTA DELLA TANA
FMTA DELLA TANA

CALLE COLTRERA

Rio di FMTA SANT'ANNA

Sant' Anna

Via Giuseppe Garibaldi (p129)

START FINISH

VIA GIUSEPPE GARIBALDI

John Cabot Home

RIVA DEI SETTE MARTIRI

CALLE SCHIAVONA

CALLE SAN DOMENICO

VIALE GARIBALDI

CALLE STUA

CALLE CORRERA

CALLE CATAPAN

SECCO

Garibaldi Monument

San Giusep

FONDAMENTA SAN GIUSEPPE

CAMPO S. GIUSEPPE

The first house on the right was **the home of John Cabot** *and his son Sebastian, the Italian navigators who in 1497 found what they thought to be the coast of China (it was actually the Labrador coast of Newfoundland).*

A bronze **monument of Garibaldi** *by Augusto Benvenuti (1885) marks the northern end of the Viale Garibaldi, which leads to the public gardens.*

Giardini

La Donna Partigiana

Giardini Pubblici

RIVA DEI PARTIGI

La Donna Partigiana *is a bronze memorial to all the women who lost their lives fighting in World War II. It can only be seen at low tide.*

The Church of **San Giuseppe.** *On the rare occasions it is open you can see Vincenzo Scamozzi's monument to Doge Marino Grimani.*

← Plant lovers adore the lush interior of the historic greenhouse in the Giardini Pubblici

The old church of **San Pietro di Castello** (p130) and its tilting campanile overlook a grassy square.

↑ Quiet backwaters of Canale di San Pietro di Castello

Basilica di San Pietro di Castello

Palazzo Patriarcale

Isola San Pietro di Castello

🚊 San Pietro di Castello

Beside the church, the **Palazzo Patriarcale** (Bishop's Palace) was turned into barracks by Napoleon.

CAMPO SAN PIETRO

onte San Pietro

Canale di San Pietro

FMTA QUINTAVALE

CAMPO DEI POMERI

Ponte de Quintavale

ant'Anna lonastery

ARINA

in San Giuseppe

RIO TERA SAN GIUSEPPE

Rio dei Giardini

ILUDO SANT'ANTONIO

VIALE 24 MAGGIO

Ponte de la Biennale

Ponte de Quintavale, a wooden bridge with good views of brightly coloured boats anchored on either side of the waterway, connects the island of San Pietro di Castello with the other islands.

The large and semi-derelict building at the foot of the bridge is the ex-church and monastery of **Sant'Anna**.

A small footbridge crosses over the **Rio dei Giardini**.

0 metres 200
0 yards 200
N ↑

Giardini della Biennale

CALLE DEL PASUBIO

VIALE QUATTRO NOVEMBRE

CALLE DEL SABOTINO

CALLE OSLAVIA

C PODGORA

VIALE PIAVE

Stadio

Ponte del Giardini

CALLE DUCA D'AOSTA

CALLE CONI ZUGNA

FMTA SANT'ELENA

CAMPO DELLA CHIESA

Sant'Elena is a pretty Gothic church founded in the 13th century.

VIALE SANT'ELENA

Church of Sant'Elena

VIALE QUATTRO NOVEMBRE

C BUCCARI

Rio di Sant'Elena

VIALE VITTORIO VENETO

🚊 Sant'Elena

Parco delle Rimembranze

Campo Sportivo

135

DORSODURO

Dorsoduro is named after the solid subsoil on which this area has been built up – the name translates from Italian to "hard backbone". Venice's first settlers selected this spot to build their homes precisely due to its comparatively high land, which formed the island now known as Giudecca, and the firm silt beneath the lagoon. Dorsoduro was originally centred around the Giudecca Canal, and domestic dwellings sprung up along both its banks from the 6th century. Settlement had spread across to the Grand Canal by the turn of the 11th century, and the Zattere, the long quayside looking across to Giudecca, became a focal point of Venetian daily life.

The later establishment of the Accademia, linked to the much sought-after *sestiere* of San Marco via the Ponte dell'Accademia, brought prosperity and foreign interest to the immediate area, while the western quarter and Giudecca remained much less refined and heavily industrialised until the end of World War II, when factories and shipyards went into decline. Giudecca is now a quiet residential neighborhood.

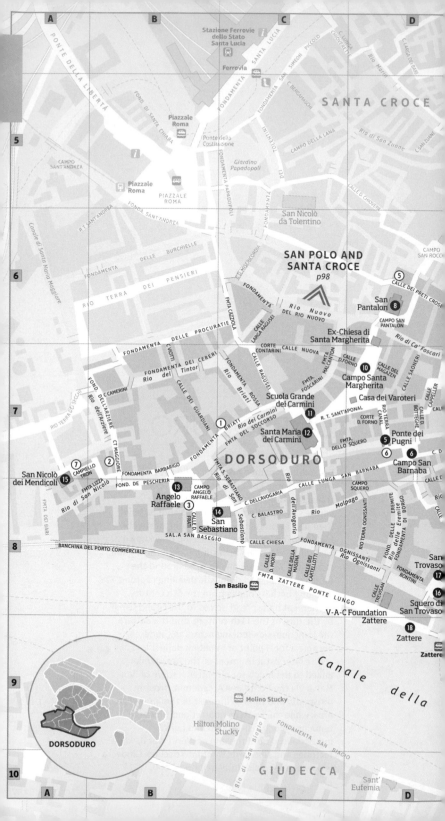

A B C D

5

STAZIONE FERROVIE dello Stato Santa Lucia
Ferrovia

SANTA CROCE

Piazzale Roma

Ponte della Costituzione

Giardino Papadopoli

San Nicolò da Tolentino

CAMPO DELLA LANA

Rio di San Zuane

CAMPO SAN ROCCO

CAMPO SANT'ANDREA

Piazzale Roma

PIAZZALE ROMA

Canale di Santa Maria Maggiore

6

SAN POLO AND SANTA CROCE
p98

Rio Nuovo DEL RIO NUOVO

San Pantalon **8**

5

CALLE DEI PRETI, CROSE

RIO TERRA DEI PENSIERI

FONDAMENTA DELLE BURCHIELLE

CAMPO SAN PANTALON

Ex-Chiesa di Santa Margherita

Rio di Ca' Foscari

7

FONDAMENTA DELLE PROCURATIE

FONDAMENTA DEI CERERI

CORTE CONTARINI

CALLE NUOVA

Campo Santa Margherita

Rio del Tintor

CALLE DEI GUARDIANI

Scuola Grande dei Carmini **11**

Casa dei Varoteri

Santa Maria dei Carmini **12**

Ponte dei Pugni **5**

DORSODURO

Campo San Barnaba **6**

San Nicolò dei Mendicoli **15** **7**

CAMPIELLO TRON **2**

FONDAMENTA BARBARIGO

CALLE LUNGA SAN BARNABA

CAMPO SQUERO

8

Angelo Raffaele **3** **13**

CAMPO ANGELO RAFFAELE

San Sebastiano **14**

Rio Malpaga

BANCHINA DEL PORTO COMMERCIALE

SAL. A SAN BASEGIO

CALLE CHIESA

FONDAMENTA OGNISSANTI

Rio Ognissanti

San Trovaso **17**

San Basilio

FMTA ZATTERE PONTE LUNGO

Squero di San Trovaso **16**

V-A-C Foundation Zattere

Zattere **18**

Zattere

9

Canale della

DORSODURO

Molino Stucky

Hilton Molino Stucky

FONDAMENTA SAN BIAGIO

10

GIUDECCA

Sant' Eufemia

A B C D

DORSODURO

Must Sees
1. Accademia
2. Peggy Guggenheim Collection

Experience More
3. Santa Maria della Salute
4. Campiello Barbaro
5. Ponte dei Pugni
6. Campo San Barnaba
7. Punta della Dogana
8. San Pantalon
9. Ca' Rezzonico
10. Campo Santa Margherita
11. Scuola Grande dei Carmini
12. Santa Maria dei Carmini
13. Angelo Raffaele
14. San Sebastiano
15. San Nicolò dei Mendicoli
16. Squero di San Trovaso
17. San Trovaso
18. Zattere
19. Santa Maria della Visitazione
20. Gesuati

Eat
1. Da Codroma
2. Osteria Bakan
3. Trattoria Anzolo Raffaele

Drink
4. Cantine del Vino già Schiavi
5. Malvasia all'Adriatico Mar
6. Osteria ai Pugni

Stay
7. B&B Le Terese
8. Pensione Accademia Villa Maravegie

❶ ⊘ ⊘ 🛍

ACCADEMIA

📍E8 🏛Campo della Carità 🚏Accademia 🕐8:15am–7:15pm daily
(to 2pm Mon); last adm 1 hour before closing 📅1 Jan, 1 May, 25 Dec
🌐gallerieaccademia.it

**A dazzling collection of masterpieces spanning the full development
of Venetian art from Byzantine to Renaissance, Baroque and Rococo,
the Accademia is Venice's answer to the Uffizi in Florence – and with
works by Titian, Bellini and Giorgione, it is equally unmissable.**

The largest collection of Venetian art in existence, the Gallerie
dell'Accademia is housed in three former religious buildings.
The basis of the collection was the Accademia di Belle Arti,
founded in 1750 by the painter Giambattista Piazzetta, who
started the collection to serve as models for the art school;
in 1807 it was boosted by Napoleon with the addition of many
masterpieces salvaged from the churches and monasteries
that he suppressed. That same year the collection was moved
to its present premises.

The opening of the downstairs galleries in 2015 was the
first stage of an ambitious expansion plan. These interactive
galleries present the art of the 17th, 18th and 19th centuries,
grouped around themes such as portraiture, with rooms devoted
to the work of Hayez, Canova and Palladio, as well as a room
on ceiling paintings including a masterpiece by Veronese.

Did You Know?

Entry to the gallery is
free on local public
holidays and during
National Museum
Week in March.

→
Crowds gather to see
Veronese's *Feast in the
House of Levi* (1573)

1507
▽ The unknown meaning of Giorgione's *Tempest* has been vexing art historians for centuries.

1496
△ Though his *St Ursula* cycle is the Accademia's real treasure, Carpaccio's *Miracle of the Cross at the Rialto* is remarkable for its depiction of a black gondolier.

1530
△ Another famously haunting piece is Lorenzo Lotto's *Portrait of a Young Man*, known for his penetrative stare.

1534
△ Commissioned by the fraternity of the Scuola Grande di Santa Maria della Carita, Titian's magnificent *Presentation of the Virgin* still hangs proudly in its original home.

GALLERY GUIDE

The current programme of restoration work is ongoing, so be prepared for potentially absent paintings or sections of the gallery that are temporarily closed off. Also, bear in mind that the paintings depend on natural light, so it is best to visit on a bright morning. The additional ground-floor galleries are arranged thematically, while upstairs a second gallery (Quadreria) contains works by artists such as Bellini. Guided visits are free of charge but it is recommended to book in advance.

↑ Entrance to the Accademia Gallery on Campo della Carità

EXPLORING THE ACCADEMIA'S COLLECTION

Spanning more than five centuries, the fascinating collection of paintings in the Accademia provides a complete spectrum of the Venetian school, from the medieval Byzantine period through the Renaissance to the Baroque and Rococo. Upstairs, the order is more or less chronological, while the downstairs rooms are arranged thematically.

Byzantine and International Gothic

In Room 1, Paolo Veneziano, the true founder of the Venetian school and the most important Venetian painter of the 14th century, displays a blend of Western and Eastern influences in his *Coronation of the Virgin* (1325). The linear rhythms are unmistakably Gothic, yet the glowing gold background is distinctly Byzantine. In the same room, Michele Giambono's *Coronation of the Virgin* (1448) is characterized by delicate naturalistic detail.

↑ *Coronation of the Virgin in Paradise* (1450) by da Venezia in Room 1

Early Renaissance

Central to Venetian art in the 15th century was the *Sacra Conversazione*, where the Madonna is portrayed in a unified composition with saints: Giovanni Bellini's altarpiece for San Giobbe (c 1487) in Room 2 is a fine example. Giovanni, the younger Bellini, was influenced by the controlled rational style and mastery of perspective in the works of his brother-in-law, Andrea Mantegna, whose work *St George* (c 1460) is in Room 23. To Mantegna's rationality and harsh realism Giovanni added humanity. This is seen in his Madonna paintings (Rooms 4 and 23).

Out on a limb from the main 16th-century Venetian tradition was the enigmatic Lorenzo Lotto, best known for portraits conveying moods of psychological unrest, such as his melancholic *Portrait of a Gentleman* (c 1525) in Room 7. More in the Venetian tradition, Palma il Vecchio's sumptuous *Sacra Conversazione* in Room 8, painted around the same time, shows the influence of the early work of Titian.

High Renaissance

Occupying an entire wall of Room 10, the *Feast in the House of Levi* by Paolo Veronese (1573) was commissioned as *The Last Supper*. However, the hedonistic details in the painting was not well received and Veronese was ordered to remove the profane content of the picture. Instead, he simply changed the title.

Jacopo Tintoretto made his reputation with *The Miracle of the Slave* (1548), also in Room 10. This was the first of a series of works painted for the Scuola Grande di San Marco (p127). In the same room, see Veronese's use of colour in the *Mystical Marriage of St Catherine* (c 1575).

ROSALBA CARRIERA

Venetian artist Rosalba Carriera's career took off in the 17th-century, when her pastel portraits earned her international acclaim throughout Europe, particularly in Vienna and Paris. It was here that she painted fellow painter Antoine Watteau among many others. She remains the most successful female artists of her time.

Baroque, Genre and Landscapes

Venice suffered from a distinct lack of native Baroque painters, but a few non-Venetians kept the Venetian school alive during the 17th century. The most notable among these artists was celebrated Genoese painter Bernardo Strozzi (1581–1644). The artist was a great admirer of the work of Veronese, as can be seen in his *Feast at the House of Simon* (1629) in Room 11. Also represented in this room is Giambattista Tiepolo, the greatest Venetian painter of the 18th century.

Ceremonial Paintings

Rooms 20 and 21 feature two great cycles of paintings from the late 16th century. Room 20 houses *The Stories of*

↑ Tintoretto's *Miracle of the Slave* (1548) depicting St Mark's benevolence

the *Cross* by many of Venice's leading artists, commissioned by the Scuola di San Giovanni Evangelista, including *The Procession in St Mark's Square* (1496) by Gentile Bellini. Another, Vittore Carpaccio's *Healing of the Madman* (c 1496), depicts the Rialto Bridge, which collapsed in 1524. The second series, which features detailed *Scenes from the Legend of St Ursula* (1490s) by Carpaccio in Room 21, provides a fascinatingly poignant kaleidoscope of life.

Masterpieces

Room 23 brings together some of the most famous masterpieces of the collection.

These include Andrea Mantegna's *St George* (c 1460), Bellini's *Madonna of the Little Trees* (c 1487), and Giorgione's famous *Tempest* (c 1507). The inventive young Giorgione was influenced by Bellini, but went way beyond his master. In the atmospheric *Tempest*, this treatment of the landscape and the use of the figures to intensify that mood was an innovation that was replicated by many artists working in the 16th century and well beyond.

Sala dell'Albergo

When the Scuola della Carità became the site of the Academy of Art in the early 19th century, the Scuola's albergo (where students lodged) retained its original panelling and 15th-century ceiling. The huge *Presentation of the Virgin* (1538) is one of surprisingly few Titians in the gallery. The walls are also adorned with a grandiose triptych (1446) by Antonio Vivarini and Giovanni d'Alemagna.

💬 INSIDER TIP
Skip the Queue

Skip the queues during the summer months by booking online in advance (subject to a €1.50 booking fee). Admission to the Accademia gallery is free on the first Sunday of the month.

↑ The colourful triptych (1446) adorning the walls of the Sala d'Albergo

→ Cubist works in the dining room at the Peggy Guggenheim *(inset)*

2

PEGGY GUGGENHEIM COLLECTION

♀F8 🏠Palazzo Venier dei Leoni 🚤Accademia 🕙10am–6pm Wed–Mon 🚫25 Dec 🌐guggenheim-venice.it

The light-filled rooms and the modern canvases of the Peggy Guggenheim Collection stand in stark contrast to the Renaissance paintings of Venice's churches and museums. One of the city's most visited sights, it houses works by more than 200 modern and contemporary artists representing avant-garde movements such as Cubism, Futurism and Surrealism.

Intended as a four-storey palace, the Palazzo Venier dei Leoni never rose beyond the ground floor – hence its nickname, Il Palazzo Nonfinito. In 1949 it was bought by American millionairess Peggy Guggenheim, a collector, dealer and patron of the arts. A perspicacious and high-spirited woman, she befriended and furthered the careers of many Abstract and Surrealist artists. She bequeathed her vast collection of modern European and American art to her uncle Solomon R Guggenheim's foundation in 1979, stipulating that it remain in Venice. The museum was inaugurated in 1980.

The collection is one of Europe's leading modern art galleries. It consists of 200 pieces, representing almost every modern art movement, by artists such as Picasso, Braque, Miró, de Chirico, Magritte, Dalí, Kandinsky, Balla, Severini, Picabia, Delaunay, Pollock, Duchamp, Klee, Mondrian, Malevich, Calder and Rothko.

Sculpture features prominently throughout the house and garden. The most provocative piece is Marino Marini's *Angelo della Città* (Angel of the City, 1948), a prominently displayed man sitting on a horse, erect in all respects.

EXPERIENCE MORE

3 🖼

Santa Maria della Salute

📍G8 🏛Campo della Salute 🚤Salute 🕐9am–noon, 3–5:30pm daily 🌐basilica salutevenezia.it

This great Baroque Church standing at the entrance of the Grand Canal is one of the most imposing architectural landmarks of Venice. Henry James likened it to "some great lady on the threshold of her salon".

The church was built in thanksgiving for the city's deliverance from the plague of 1630, hence the name *Salute*, meaning "health and salvation". Every 21 November, in celebration of the occasion, worshippers approach across a bridge of boats spanning the mouth of the canal. Baldassare Longhena began the church in 1630. It was completed in 1687, five years after his death.

The interior consists of a large octagonal space and six chapels radiating from the ambulatory. The altar's sculptural group by Giusto Le Corte represents the Virgin and Child protecting Venice from the plague. Some of the best works, such as Titian's ceiling

paintings of *Cain and Abel*, *Abraham and Isaac* and *David and Goliath* (1540–49), are beyond the altar, where visitors are not allowed. The Pinacoteca Manfrediniana, next door to the sacristy, is home to a number of works by Veronese and Titian.

4

Campiello Barbaro

📍F8 🚤Salute

This enchanting little square is flanked on one side by the wisteria-clad walls of Ca' Dario. Throughout the history of this Grand Canal palace, its owners have been plagued by suicides, accidents, and bankruptcy, from Giovanni Dario, who commissioned the building in 1479, to the industrialist Raul Gardini, who shot himself in 1993.

170

The total number of canals that crisscross the city of Venice.

PEGGY GUGGENHEIM

Peggy Guggenheim (1898–1979) came to Europe in 1921, quickly fitting into Bohemian Paris. Resolving to "buy a picture a day", she amassed an extensive collection before she made Venice her home in 1947. She is fondly remembered by locals for her faithful dogs and for owning the city's last private gondola.

↑ The sun sinking behind the spectacular walls of Santa Maria della Salute

DRINK

Cantine del Vino già Schiavi

This outstanding vintner's doubles as a wine bar, and it's one of the best in town. There are no seats, so you're served where you stand.

🟠E8 🏠Fondamenta Priuli 992 🕐Sun ⓦcantinaschiavi.com

Malvasia all'Adriatico Mar

This tiny bar squeezes in delicious snacks, light meals and unusual wines – ask Francesco to guide you through the exceptional list.

🟠D6 🏠Calle Crosera 3771 📞041 476 43 22

Osteria ai Pugni

A lively bar beloved of locals and offering over 50 different wines to choose from. Tasty snacks are also served.

🟠D7 🏠Fondamenta Gherardini 2856 ⓦosteriaaipugni.com

⑤ Ponte dei Pugni

🟠D7 🏠Fondamenta Gherardini 🚏Ca' Rezzonico

Venice has several Ponti dei Pugni ("bridges of fists"), but this is the most famous. Spanning the peaceful Rio San Barnaba, the small bridge is distinguished by two pairs of footprints that are set in white stone on the top of the bridge. These mark the starting positions for the fights that took place between rival factions. Formerly there were no balustrades and contenders hurled each other straight into the water. The battles became so bloodthirsty that they were banned in 1705.

⑥ Campo San Barnaba

🟠D7 🚏Ca' Rezzonico

The Parish of San Barnaba, with its central canalside square, was known in the 18th century as the home of impoverished Venetian patricians who were lured by the low rents. Some relied on state support or begging, while others worked in the state gambling house.

Today the square and canal, with its vegetable barge, are

quietly appealing. The church (open Mon–Sat mornings) is fairly unremarkable, apart from a Tiepolesque ceiling.

⑦ Punta della Dogana

🟠G8 🏠Campo della Salute 🚏Salute 🕐10am–7pm daily 🕐25 Dec ⓦpalazzograssi.it

The building that housed the sea customs post was originally constructed in the 15th century to inspect the cargo of ships that intended to enter Venice. However, the customs house that visitors see today was built in the late 17th century and replaced a tower that guarded the entrance to the Grand Canal. On the corner tower of the house, two bronze Atlases support a striking golden ball.

The Punta della Dogana continued to serve as a customs house until the 1980s. After standing empty for many years, it was bought in 2007 by French billionaire François Pinault, owner of the famous Palazzo Grassi (p93), and now hosts temporary displays of modern art.

⑧ San Pantalon

🟠D6 🏠Campo San Pantalon 🚏San Tomà, Piazzale Roma 🕐Times vary, check website ⓦsanpantalon.it

The overwhelming feature of this late 17th-century church is the painted ceiling, remarkable for its illusionistic effects. It comprises a total of 40 scenes (admirers claim it as the world's largest work of art on canvas), depicting the martyrdom of the physician St Pantalon. The artist, Gian Antonio Fumiani, took 24 years (1680–1704) to achieve this masterpiece, but then allegedly fell to his death from the scaffolding.

↑ The canal that cuts through picturesque Campo San Barnaba

↑ Visitors exploring the exquisite marble halls of Ca' Rezzonico

Paolo Veronese's emotive painting *St Pantalon Healing a Boy* was his final work of art (1587). To see Antonio Vivarini and Giovanni d'Alemagna's *Coronation of the Virgin* (1444) and *The Annunciation* (1350), attributed to Paolo Veneziano, ask the custodian for access to the Chapel of the Holy Nail (Cappella del Sacro Chiodo).

Ca' Rezzonico

📍 D7 🏛 Fondamenta Rezzonico 3136 🚤 Ca' Rezzonico ⏰ 10:30am-6pm Wed-Mon (Nov-Mar: to 4:30pm) 🌐 carezzonico.visitmuve.it

This richly furnished Baroque palace is one of the most splendid in Venice. It is also one of the few palaces in the city that opens its doors to the public, and since 1934 it has housed the museum of 18th-century Venice.

The building was begun by Baldassare Longhena (architect of the Salute, *p145*) in 1667, but the funds of the Bon family, who commissioned it, ran dry before the second floor was started. In 1712, the unfinished palace was bought by the Rezzonicos, a Genoese family of merchants-turned-

bankers. A large portion of their fortune was spent on the purchase, construction and decoration of the palace. By 1758 it was in a fit state for the Rezzonicos to throw the first of the huge parties for which they later became renowned.

In 1888 the palace was bought by the poet Robert Browning and his son, who was married to an American heiress. Browning had little time to enjoy the enormous rooms, as he died of bronchitis in 1889.

The outstanding attraction in the palace today is Giorgio Massari's ballroom, which occupies the entire breadth of the building. It has been beautifully restored and is embellished with gilded chandeliers and a ceiling with trompe l'oeil frescoes.

Eighteenth-century paintings occupy the *piano nobile* (second floor). A whole room is devoted to Pietro Longhi's portrayals of everyday Venetian life. Other paintings worthy of note are Francesco Guardi's *Nuns' Parlour* (1768) and one of the few Canalettos in Venice, his *View of the Rio dei*

Mendicanti (1725). On the floor above is a reconstructed 18th-century apothecary's shop and a puppet theatre.

---

⑩
Campo Santa Margherita

📍 D7 🚤 Ca' Rezzonico

The sprawling square of Santa Margherita, lined with houses from the 14th and 15th centuries, is the lively hub of western Dorsoduro. Market stalls, offbeat shops and cafés attract many young people.

The former church of Santa Margherita, now an auditorium owned by the university, lies to the north of the square. Visitors can see sculptural fragments from the original 18th-century church, including gargoyles, on the truncated campanile and adjacent house. The Scuola dei Varotari (Scuola of the Tanners), in the centre of the square, has a faded relief of the Madonna della Misericordia protecting the tanners.

> **The sprawling square of Santa Margherita, lined with houses from the 14th and 15th centuries, is the lively hub of western Dorsoduro.**

↑ A frescoed ceiling within Scuola Grande dei Carmini, painted by Giambattista Tiepolo

EAT

Da Codroma

Expect quality cooking at this neighbourhood fish restaurant.

📍C7 🏠Fondamenta Briati 2540 📞041 524 6789 🕐10am-4pm, 6-11pm Tue-Sat

€€€

Osteria Bakan

Behind the humble exterior lies a fabulous (and quirky) restaurant.

📍B7 🏠Corte Maggiore 2314a 📞041 564 76 58 🕐8am-3pm, 6-10pm Wed-Mon

€€€

Trattoria Anzolo Raffaele

Head here for meat-heavy mains and a superb regional wine list.

📍B8 🏠Campo de l'Anzolo Rafael 1722 🕐Thu-Tue 🌐trattoria anzoloraffaele.it

€€€

Scuola Grande dei Carmini

📍C7 🏠Campo Carmini 🚌Ca' Rezzonico 🕐11am-5pm daily 🚫1 Jan, 25 Dec 🌐scuolagrandecarmini.it

The headquarters of the Carmelite confraternity was built beside their church in 1663. In the 1740s Giambattista Tiepolo was commissioned to decorate the ceiling of the *salone* (hall) on the upper floor. The nine ceiling paintings that he produced so impressed the Carmelites that Tiepolo was promptly made an honorary member of the brotherhood. The ceiling shows *St Simeon Stock Receiving the Scapular of the Carmelite Order from the Virgin*. The Carmelites honoured St Simeon Stock because he re-established the order in Europe after its 13th-century expulsion from the Holy Land.

The archive rooms also contain remarkable art and elaborate woodwork, with ceiling and wall paintings by Giustino Menescardi and caryatids by Giacomo Piazzetta.

Santa Maria dei Carmini

📍C7 🏠Campo Carmini 📞041 522 65 53 🚌Ca' Rezzonico, San Basilio 🕐11am-5pm daily 🚫1 Jan, 25 Dec

Known also as Santa Maria dei Carmelo, this church was built in the 14th century but has since undergone extensive alterations. The most prominent external feature is the lofty campanile, whose perilous tilt was skilfully rectified in 1688. The interior is large, sombre and richly decorated, with the nave adorned with gilded statues, and a series of paintings illustrating the history of the Carmelite Order.

There are two interesting paintings in the church's side altars. Cima da Conegliano's *Adoration of the Shepherds* (c 1509) is in the second altar on the right (coins in the light meter are essential). In the second altar on the left is Lorenzo Lotto's *St Nicholas of Bari with Saints Lucy and John the Baptist* (c 1529). This painting demonstrates the artist's religious devotion and his love of nature. On the right-hand side of this highly detailed landscape, there is a tiny depiction of St George killing the dragon. To the right is a *Holy Family* by Paolo Veronese.

> Contrasting with the remote and run-down area that surrounds it, San Nicolò dei Mendicoli is one of the most charming and delightful churches in Venice.

⓭
Angelo San Raffaele

📍 B8 🏛 Campo Angelo Raffaele 📞 041 522 85 48 🚤 San Basilio 🕐 10am-noon, 3-5:30pm Mon-Sat, 9am-noon Sun & pub hols

The main attraction of this 17th-century church is the series of panel paintings on the organ balustrade. These were executed in 1749 by Antonio Guardi, brother of the more famous Francesco, and tell the tale of Tobias, the blind prophet cured by the archangel Raphael, after whom the church is named.

⓮
San Sebastiano

📍 C8 🏛 Campo San Sebastiano 🚤 San Basilio 🕐 10:30am-4:30pm Mon-Sat 🚫 1 Jan, Easter, 15 Aug, 25 Dec 🌐 chorusvenezia.org

This 16th-century church has one of the most colourful interiors of Venice. Veronese, who was commissioned to decorate the sacristy ceiling,

> ### SCUOLE
>
> The *scuole* were educational institutions unique to Venice. Founded mainly in the early 13th century, they were lay confraternities that ostensibly existed for the charitable benefit of the neediest groups of society, the professions or resident ethnic minorities (such as the Scuola degli Schiavoni, *p128*). Some became extremely wealthy, spending large sums on building decor and commissioning extravagant works of art, often to the disadvantage of their declared beneficiaries.

the nave ceiling, the frieze, the east end of the choir, the high altar, the doors of the organ panels and the chancel – in that order. The paintings are typical of Veronese: rich and radiant, with sumptuous costumes and colours. Among the finest of his works are the three ceiling paintings of Esther, Queen of Xerxes I of Persia. Appropriately, Veronese is buried here, alongside the organ.

⓯
San Nicolò dei Mendicoli

📍 A7 🏛 Campo San Nicolò 📞 041 270 24 64 🚤 San Basilio 🕐 10am-noon, 3-5.30pm Mon-Sat, 9am-noon Sun & pub hols

Contrasting with the remote and run-down area that

The walls and ornately carved interiors *(inset)* of San Nicolo dei Mendicoli
↓

surrounds it, San Nicolò dei Mendicoli is one of the most charming and delightful churches in Venice. Originally constructed in the 12th century, it has been rebuilt extensively over the centuries; the porch on the north flank dates from the 15th century.

Thanks to the Venice in Peril Fund, in the 1970s the church underwent one of the most comprehensive restoration programmes since the floods of 1966. The floor, which was 30 cm (1 ft) below the level of the canals, was rebuilt and raised slightly to prevent further damage; the roofs and lower walls were reconstructed; and paintings and statues restored.

The interior is richly embellished, especially the nave with its 16th-century gilded wood statues, which included the figure of San Nicolò himself. On the upper walls is a series of paintings of the life of Christ by Alvise dal Friso and other pupils of Veronese.

16

Squero di San Trovaso

📍 D8 🚏 Rio San Trovaso
🚤 Zattere

This is one of the few surviving gondola workshops in Venice, and the most picturesque. Its Tyrolean look dates from the days when craftsmen came down from the Cadore area of the Dolomites (p246).

Tours run during the week and must be booked in advance, but from the far side of the Rio San Trovaso it is possible to watch the upturned gondolas being given their scraping and tarring treatment. Nowadays, only around 10 boats are made each year, but there is still plenty to see.

 PICTURE PERFECT
Shipyard Snaps

The Squero San Trovaso boatyard has to be one of the most photo-graphed spots in Venice. For the best results, go in the morning when the sun is shining on the boatyard and stand on Fondamenta Priuli.

17

San Trovaso

📍 D8 🏛 Campo San Trovaso
📞 041 522 21 33 🚤 Zattere or Accademia 🕐 2:30–5:30pm Mon–Sat

The church of Santi Gervasio e Protasio, which in the Venetian dialect is slurred to "San Trovaso", was built in 1590. It has two identical façades, one overlooking a canal, the other a quiet square. The church stood on neutral ground between the parishes of the rival factions of the Castellani and Nicolotti families, and tradition has it that this necessitated a separate entrance for each party.

The interior houses some late paintings by Jacopo Tintoretto, and Michele Giam-bono's 15th-century work, *St Chrysogonus on Horseback*, is situated in the chapel.

18

Zattere

📍 D9 🚤 Zattere or San Basilio

Stretching along the southern part of the *sestiere*, the Zattere is the long quayside looking across to the island of Giudecca. The name derives from the rafts (*zattere*) made of and carrying timber from the Republic's forests. After skilful navigation along the River Piave, the rafts were dismantled on arrival in Venice. On a sunny day it is a pleasure to sit at a waterside café here, looking across to the Church of the Redentore or watching the waterbuses as they cross back and forth between the shores.

Overlooking the Giudecca Canal is the Russian-run **V-A-C Foundation Zattere** is a space for contemporary art events with a focus on engaging with the Venetian population. Throughout the year, exhibitions, workshops and film screenings take place – all free of charge – in this well-restored palace. On the ground floor is the sudest 1401 restaurant, run by refugees, and a garden that reproduces the Venetian lagoon habitat.

V-A-C Foundation Zattere

🏷 📍 D8 🏛 Fondamenta Zattere al Ponte Longo 🕐 11am–5pm Sat–Tue, 11am–9pm Fri
🌐 v-a-c.ru

→ The picturesque canalside Squero di San Trovaso

⑲

Santa Maria della Visitazione

⑨ E9 🏠 Fondamenta delle Zattere 📞 041 522 21 71 🚤 Zattere 🕙 10:30am–4:30pm Mon-Sat

Situated beside the Gesuati, this Renaissance church was built between 1494 and 1524 by the Order of the Gesuati. Inside the church is a fine wooden ceiling painted by 16th-century Umbrian and Tuscan artists. The exterior *bocca di leone* to the right of the façade is one of several "lion's mouth" denunciation boxes surviving from the rule of the Council of Ten *(p85)*; this one was used to complain about the state of the streets.

↑ The decorative façade of Gesuati church, looking out over the turquoise water

⑳ 🎨

Gesuati

⑨ E9 🏠 Fondamenta delle Zattere 🚤 Zattere 🕙 10:30am–4:30pm Mon-Sat 🚫 1 Jan, Easter, 15 Aug, 25 Dec 🌐 chorusvenezia.org

Not to be confused with the Gesuiti *(p166)*, this church was built by the Dominicans, who took possession of the site in the 17th century when the Gesuati Order was suppressed. Work began in 1726 and the stately façade reflects that of Palladio's Redentore church across the Giudecca. It is the most conspicuous landmark of the long Zattere quayside. The interior of the church is richly decorated. Tiepolo's frescoed ceiling, *The Life of St Dominic* (1737–39), demonstrates the artist's mastery of light and colour. Just as impressive (and far easier to see) is his *Virgin with Saints* (1740), which is situated in the first chapel on the right. The church also boasts two altar paintings by Sebastiano Ricci and Giambattista Piazzetta.

STAY

B&B Le Terese
Run by a couple of architects, this B&B has two guestrooms with a shared bathroom, all stylishly decorated.

⑨ A7 🏠 Campiello Tron 1902 🌐 leterese.com

€€€

Pensione Accademia Villa Maravegie
Once the Russian embassy, this 17th-century villa is a tranquil haven away from the bustle of central Venice.

⑨ E8 🏠 Fondamenta Bollani 1058 🌐 pensione accademia.it

€€€

A SHORT WALK
DORSODURO

Distance 1.5 km (1 miles) **Time** 25 minutes
Nearest Vaporetto Ca' Rezzonico

Lively Campo Santa Margherita is at the heart of the *sestiere* of Dorsoduro. The square bustles with activity, particularly in the morning, when the market stalls are open, and in the evening when it is the haunt of students from nearby Ca' Foscari, now part of the University of Venice. The surrounding streets contain several spectacular buildings, most notably Ca' Rezzonico and the Scuola Grande dei Carmini, which has decorations by Tiepolo. Of the area's waterways, the delightful Rio San Barnaba is best appreciated from the Ponte dei Pugni, near the barge selling fruit and vegetables – itself a time-honoured Venetian sight. To discover the quieter part of the *sestiere*, travel east of the Peggy Guggenheim Collection for shaded squares and picturesque residences.

Campo Santa Margherita *is an ideal place for relaxing in a café.*

Scuola Grande dei Carmini (p148) *contains nine ceiling panels in the hall on the upper floor, painted by Tiepolo for the Carmelite confraternity.*

Palazzo Zenobio (p148), *built at the end of the 17th century, is used for temporary exhibitions. With permission, visitors can see the fine 18th-century ballroom.*

The church of **Santa Maria dei Carmini** *has a Gothic side porch carved with Byzantine reliefs.*

Fondamenta Gherardini *runs beside the Rio San Barnaba, one of the prettiest canals in the sestiere.*

RIO DI SANTA MARGHERITA

C DEL PISTOR

C DELLA

C D CAFFETTIER

C DEL FORNO

CAMPO SANTA MARGHERITA

R T SANT APONAL

CAMPO DEI CARMINI

START

CALLE D PAZIENZA

R T SCOAZZERA

FMTA D SQUERO

RIO SAN BARNABA

FONDAMENTA GHERARDINI

C LUNGA SAN BARNABA

0 metres 75
0 yards 75
N ↑

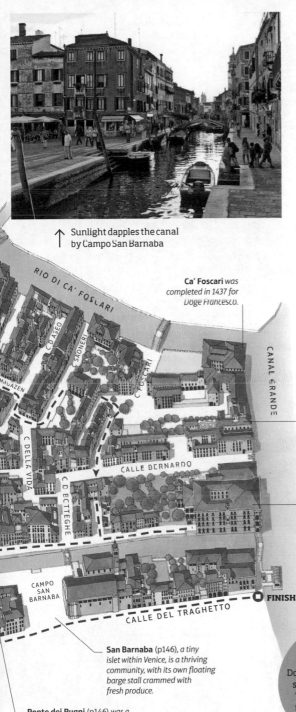

↑ Sunlight dapples the canal by Campo San Barnaba

Locator Map
For more detail see p138

Ca' Foscari *was completed in 1437 for Doge Francesco.*

RIO DI CA' FOSCARI

C D'AZEO

SAONERI

MAGAZEN

C FOSCARI

CANAL GRANDE

C DELLA VIDA

C D. BOTTEGHE

CALLE BERNARDO

Palazzo Giustinian *was home to Wagner in 1858*

The ballroom of Ca' Rezzonico covers the width of the palazzo.

CAMPO SAN BARNABA

🔵 **FINISH**

CALLE DEL TRAGHETTO

San Barnaba (p146), *a tiny islet within Venice, is a thriving community, with its own floating barge stall crammed with fresh produce.*

Ponte dei Pugni (p146) *was a traditional setting for fist fights between rival factions. They were finally banned in 1705 for being too violent.*

Did You Know?

Dorsoduro is built on solid subsoil, unlike much of Venice. This accounts for its name, meaning "hard backbone".

CANNAREGIO

The city's most northerly *sestiere*, Cannaregio, stretches in a large arc from the 20th-century Santa Lucia train station in the west to one of the oldest quarters of Venice in the east. The northern quays look out towards the islands in the lagoon, while to the south the *sestiere* is bounded by the upper sweep of the Grand Canal.

The name of the quarter derives either from the red-coloured Italian *canne*, meaning canes or reeds, which grew here centuries ago, or perhaps from "Canal Regio" or Royal Canal – the former name of what is now the Canale di Cannaregio. This waterway was the main entry to Venice prior to the advent of the rail link with the mainland. During the 11th century, major development took place, and the main canal was drained to allow the adjoining waterways to be dredged. Elegant palazzos faced the Grand Canal, but this area was primarily working class and residential, with some manufacturing buildings. In 1516, Venice's Jewish population was confined to an enclosed area known as the Ghetto. Such restrictions continued for more than 270 years, until Napoleon Bonaparte conquered the Republic in 1797, ridding the area of all its gates and allowing residents the freedom to live where they chose.

Today, over a third of the city's population lives in Cannaregio. For the most part it is an unspoiled area, divided by wide canals, crisscrossed by alleys, and characterized by small stores, simple bars and artisans' workshops.

CANNAREGIO

Must Sees

1 Ca' d'Oro
2 The Ghetto
3 Santa Maria dei Miracoli

Experience More

4 Campo dei Mori
5 Madonna dell'Orto
6 Fondamenta della Sensa
7 San Marziale
8 Gesuiti
9 Fondamente Nuove
10 Oratorio dei Crociferi
11 San Giovanni Grisostomo
12 Scalzi
13 Santi Apostoli
14 Palazzo Labia
15 Teatro Malibran
16 San Giobbe

Eat

1 Al Timon All'Antica Mola
2 Osteria Al Cicheto
3 Osteria Da Rioba
4 Paradiso Perduto

Drink

5 Un Mondo di Vino
6 Osteria ai Tronchi
7 Hostaria Bacanera

Shop

8 Codex
9 Mori & Bozzi
10 Nicolao Atelier
11 Sullaluna

F G H J

0 metres 250
0 yards 250
N

1

Canale delle Fondamente Nuove

🚉 Orto

CAMPIELLO PIAVE

5 Madonna dell'Orto

Palazzo Mastelli

4 Campo dei Mori

Casa del Tintoretto

Sacca della Misericordia

FOND GASPARO CONTARINI

2

10 **3**

4 **11**

FONDAMENTA DELLA MISERICORDIA

Santa Maria della Misericordia

CAMPO DELL'ABBAZIA

7 San Marziale

FONDAMENTA NUOVE

Fondamente Nuove

9

🚉 Fondamente Nove

ADDALENA

Oratorio dei Crociferi **10**

Gesuiti **8**

CAMPO DEI GESUITI

VIA VITTORIO EMANUELE

Santa Caterina

6

Ca' d'Oro **1**

🚉 Ca' d'Oro

CAMPO SANTA SOFIA

Palazzo Sagredo

13 Santi Apostoli

CAMPO DEI SANTI APOSTOLI

7

5

3 Santa Maria dei Miracoli

Santi Giovanni e Paolo

4

Ca' Pesaro

CAMPO SAN STAE

CAMPO SAN CASSIANO

🚉 Rialto Mercato

Fabbriche Nuove

11 San Giovanni Grisostomo

CORTE 2a D. MILION

15 Teatro Malibran

CASTELLO *p116*

5

SAN POLO

Ponte di Rialto

🚉 Rialto

SAN MARCO *p72*

CASTELLO

CANNAREGIO

6

🚉 San Silvestro

San Salvatore

Palazzo Grimani

🚉 Sant'Angelo

SAN MARCO

CAMPO SANT'ANGELO

PIAZZA SAN MARCO

7

F G H J

① ⟨◈⟩ ⟨🛍⟩

CA' D'ORO

📍G4 🚶Canal Grande (Calle Ca' d'Oro) 🚤Ca' d'Oro 🕐8:15am–2pm
Mon, 8:15am–7:15pm Tue–Sun 🚫1 Jan, 1 May, 25 Dec 🌐cadoro.org

The original lapis lazuli, vermilion and gold façade has long faded, but the breathtaking Gothic delicacy of this "golden palace" is intact, with exquisite marble tracery and arcaded loggias crafted by 15th-century stonemasons.

One of the great showpieces of the Grand Canal, the Ca' d'Oro (or House of Gold) is the finest example of Venetian Gothic architecture in the city. The façade, with its finely carved ogee windows, Oriental pinnacles and exotic marble tracery, has an unmistakable flavour of the East.

In the course of the 16th century the house was remodelled by a succession of owners, and by the early 18th century was semi-derelict. In 1846 the Russian Prince Troubetzkoy bought it for the famous ballerina Marie Taglioni. Under her direction, the Ca' d'Oro suffered barbaric remodelling in 1894. It was finally rescued by Baron Giorgio Franchetti who lovingly restored it to its former glory. Restoration of the façade is now complete, revealing the building's intricate design.

Behind the palace's beautiful Gothic tracery is a courtyard paved with coloured tesserae. Inside is the Galleria Giorgio Franchetti, a collection of paintings, sculptures and ceramics donated to the state by Baron Franchetti in 1916, along with the building. One highlight is Andrea Mantegna's painting *St Sebastian* (1506) in the portico leading to a loggia overlooking the Grand Canal. An ornate 15th-century staircase leads to 16th-century Flemish tapestries on the second floor.

Did You Know?

"Ca'" is an abbreviation of *casa*, meaning home. This is used to denote grand palazzos, not humble dwellings.

→
Glorious sunset over the Grand Canal and Ca' d'Oro

① Ca' d'Oro's intricately carved balcony overlooking the Grand Canal.

② Visitors exploring the Ca' d'Oro Art Gallery.

③ Detail of the impressive mosaic tiling inside the ground floor loggia.

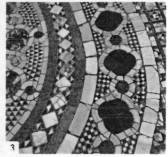

GALLERY GUIDE

On the first floor, pride of place is given to Andrea Mantegna's *St Sebastian* (1506). The *portego* (gallery) opening on to the Grand Canal is a showroom of sculpture. Among the finest pieces are bronze reliefs by the Paduan sculptor Il Riccio (1470–1532), and Tullio Lombardo's marble *Double Portrait* (c 1493). The upper floor houses paintings by numerous Venetian masters, including a Venus by Titian, two Venetian views by Guardi and fresco fragments by Titian.

SHOP

Codex
Delicate ink drawings
are sold in this store.

🏠 Fondamenta degli
Ormesini 2799
🌐 codexvenezia.it

Mori & Bozzi
A haven for
fashionistas.

🏠 Rio Terà de la
Maddalena 2367
📞 041 715 261

Nicolao Atelier
The place to go for
Carneval costumes.

🏠 Fondamenta de la
Misericordia 2590
🌐 nicolao.com

Sullaluna
Quirky bookshop
and cafè.

🏠 Fondamenta de la
Misericordia 2535
📞 041 722 924

❷ 🛍

THE GHETTO

📍 D2, D3   🚏 Ponte Guglie

Once home to a thriving Jewish population, the Ghetto lost its
importance after the Jews were granted citizenship and dispersed. It
is now packed with independent shops and local restaurants and, with
five synagogues, it remains the centre of Venice's Jewish community.

In 1516 the Council of Ten decreed that all Jews in Venice be confined to an islet of Cannaregio. The quarter was cut off, its entrances manned by Christian guards. By day Jews were allowed out of the Ghetto, but at all times they were made to wear identifying badges and caps. The rising number of Jews forced the Ghetto to expand. Buildings rose vertically and spread into the Ghetto Vecchio and the neighbouring Ghetto Nuovo. By the mid-17th century the population numbered over 5,000. It wasn't until 1866 that they were granted their freedom.

The Museo Ebraico houses a collection of artifacts from the 17th to 19th centuries. A guided tour of the quarter's synagogues departs from the museum daily (except on Saturdays), allowing a fascinating glimpse into the past life of the Ghetto.

Museo Ebraico
♿🕑📷🏠 Campo del Ghetto Nuovo
🕐 10am-7pm Sun-Fri (Oct-May: to 5:30pm)
🚫 1 Jan, 1 May, 25 Dec, Jewish hols
🌐 museoebraico.it

Did You Know?

The area was named after a foundry (*geto*), a term later applied to other Jewish enclaves around the world.

↑ A quiet evening on Fondamenta Ormesini, Ghetto Nuovo

↑ A tailor embroidering detail on a carnival costume at Nicolao Atelier

LEONE DA MODENA

Leone da Modena (1571–1648) was a respected rabbi, musician and printer with a penchant for gambling. A fiery opponent of the mystical approach to Judaism, he was not too keen on Christian interpretations of Hebrew scriptures either. His account of Jewish customs and rituals paved the way for the Jews' eventual resettlement in England.

③ 🖉

SANTA MARIA DEI MIRACOLI

📍 H5 **🏠 Campiello dei Miracoli** **🚏 Fondamente Nuove or Rialto**
🕐 10:30am–4:30pm Mon–Sat **🚫 1 Jan, Easter, 15 Aug, 25 Dec**
🌐 chorusvenezia.org

A "jewellery box" of marble slabs and exquisite bas-reliefs, this Renaissance church was named after an alleged miracle-working icon from 1409, which reputedly brought a drowned man back to life and erased a woman's fatal wounds. The sculpture is now enshrined on the main altar.

An exquisite masterpiece of the early Renaissance, Santa Maria dei Miracoli is the favourite church of many Venetians, and was the subject of a major restoration programme funded by the American Save Venice organization in the early 1990s. Tucked away in a winding maze of alleys and waterways in eastern Cannaregio, it is small and somewhat elusive, but well worth the trip.

The façade is decorated in various shades of marble, with fine bas-reliefs and sculpture. It was built in 1481–9 by the architect Pietro Lombardo and his sons to enshrine *The Virgin and Child* (1408), a painting believed to have miraculous powers. The picture, by Nicolò di Pietro, can still be seen high above the altar.

The stunning interior of the Miracoli, which ideally should be visited in the morning when pale shafts of light stream in through the windows, is embellished by pink, white and grey marble and crowned by a barrel-vaulted ceiling, featuring portraits of saints and prophets. Tullio Lombardo's balustrade is decorated by carved figures of St Francis, Archangel Gabriel, the Virgin and St Clare. The screen around the high altar and the medallions of the Evangelists in the cupola spandrels are also by Lombardo.

↑ Banding in this stone carving gives the impression that the Madonna is weeping

EARLY RENAISSANCE ARCHITECTURE

One of the best examples of the early Venetian Renaissance, the Miracoli's façade is a harmonious tapestry of decorated panels and multicoloured polished stone. Inside, the ceiling gleams with gilt miniatures of holy figures.

The semicircular crowning lunette emphasizes the church's jewel-box appearance.

A false loggia is formed of Ionic arches, inset with windows.

The marble panels are fixed to the bricks by metal hooks. This method, which prevents the build-up of damp and salt water behind the panels, dates from the Renaissance.

→
Ornate façade of the Santa Maria dei Miracoli

The Miracoli *(inset)* and its impressive barrel-vaulted ceiling, featuring over 50 frescoed portraits
↓

A statue known for its intriguing metal nose in the corner of the Campo dei Mori ↑

EXPERIENCE MORE

4

Campo dei Mori

F2 **Madonna dell'Orto**

According to popular tradition, the "Mori" were the three Mastelli brothers who came from the Morea (the Peloponnese). The brothers, who were silk merchants by trade, took refuge in Venice in 1112 and built the Palazzo Mastelli, visible from Fondamenta Gasparo Contarini and recognizable by its camel bas-relief. The brothers' stone figures are embedded in the wall of the *campo* on its eastern side. The corner figure with the makeshift rusty metal nose (added in the 19th century) is "Signor Antonio Rioba", who, like the Roman Pasquino, was the focus of malicious fun and satire. A fourth Oriental merchant with a large turban faces the Rio della Sensa on the façade of Tintoretto's house (p170).

5

Madonna dell'Orto

F2 **Campo Madonna dell'Orto** **Madonna dell'Orto** **10am-5pm Mon-Sat, noon-5pm Sun & pub hols** **1 Jan, 25 Dec** **madonnadellorto.org**

This lovely Gothic church is frequently referred to as the English Church in Venice, for it was British funds that helped restore the building after the 1966 floods. The original church, founded in the mid-14th century, was dedicated to St Christopher, patron saint of travellers, to protect the boatmen who ferried passengers to the islands in the northern lagoon. The dedication was changed and the church reconstructed in the early 15th century following the discovery, in a nearby garden (*orto*), of a statue of the Virgin Mary said to have miraculous powers. A 15th-century statue of St Christopher still stands above the portal, however.

The interior is large, light and uncluttered. The greatest treasures are the works of art by Tintoretto, who was a parishioner of the church. His tomb lies in the chapel to the

> **According to popular tradition, the "Mori" were the three Mastelli brothers who came from the Morea (the Peloponese).**

right of the chancel. The most dramatic of his works are the towering paintings in the chancel (1562–4). In the painting *The Adoration of the Golden Calf* on the left wall, the figure carrying the calf, fourth from the left, is said to depict Tintoretto himself.

Inside the chapel of San Mauro visitors can see the radically restored statue of the Madonna that inspired the reconstruction of the church. The vacant space opposite the entrance belongs to Giovanni Bellini's *Madonna with Child* (c 1478), which was stolen for the third time in 1993.

6
Fondamenta della Sensa

◐E2 ▦Madonna dell'Orto

When the marshy lands of Cannaregio were drained in the Middle Ages, three long, straight canals were created, running parallel to each other. The middle of these is the Rio della Sensa, which stretches from the Sacca di Sant'Alvise at its western end to the Canale della Misericordia In the east. The Fondamenta cuts through a quiet quarter of Cannaregio. With its small grocery shops, and simple local bars and *trattorie*, the neighbourhood feels far removed from San Marco.

This is one of the poorer areas of the city, though it is interspersed with fine (but neglected) palaces that once belonged to wealthy Venetians.

7
San Marziale

◐F3 ▣Campiello San Marziale ☎041 71 99 33 ▦San Marcuola ◷By appt

A Baroque church on medieval foundations, San Marziale was rebuilt between 1693 and 1721. It is visited mainly for the ceiling frescoes by Sebastiano Ricci, a painter of the decorative Rococo style. Executed between 1700 and 1705, relatively early in Ricci's career, these foreshortened frescoes combine the Venetian tradition with flamboyant Rococo flourishes. Sadly, though, the vivid colours for which Ricci was known have been sullied by decades of grime. The central painting shows *The Glory of Saint Martial*, while the side paintings relate to the Image of the Virgin.

←

Visitors paddling the canal in front of the brick façade of the Madonna dell'Orto

↑ The spectacular interiors and imposing façade *(inset)* of the Gesuiti

⑧
Gesuiti

▣ H3 ⌂ Salizada dei Spechieri, 4877 ☎ 041 528 1610 ⛴ Fondamente Nuove ⊙ 10am–noon, 4–6pm daily

The Jesuits' close links with the papacy provoked Venetian hostility during the 17th century, and for 50 years they were refused entry to the city. However, in 1714 they were given permission to build this church in the north of Venice, on the site of a 12th-century church that had originally belonged to the Order of the Crociferi. Consecrated as Santa Maria Assunta, the church is always referred to simply as the Gesuiti; thus it is often confused with the Gesuati in Dorsoduro *(p151)*.

Domenico Rossi's imposing Baroque exterior gives only a hint of the opulence inside. The proliferation of green and white marble, carved in parts like great folds of fabric, gives the dramatic impression that the interior of the church is clothed in damask.

Titian's *Martyrdom of St Lawrence* (c 1555), which hangs above the first altar on the left, is worth a closer look, and has been described by the art historian Hugh Honour as "the first successful nocturne in the history of art".

---

⑨
Fondamente Nuove

▣ H3 ⛴ Fondamente Nuove

The Fondamente Nuove or "New Quays" are actually over 400 years old. This chain of waterside streets borders the northern lagoon for one kilometre (over half a mile), from the solitary Sacca della Misericordia to the Rio di Santa Giustina in Castello on the eastern side.

Before the construction of the quays in the 1580s, this was a desirable residential area where the air was said to be healthy and the houses had gardens sloping down to the lagoon.

One of the residents of this neighbourhood was Titian, who lived from 1531 until his death in 1576 in a now demolished house at Calle Larga dei Botteri No. 5182–3 (an ornately carved plaque marks the site).

Today the quaysides are aesthetically uninspiring but they do provide splendid views of the northern lagoon and – on a clear day – the spectacular peaks of the Dolomites. The island most easily visible from the quays is San Michele in Isola *(p182)*, with its dark, stately cypress trees rising high above the cemetery walls.

Did You Know?

Titian lived at the Vatican for six months while working on two portraits of Pope Paul III.

Oratorio dei Crociferi

📍H3 🏛Campo dei Gesuiti, 4905 📞041 532 29 20 🚊Fondamente Nuove 🕙10am-1pm & 2-5pm Thu-Sun

Founded in the 13th century as a hospital for returning Crusaders, the Oratorio dei Crociferi (built for the order of the Bearers of the Cross) was turned into a charitable institution for old people in the 15th century.

Between 1583 and 1591 the artist Palma il Giovane, commissioned by the Crociferi, decorated the chapel with a cycle of paintings depicting crucial events in the history of this religious order. The paintings suffered terrible damage in the floods of 1966, but were successfully restored and the chapel reopened in 1984. The inscriptions on the walls of some of the surrounding houses in the square are those of art and craft guilds, such as silk weavers and tailors, whose works formerly occupied the buildings.

San Giovanni Grisostomo

📍H5 🏛Campo San Giovanni Grisostomo 📞041 522 71 55 🚊Rialto 🕙8:15am-12:15pm, 3-7pm daily 🕙During Mass

This pretty terracotta-coloured church is found near the Rialto. Built between 1479 and 1504, the church was the last work of Mauro Coducci.

The interior, built on a Greek-cross plan, is dark and intimate. Notable works of art that hang here include Giovanni Bellini's *St Jerome with Saints Christopher and Augustine* (1513), which is found above the first altar on the right. Influenced by Giorgione, this was probably Bellini's last painting. Another artist inspired by Giorgione was Sebastiano del Piombo, whose *St John Chrysostom and Six Saints* (1509–11) hangs above the high altar. Some believe that the figures of St John the Baptist and St Liberal were painted by Giorgione himself.

DRINK

Un Mondo di Vino
This compact spot is usually packed, and deservedly so. Elbow your way to the bar for a scrumptious *cichetto*. There are also dozens of wines available by the glass.

📍H5 🏛Salizada San Canzian 5984/a 📞041 521 10 93

Osteria al Tronchi
Visitors here can choose between a bargain glass of delicious house wine for around €1, or the myriad more sophisticated options. If you're peckish, dig in to snacks and sandwiches.

📍H4 🏛Calle del Spezier 4792 📞041 528 27 27 🕙Sun

Hostaria Bacanera
This local favourite is part wine bar, part restaurant, and a formidable selection of wines are served by knowledgeable staff. On Tuesdays, head down to enjoy some live music.

📍H4 🏛Campiello de la Cason 4506 📞041 260 11 46 🕙11:30am-3pm, 6-10:30pm Tue-Sun

↑ The peach tower of San Giovanni Grisostomo, rising above the surrounding narrow streets

MARCO POLO

Born c 1254 near the Rialto, Marco Polo left Venice at the age of 18 for his voyage to the court of the Emperor Kublai Khan. He returned in 1295, bringing with him a fortune in jewels and a host of fabulous stories. While a prisoner of war in 1298 he compiled an account of his travels, which became *Le Livre des Merveilles*. Though many disbelieved his tales of the East, the book was an instant hit. His nickname became Marco Il Milione (of the million lies).

and sculptures. The impressive ceiling painting, *The Council of Ephesus* by Ettore Tito (1934), replaced Giambattista Tiepolo's fresco of *The Translation of the Holy House to Loreto* (1743–5), which was destroyed by the Austrian bombardment of 24 October 1915.

13
Santi Apostoli

G4 **Campo Santi Apostoli** **041 523 82 97** **Ca' d'Oro** **For Mass only**

The Campo Santi Apostoli is a busy crossroads for pedestrians en route to the Rialto or the railway station. Its church is architecturally unremarkable and little remains of the 16th-century building. A notable exception, however, is the enchanting late 15th-century Renaissance

12
Scalzi

C4 **Fondamenta Scalzi** **041 822 40 06** **Ferrovia** **7am-noon, 3-7pm daily**

Beside the modern railway station stands the church of Santa Maria di Nazareth, known as the Scalzi. The *scalzi* were "barefooted" Carmelite friars who came to Venice during the 1670s and commissioned their church to be built on the Grand Canal.

Designed by Baldassare Longhena, the huge Baroque interior is an over-elaboration of marble, gilded woodwork

→ Sunset behind the Scalzi, as day trippers begin to return to the train station

Corner Chapel on the right of the nave, believed to have been designed by Mauro Coducci. The chapel contains *The Communion of St Lucy* by Giambattista Tiepolo (1748), the tomb of Marco Corner, probably by Tullio Lombardo (1511), and an inscription to Corner's daughter, Caterina Cornaro, Queen of Cyprus, who was buried here before she was moved to the Church of San Salvatore *(p93)*.

14

Palazzo Labia

📍 D3 🏠 Fondamenta Labia (entrance on Campo San Geremia) ☎ 041 78 11 11 🚢 Ponte Guglie ⏰ By appt

The Labias were a wealthy family of merchants from Catalonia, who bought their way into the Venetian patrici-

ate in 1646. Towards the end of the century they built their prestigious Baroque palace, with a splendid façade, on the wide Cannaregio Canal, close to its junction with the Grand Canal.

In 1745–50 the ballroom was frescoed by Giambattista Tiepolo. The wonderfully painted scenes are taken from the life of Cleopatra but the setting is Venice, and the queen's attire is that of a 16th-century noblewoman.

Passed from one owner to another, the palace gradually lost all trace of its former grandeur and has variously served as a religious foundation, a school and a doss-house. Since 1964, the Palazzo Labia has served as the office of the Italian broadcasting network, RAI, which also undertook its restoration.

15

Teatro Malibran

📍 H5 🏠 Campiello del Teatro 5873 🌐 teatrola fenice.it

Tucked behind a bustling thoroughfare is the charming Teatro Malibran. Built on the site of Marco Polo's former home, this theatre originally went by the name of Teatro Grisostomo, after the nearby church. The theatre first opened its doors in 1678 and was one of three such venues owned by the powerful Grimani family. In 1819 the theatre was sold, lavishly restored and reopened with Rossini's *La Gazza Ladra*.

The famous soprano Maria Garcia Malibran came to perform at the theatre in 1835, and the building was renamed in her honour. When La Fenice tragically burned down in 1996, the Malibran was used as a replacement and continues to work in tandem with the renowned opera house, hosting a number of perform-ances throughout the year.

Did You Know?

Marco Polo introduced Europe to the concept of paper money, having encountered it in the Mongol empire.

16

San Giobbe

📍 C3 🏠 Campo San Giobbe 🚢 Ponte dei 3 Archi ⏰ 10:30am-2pm Mon-Sat 🚫 1 Jan, Easter, 15 Aug, 25 Dec 🌐 chorusvenezia.org

The simple church of San Giobbe stands in a remote *campo* full of cats. The early Gothic structure of the church was modified in the 1470s by Pietro Lombardo, who added Renaissance elements to the design, such as the saints over the portal. The Martini chapel, which is located second on the left, displays clear Tuscan influences and is decorated with Della Robbia-style glazed terracotta. The altarpieces by Giovanni Bellini and Vittore Carpaccio were removed when Napoleon suppressed the monastery of San Giobbe, and these highly valuable pieces are now on display in the Accademia gallery *(p140)*. The church is undergoing restoration; check the website for details.

→

A statue from San Giobbe, attributed to Pietro Lombardo

A SHORT WALK
AROUND CANNAREGIO

Distance 1.5 km (1 mile) **Time** 25 minutes
Nearest Vaporetto Madonna dell'Orto

Surprisingly few tourists find their way to this
unspoiled quarter of northern Cannaregio.
This is the more humble, peaceful side
of Venice, where clean washing is
strung over the waterways and
the streets are flanked by the
softly crumbling façades of
shuttered houses, from which
the comforting smell of
home-cooking wafts out
onto the streets, the envy
of many a passer-by.
All along the spacious
fondamente, little shops
stock basic groceries
and unassuming bars
are always crowded with
Venetians. The quarter's
cultural highlight is the
lovely Gothic church
of Madonna dell'Orto,
Tintoretto's parish church.

One of the finest Gothic churches in Venice, **Madonna dell'Orto** (p164) *has a richly decorated façade and a wealth of works by such artists as Tintoretto.* **START**

Fondamenta della Sensa (p165) *is a peaceful backwater with typically Venetian peeling façades.*

Tintoretto lived with his family in this house, **No. 3399 Fondamenta dei Mori**, *from 1574 until his death.*

Campo dei Mori (p164) *is named after the stone statues of three Moors (Mori) which are carved on its walls.*

Ceiling paintings by Sebastiano Ricci (1700–25) and a bizarre Baroque altar adorn the Baroque church of **San Marziale** (p165). **FINISH**

↑ A woman walking along Fondamenta della Sensa and Rio della Sensa in Cannaregio

0 metres 50 N
0 yards 50 ↑

↑ Quiet Campo dell'Abbazia della Misericordia and its church

Fondamenta Gasparo Contarini *is named after the cardinal, diplomat and scholar who lived at Palazzo Contarini dal Zaffo in the 16th century.*

Did You Know?

Madonna dell'Orto once held a Bellini masterpiece. Stolen in 1993, it is yet to be recovered.

La Sacca della Misericordia *is a large man-made basin opening out into the lagoon, with views of the islands of San Michele and Murano.*

Venetian oarsmen usually practise their technique on the lagoon, but they can also be seen on Cannaregio's quieter canals, such as the **Rio Madonna dell'Orto**

Campo dell'Abbazia, *a peaceful open square with decorative herringbone floor tiles, is overlooked by the Scuola Vecchia della Misericordia and a deconsecrated church.*

Fondamenta della Misericordia *was built in the Middle Ages.*

THE LAGOON ISLANDS

Shrouded in myth and superstition, the lagoon was once the preserve of fishermen and hunters. But marauders in the 5th and 6th centuries AD drove mainland dwellers to the safety of the marshy lagoon. Here, they conquered their watery environment, which was protected from the open sea by thin sandbanks (*lidi*), created from silt washed down by the rivers of the Po Delta. In the 13th century the first *murazzi* were built – seawalls of angular stone that safeguard the *lidi* from erosion. Experiments with tidal barriers continue in an effort to combat the ever-present threat of flooding caused predominantly by high tides in the Adriatic and strong sirocco winds from the south.

The thriving communities that once lived and traded here are long gone. Many of the islands, formerly used as sites for monasteries, hospitals or powder factories, are now abandoned, but a handful of them are undergoing development, one as an international university, another as an exclusive resort.

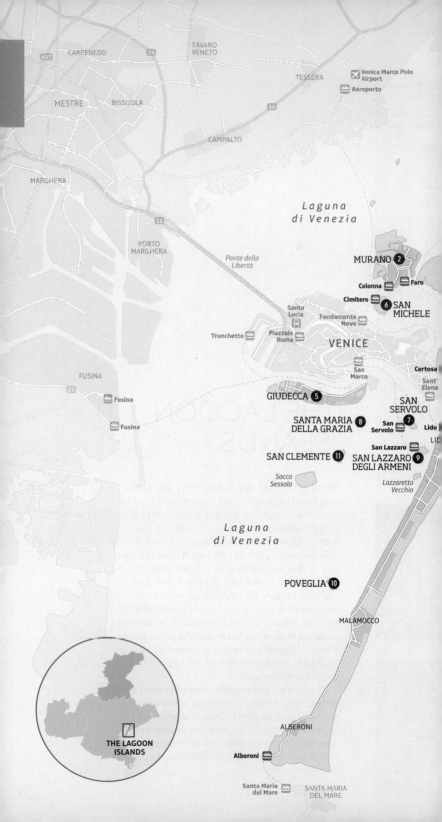

CARPENEDO

FAVARO
VENETO

TESSERA

Venice Marco Polo
Airport
Aeroporto

MESTRE   BISSUOLA

CAMPALTO

MARGHERA

*Laguna
di Venezia*

PORTO
MARGHERA

*Ponte della
Libertà*

MURANO **2**

Colonna Faro

Cimitero **6** SAN
MICHELE

FUSINA

Santa
Lucia

Fondamente
Nove

Tronchetto Piazzale
Roma

VENICE

San
Marco

Certosa

Sant'
Elena

Fusina

GIUDECCA **5**

SAN
SERVOLO

Fusina

SANTA MARIA
DELLA GRAZIA **8**

San
Servolo **7**

Lido

LID

SAN CLEMENTE **11**

San Lazzaro

SAN LAZZARO
DEGLI ARMENI **9**

*Sacca
Sessola*

*Lazzaretto
Vecchio*

*Laguna
di Venezia*

POVEGLIA **10**

MALAMOCCO

**THE LAGOON
ISLANDS**

ALBERONI

Alberoni

Santa Maria
del Mare   SANTA MARIA
DEL MARE

THE LAGOON ISLANDS

Must Sees

1 Torcello
2 Murano

Experience More

3 Burano
4 San Francesco del Deserto
5 Giudecca
6 San Michele
7 San Servolo
8 Santa Maria della Grazia
9 San Lazzaro degli Armeni
10 Poveglia
11 San Clemente
12 Lido
13 Lazzaretto Nuovo

*Golfo di
Venezia*

❶ ✎ TORCELLO

🚌 12 from Fondamenta Nuove, then 9 from Burano
📞 041 73 07 61 ⏰ Times vary, call ahead

A 40-minute ferry ride from the main islands of Venice, Torcello's green fields, tranquil canals and pastel-hued houses that sit alongside them offer a welcome escape from the swarming crowds.

Established between the 5th and 6th centuries, Torcello grew into a thriving colony, with palaces, churches and a population said to have reached 20,000. But with the rise of Venice the island went into decline. Today, Torcello is home to a handful of gardeners and fishermen, and all that remains of this once vigorous community is the Byzantine cathedral, the church of Santa Fosca, and the memory of its former glory.

The striking Basilica di Santa Maria dell'Assunta – the lagoon's oldest building – was founded in 639, but underwent radical restructuring in 1008. It retains its Romanesque form, light-brick walls and an arcaded 9th-century portico. Here, some of the most breathtaking Byzantine mosaics in the world reward those who visit.

The cathedral's 55-m (180-ft) campanile offers spectacular views over the vast expanse of the lagoon to the Adriatic Sea, Venice itself and even north to the Alps on a clear winter's day. Inside are astonishing 12th- and 13th-century Domesday Mosaic, which depict scenes of devils and angels.

ATTILA THE HUN

The King of the Huns ruled from over an empire that stretched from the Alps to the Caspian Sea. As part of his campaign against the Roman empire, Attila attacked Milan, Verona and Padua, and refugees fled to Torcello. Legend has it that a marble armchair in front of the Cathedral was his throne.

The Apse Mosaic, of a 13th-century Madonna set against a gold background, is one of the most moving mosaics in Venice.

The huge and highly decorative Domesday Mosaic, depicting the Last Judgment, covers the entire west wall.

The present basilica dates from 1008, but includes many earlier features. The marble pulpit is made of fragments from the first, 7th-century church.

The exquisite Byzantine marble panels of the Iconostasis (rood screen) are carved with peacocks, lions and flowers. A highlight is a detailed relief showing two peacocks drinking from the fountain of life.

Santa Maria dell'Assunta and the church of Santa Fosca ↑

① The elegant Santa Fosca was based on a Greek-cross design.

② Santa Fosca heightens Torcello's peaceful atmosphere.

③ The only path in Torcello runs alongside the canal.

Built in the 11th and 12th centuries on a Greek-cross plan, Santa Fosca has a lovely portico and a serene Byzantine interior.

The central dome and cross-sections are supported by columns of Greek marble with fine Corinthian capitals.

60

The tiny population of Torcello today.

It was said that Attila, the 5th-century king of the Huns, used this marble seat as his throne.

Old church treasures and archaeological fragments are housed in the fantastic Museo dell' Estuario.

GLASS-BLOWING

A main attraction of a trip to Murano is a demonstration of glass-blowing, where you can watch in amazement while a glass blower takes a blob of molten paste on the end of an iron rod and, by twisting, turning and blowing, transforms it into a vase, bird, lion, wine goblet or similar work of art. The display is usually followed by a tour of the showroom and a certain amount of pressure from the salespeople. Do bear in mind that there is no obligation to buy.

↑ Murano's handcrafted glassware makes an excellent souvenir

2

MURANO

🚤 4.1, 4.2 or 12 from Fondamente Nuove; 3 from Piazzale Roma.

Murano, like Venice, comprises a cluster of islands, connected by bridges. It has been the centre of Venetian glass-making since the 13th century.

Murano owes its prosperity entirely to glass. From the late 13th century, when the population numbered over 30,000, Murano enjoyed self-government, and in the 15th and 16th centuries it became the principal glass-producing centre in Europe. Though some of its factories are now derelict, glass is still produced here in vast quantities.

The Museo del Vetro houses a collection of antique pieces as well as a splendid section devoted entirely to modern glass.

The island's architectural highlight is the **Basilica dei Santi Maria e Donato**, whose magnificent colonnaded apse is reflected in the waters of the San Donato canal. The church's floor, or *pavimento*, incorporates fragments of ancient glass from the island's foundries into its imagery.

Basilica dei Santi Maria e Donato
🖼️🕍♿ 🏛️ Campo San Donato
📞 041 73 90 56 🕐 9am–6pm Mon–Sat

Museo del Vetro
♿🛈 🏛️ Palazzo Giustinian, Fondamenta Giustinian 🕐 Times vary, check website
🌐 museovetro.visitmuve.it

SHOP

Those looking for souvenirs will be spoilt for choice in Murano. Here are some of the best places to buy authentic Murano glassware, from hand-crafted jewellery to exquisite homewares.

Davide Penso
🏛️ Fondamenta Riva Longa 48, Murano
🌐 davidepenso.com

L'ISOLA – The Carlo Moretti Showroom
🏛️ Calle de le Botteghe 2970, Venice
🌐 lisola.com

Marina e Susanna Sent
🏛️ Fondamenta Serenella 20 🌐 marina esusannasent.com

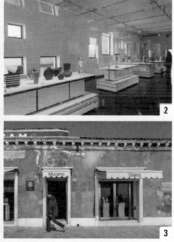

① Basilica dei Santa Maria e San Donato overlooking the square.

② Colourful exhibits on display in the Museo del Vetro.

③ Traditional Murano Glass retailer.

EXPERIENCE MORE

❸

Burano

🚢 12 from Fondamente Nuove; 14 from San Zaccaria via Lido and Punta Sabbioni

Burano is the most colourful of the lagoon islands. Lying in a lonely expanse of the northern lagoon, it is distinguished from a distance by the tall, dramatically tilted tower of its church. In contrast to the desolate Torcello (p176), the island is densely populated, its waterways lined by brightly painted houses.

A tour of the island's sights will take an hour or so. The street from the ferry stop takes visitors to the main thoroughfare, Via Baldassare Galuppi, named after the Burano-born composer (1706–85). The street is lined with traditional lace and linen stalls and open-air trattorias serving fresh fish.

PICTURE PERFECT
Burano's Houses

As the strict laws governing the colour of Venetian houses do not apply to Burano, the islanders have run amok with their paint choices. The result is a glorious riot of colour reflected in the canals and lagoon – a photographer's delight.

---

❹

San Francesco del Deserto

🚤 Access via private boat from the landing stage in Burano 🌐 sanfrancesco deldeserto.it

This little oasis of lush greenery, inhabited by nine friars, lies just south of the island of Burano. There is no vaporetto service and in order to get there you must bargain with the boatmen on Burano's quayside. Book a trip on Massimiliano's Laguna Fla boat (www.lagunaflaline.it) or take a water taxi.

> The name Giudecca, once thought to have referred to the Jews, or *giudei*, who lived here in the 13th century, is more likely to have originated from the word *giudicati*, meaning "the judged".

The multilingual friars give tours of the island's old church and the lovely gardens, which contain a tree said to have sprouted from the staff of St Francis of Assisi.

---

❺

Giudecca

🚢 2, 4.1 or 4.2

In the days of the Republic, the island of Giudecca was a pleasure ground of palaces and gardens. Today it is very much a suburb of the city, with its dark, narrow alleys flanked by apartments, its

←

Visitors admiring the
vibrant houses that fringe
Burano's waterways

TOP 3 CULTURAL SPACES IN GIUDECCA

Libreria Marco Polo
⌂ Giudecca 282 🔲 libreria
marcopolo.com
The first bookstore on
the island sells texts in
multiple languages.

Galleria Michela Rizzo
⌂ Fondamenta S. Biagio
🔲 galleriamichelarizzo.net
International and
Venetian artists are
championed at this
fabulous gallery.

Spazio Punch
⌂ Giudecca 800
🔲 spaziopunch.com
Spazio Punch stages
live events in this
former brewery.

squares overgrown and its palazzos neglected. Many of its old factories have been converted into modern housing. However, the long, wide quayside skirting the city side of the island makes a very pleasant promenade and provides stunning views of Venice across the water.

The island was originally named Spinalunga (long spine) on account of its shape. The name Giudecca, once thought to have referred to the Jews, or *giudei*, who lived here in the 13th century, is more likely to have originated from the word *giudicati*, meaning " the judged". This referred to troublesome aristocrats who, as early as the 9th century, were banished to the island.

Hotel Cipriani, among the most luxurious places to stay in Venice, is discreetly located at the tip of the island. At Giudecca's western end looms the massive Neo-Gothic ruin of the Mulino Stucky. It was built in 1895 as a flour mill by the Swiss entrepreneur Giovanni Stucky, an unpopular employer who was murdered by one of his workers in 1910. The mill ceased functioning in 1954. Following extensive renovations, it reopened in 2007 as a luxury hotel with a rooftop pool.

Giudecca's main monument is Palladio's church of Il Redentore (The Redeemer). It was built in 1577–92 in thanksgiving for the end of the 1576 plague, which wiped out a third of the city's population. The Classical interior presents a marked contrast to the ornate style of most Venetian churches. The main paintings, by Paolo Veronese and Alvise Vivarini, are in the sacristy to the right of the choir.

Il Redentore
⊕ ⌂ Campo Redentore
🚤 Redentore 🕐 10am–
4:30pm Mon-Sat 🚫 1 Jan,
25 Dec 🔲 chorusvenezia.org

↑ A bustling restaurant in Giudecca, packed
with diners as the sun begins to set

6

San Michele

🚤 **4.1 or 4.2 from Fondamente Nuove**

Studded with dark cypresses and enclosed within high terracotta walls, the cemetery island of San Michele lies just across the water from Venice's Fondamente Nuove (p166). The bodies of Venetians were traditionally buried in church graveyards in Venice, but, for reasons of hygiene and space, San Michele and its neighbour were designated cemeteries in the 19th century.

The church of San Michele in Isola stands by the landing stage. Designed by Mauro Coducci, it was the first church in Venice to be faced in white Istrian stone. With its carved tombstones and chapels, the cemetery holds a curious

---

FRA MAURO

The monastery of San Michele was home to Camaldolese monks from 1212, before being handed over to the Franciscan Order. One of the monastery's most famous residents was Fra Mauro, who in about 1450 created one of the most beautiful and detailed maps of the world without ever having left his island home. Thanks to the constant flow of merchants and seamen arriving in Venice from all over the world, Fra Mauro was able to piece together their accounts of the countries and regions they had seen on their travels, and thus produce his world map. This magnificent example of medieval cartography has undergone painstaking restoration and today is housed at the Biblioteca Nazionale Marciana (p87) in Piazza San Marco.

---

fascination. Some graves have suffered neglect, but most are well-tended and enlivened by a riot of flowers.

The most famous graves are those of foreigners: Ezra Pound (1885–1972), in the Evangelisti (Protestant) section, and Sergei Diaghilev (1872–1929) and Igor Stravinsky (1882–1971) in the Greci or Orthodox section. These bodies have been allowed to rest in peace. Most others are

Bright floral offerings (inset) and the grand
↓ arched gates of San Michele's cemetery

dug up after about 10 years to make way for new arrivals, and the bones taken to the ossuary island of Sant'Ariano. Today, however, due to an increasing lack of space, most are buried on the mainland.

7

San Servolo

🚤 **20 from San Zaccaria**

Halfway between San Marco (p76) and the Lido (p184) is the island of San Servolo. Now a centre for teaching traditional crafts, and home to the **Venice International**

→ Inside the library at San Lazzaro degli Armeni, which houses over 40,000 texts

University, it started life as one of the original monastery islands of Venice. Benedictine monks established a monastery here in the 8th century, and later added a hospital.

In 1725 the island became an asylum and a new hospital was built to house the patients. The Council of Ten (*p84*) declared that this was to be strictly a shelter for "maniacs of noble family or comfortable circumstances". Meanwhile, the poor were imprisoned or left to their own devices. In 1797 Napoleon scrubbed this discriminatory decree and the asylum became free to all.

In 1980 this spartan island was taken over by the Venice European Centre for the Trades and Professions of Conservation, and in 1996 Venice International University opened its doors here. The historic buildings and the park in which they are set have been extensively restored.

Venice International University

🏠 Isola di San Servolo
🚤 20 from San Zaccaria
🌐 univiu.org

---

⑧

Santa Maria della Grazia

Originally called La Cavana or Cavanell, the island lies a short distance from San Giorgio Maggiore (*p94*). Once a shelter for pilgrims journeying to the Holy Land, it became a monastery island in the 15th century. Its name was changed when a church was built to enshrine an allegedly miraculous image of the Virgin, brought from Constantinople. The religious buildings, including a Gothic church with some fine paintings, were secularized

> **San Lazzaro degli Armeni served as an asylum in the 12th century and later became a hospital island for lepers, named after their patron saint, Lazarus.**

under Napoleon. The island became a military zone under his rule, but the buildings were destroyed in the 1848 revolutionary uprising (*p51*).

Until the end of the 20th century, the island was home to a hospital for infectious diseases; after it moved to mainland Venice, the island was sold. It is currently closed to the public.

---

⑨

San Lazzaro degli Armeni

☎ 041 526 01 04 🚤 20
(leaves San Zaccaria daily at 2:45pm)

Lying just off the Lido, San Lazzaro degli Armeni is a small monastery island, recognizable by the onion-shaped cupola of its white campanile. The buildings are surrounded by gardens and groves of cypress trees.

This island served as an asylum in the 12th century and later became a hospital island for lepers, named after their patron saint, Lazarus. In 1717 an Armenian monk was

forced to flee his homeland, the Morea, when the Turks invaded. Venetian rulers gave him this island as a place of shelter, and he established a religious order here. The Armenians rebuilt the island, setting up a monastery, church and library amid gardens and orchards, and it has remained a centre of learning ever since.

Today, multilingual monks give visitors guided tours of the church, the art collection, the library and the museum, which houses Armenian, Greek, Indian and Egyptian artifacts. The most impressive exhibit is the printing hall where, over 200 years ago, a press produced works in 36 languages. A polyglot press is still in use, producing postcards, maps and prints for visitors.

Did You Know?

Renowned 19th-century poet Lord Byron studied at San Lazzaro degli Armeni's monastery.

↑ A group of small motorboats cruising in the turquoise waters just off Poveglia

⑩ Poveglia

Formerly called Popilia on account of its many poplar trees, this island was once a thriving community with its own government. After the 1380 war with Genoa, it fell into decline, and over the centuries became a refuge for plague victims, an isolation hospital and a home for the aged. Today the land is used for growing crops and vines.

⑪ San Clemente

Founded in 1131 as a refuge for pilgrims and soldiers en route to the Holy Land, the crescent-shaped island of San Clemente became the site of a monastery, home to a succession of religious orders. During the Republic, doges frequently met distinguished visitors here, but from 1630, when it was hit by the plague, it served as a military depot. In the 19th century the island was turned into an asylum; most of the buildings date from that time. Today San Clemente is a peaceful island with a beautiful hotel, which is currently closed and awaiting new buyers.

---

⑫ Lido

🚢 1, 2, 5.1, 5.2 and 6 (summer) to Santa Maria Elisabetta; 17 from Tronchetto to San Nicolò

The Lido is a slender sandbank 12 km (8 miles) long, which forms a natural barrier between Venice and the open sea. It is both a residential suburb of the city and – more importantly for tourists – the city's seaside resort. The only island in the lagoon with roads, it is linked to the Tronchetto island car park by car ferry. From Venice, the Lido is served by regular vaporettos.

The Lido's main season runs from June to September, the most crowded months being July and August. In winter most hotels are closed.

In the 19th century, before the Lido was developed, the island was a favourite haunt of celebrated English poet Lord Byron, author Mary Shelley and other literary figures. Legend has it that Byron swam from the Lido to Santa Chiara via the Grand Canal in under four hours.

Bathing establishments were gradually opened and by the turn of the 20th century the Lido had become one of Europe's most fashionable seaside resorts, frequented by royalty, film stars and leading lights of the literati. They stayed in the grand hotels, swam in the sea or sat in deckchairs on the sands by the striped *cabanas*. Life in the Lido's heyday was brilliantly evoked in Thomas Mann's book *Death in Venice* (1912). The Hôtel des Bains, where the melancholic character of Von Aschenbach resides, appears in the novel and in Visconti's 1970 film, and is still a prominent landmark, although it has since been converted into private apartments.

The Lido is no longer the prestigious resort it was in the 1930s. Beaches are crowded and ferries packed with day trippers, but the sands, sea and sporting facilities nevertheless provide a welcome break from city culture.

The Lido can be covered by bus but a popular form of transport is the bicycle. Visitors can hire one from the shop almost opposite the vaporetto stop at Santa Maria Elisabetta.

The east side of the island is fringed by sandy beaches. For passengers arriving by ferry at the main landing stage, these beaches are reached by bus, taxi or on foot along the Gran Viale Santa Maria Elisabetta. This is the

---

A mere stone's throw from Sant'Erasmo, in the northern lagoon, Lazzaretto Nuovo is one of the few uninhabited islands that can still be visited by the public.

→

One of the many luxury hotels that are dotted across the Lido

main shopping street of the Lido. At the end of the Gran Viale, turn left for the beaches of San Nicolò or right along the Lungomare G Marconi, which boasts the most opulent hotels and by far the best beaches. However, the hotels control the beaches in this area, and levy rather exorbitant charges (except to hotel residents) for the use of their beach facilities.

The long straight road parallel to the beach leads southwest to the village of Malamocco. There are some good fish restaurants here, but visitors will find little evidence to suggest that this was once an 8th-century political powerhouse and former seat of the lagoon's government.

The Lido's main quarter of cultural interest is San Nicolò in the north. Across the Porto di Lido, it is possible to see the fortress of Sant'Andrea on the island of Le Vignole, built by Michele Sanmicheli between 1435 and 1449 to guard the main entrance of the lagoon.

It was to the Porto di Lido that the doge was rowed annually to cast a ring into the sea in symbolic marriage each spring. After this he would visit the nearby church and monastery of San Nicolò, which was founded in 1044 and rebuilt in the 16th century.

The nearby **Jewish cemetery** dates from 1386. The rest of this area is given over to an airfield. The aeroclub located

INTERNATIONAL FILM FESTIVAL

Movie fans flock to the Lido every year for the International Film Festival. First held in 1932, the festival has long attracted big names in the film world; but it has also been plagued by bureaucracy and political in-fighting. There are signs that the event is making a comeback, however, and famous names are now returning. The event takes place in late August/early September, with films shown day and night across the island.

there can organize private flying lessons.

Jewish Cemetery
⊘ ⊗ **☎** 041 71 53 59 (call in advance for a guided visit)

13 ⊗ ⊗
Lazzaretto Nuovo
🚢13 ⏱ Apr–Oct: 9:45am & 4:30pm Sat & Sun
🌐 lazzarettonuovo.com

A mere stone's throw from Sant'Erasmo, in the northern lagoon, Lazzaretto Nuovo is one of the few uninhabited islands that can still be visited by the public. Archaeologists here continue to unearth medieval structures dating back to the late 15th century, when the island was used as a quarantine station for crews of ships hailing from distant lands where the plague was rife. Cargoes would be fumigated with rosemary and juniper. During the pestilence that afflicted Venice in 1576, the island was home to around 10,000 victims.

THE VENETO PLAIN

The Veneto Plain sweeps round from the Po river delta in the southwest to the mountains that form the border between Italy and Slovenia. The whole region is crossed by a series of rivers, canals and waterways, all of which converge in the Adriatic Sea. The river-borne silt deposits that created the Venetian Lagoon cover the Veneto, making the land extremely fertile. The Romans established their frontier posts here, and these survive today as the great cities of Vicenza, Padua and Treviso. Their strategic position at the hub of the empire's road network enabled them to prosper under Roman rule, as they continued to do under the benign rule of the Venetian empire more than 1,000 years later.

Wealth from agriculture, commerce and the spoils of war paid for the beautification of these cities through the construction of Renaissance palaces and public buildings, many of them designed by the region's great architect, Andrea Palladio. His villas can be seen all over the Veneto, symbols of the idyllic and leisured existence once enjoyed by the region's aristocrats.

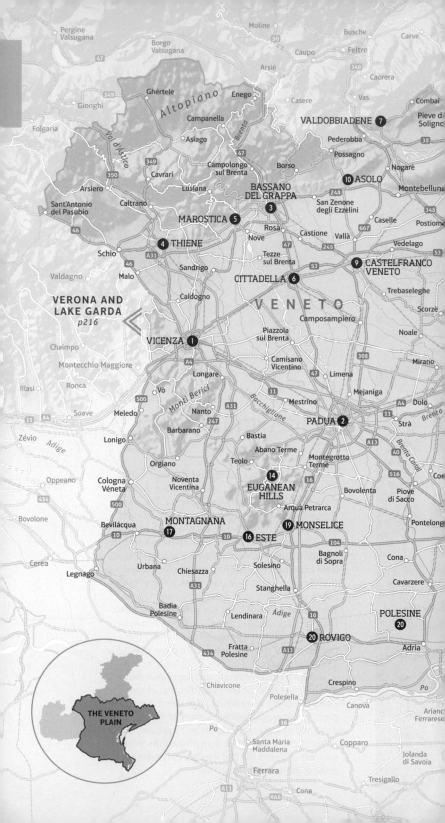

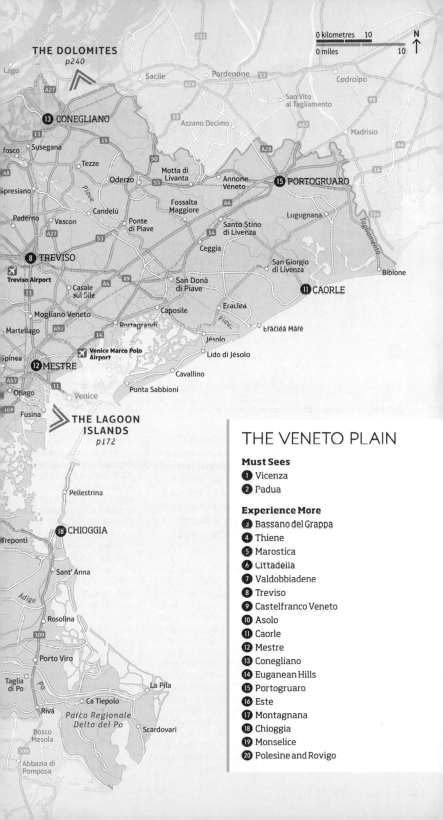

THE DOLOMITES
p240

0 kilometres   10
0 miles   10

N

13 CONEGLIANO

Lago

Sacile

Pordenone

Codroipo

San Vito
al Tagliamento

Azzano Decimo

Madrisio

fosco   Susegana

Tezze

Oderzo

Motta di
Livanta

Annone
Véneto

15 PORTOGRUARO

spresiano

Candelú

Ponte
di Piave

Fossalta
Maggiore

Lugugnana

Paderno   Vascon

Santo Stino
di Livenza

Ceggia

San Giorgio
di Livenza

Bibione

8 TREVISO

San Donà
di Piave

Treviso Airport

Casale
sul Sile

11 CAORLE

Caposile

Eraclea

Mogliano Veneto

Portegrandi

Eraclea Mare

Martellago

Jésolo

Venice Marco Polo
Airport

Lido di Jésolo

spinea   **12** MESTRE

Cavallino

Oriago

Venice

Punta Sabbioni

Fusina

THE LAGOON
ISLANDS
p172

Pellestrina

18 CHIOGGIA

Treponti

Sant' Anna

Adige

Rosolina

Porto Viro

Taglia
di Po

La Pila

Ca Tiepolo

Rivá

*Parco Regionale
Delta del Po*

Scardovari

Bosco
Mesola

Abbazia di
Pomposa

THE VENETO PLAIN

Must Sees
1 Vicenza
2 Padua

Experience More
3 Bassano del Grappa
4 Thiene
5 Marostica
6 Cittadella
7 Valdobbiadene
8 Treviso
9 Castelfranco Veneto
10 Asolo
11 Caorle
12 Mestre
13 Conegliano
14 Euganean Hills
15 Portogruaro
16 Este
17 Montagnana
18 Chioggia
19 Monselice
20 Polesine and Rovigo

Visitors exploring the
Basilica Palladiana,
Piazza dei Signori.

❶
VICENZA

🚉🚌 **Piazza Stazione** ℹ️ **Piazza Matteotti 12;**
www.vicenzae.org

Vicenza is known as the adoptive city of Andrea
Palladio (1508–80), who started out as a stonemason
and became one of the most influential architects of
all time. One of the wealthiest cities in the Veneto,
Vicenza is celebrated the world over for its splendid
and varied architecture, which shows the extraordinary
evolution of Palladio's distinctive style. It also offers a
dazzling array of elegant shops and cafés to visit.

①
Piazza dei Signori

At the heart of Vicenza, the
bustling square of Piazza dei
Signori is home to a number
of architectural landmarks,
but it is dominated by the
startling bulk of the Palazzo
della Ragione, often referred
to as the "Basilica Palladiana".
Open to the public, its green,
copper-clad roof is shaped
like an upturned boat with
a balustrade that bristles
with the statues of beloved
Greek and Roman gods. The
elegant colonnades were

designed by Palladio in 1549
to support the Vicenza's 15th-
century town hall, which had
begun to subside. This was his
first public commission, and
his aesthetically pleasing yet
practical solution ensured the
survival of the building for
many generations to come.

The astonishingly slender
Torre di Piazza alongside has
stood since the 12th century.
Opposite is the elegant café
Gran Caffè Garibaldi, which is
next to Palladio's Loggia del
Capitaniato (1571). The Loggia's
upper rooms contain the city's
council chamber.

②
Contrà Porti

Contrà (an abbreviation of
contrada, or "district") is the
local dialect word for "street".
On the western side is a series
of pretty Gothic buildings
with painted windows and
ornate balconies, including
Palazzo Porto-Colleoni (No.
19). In many ways, these
opulent houses reflect
Venice's distinctively ornate
architecture, a reminder that
Vicenza was once part of
the Venetian empire.

Several fine Palladian
palazzos stand on this street.
The Palazzo Thiene (No. 12) of
1545–50, the Palazzo Porto
Barbarano (No. 11) of 1570
and the Palazzo Iseppo da
Porto (No. 21) of 1552 all
illustrate the sheer variety of
Palladio's style – Classical
elements are common to all
three, but each is unique in its
architectural execution. The
Palazzo Thiene reveals some
intriguing details of Palladio's
methods: though the building
appears to be
of stone, close inspection
reveals that it is built of cheap
lightweight brick, cleverly
rendered to look like masonry.

the sun, who appears to fly over the ceiling of the entrance hall. In the upstairs rooms are many Gothic altarpieces, such as Hans Memling's *Crucifixion* (1468–70), the central panel of a triptych whose side panels are now in New York.

In the later rooms are works by the local artist Bartolomeo Montagna (c 1450–1523), including his *Virgin Enthroned with Child, St John the Baptist and Saints Bartholomew, Augustine and Sebastian*.

④

Santa Corona

🏠 Contrà Santa Corona
📞 0444 22 28 11 🕘 9am-5pm Tue-Sun

This Gothic church was built in 1261 to house what was thought to be a thorn from Christ's Crown of Thorns, donated by Louis IX of France. In the Porto Chapel are numerous notable paintings and the tomb of Luigi da Porto, author of the novel *Giulietta e Romeo*, upon which Shakespeare based his famous play. In the cloister the Museo Naturalistico-Archeologico exhibits natural history and archaeology.

③

Museo Civico

🏠 Piazza Matteotti 37-9
🕘 Jul-Aug: 10am-6pm Tue-Sun; Sep-Jun: 9am-5pm Tue-Sun 🌐 museicivici vicenza.it

This fine museum is housed in Palladio's Palazzo Chiericati, built in 1550. Inside is a fresco by Domenico Brusazorzi of a naked charioteer, representing

Must See

EAT

Antica Casa della Malvasia
This friendly eatery has an imaginative menu, including spaghetti with duck sauce.

🏠 Contrà Morette 5
📞 0444 54 37 04

€€€

Antico Guelfo
This upmarket restaurant is known for its traditional Veneto and modern dishes.

🏠 Contrà Pedemuro San Biagio 90 📞 0444 54 78 97

€€€

Trattoria Il Cursore
Local and seasonal produce is the order of the day here, paired with authentic regional dishes.

🏠 Stradella Pozzetto 10
📞 0444 02 05 04

€€€

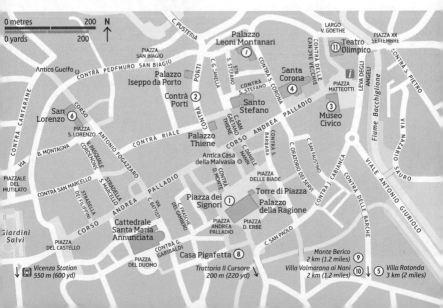

INSIDER TIP
Vicenza Card

This combined museum entry ticket is available from the tourist office, the Palladio Museum, the Museo Diocesano and Palazzo Leoni Montanari. It is valid at numerous other Vicenza sights for seven days.

terracotta roof tiles. Built between 1550 and 1552, it has inspired lookalikes in cities as far away as Delhi and St Petersburg. Fans of *Don Giovanni* will recognize locations used in Joseph Losey's 1979 film. The villa can be reached by bus from town, or on foot, following the path that passes the Villa Valmarana.

there are fine tombs. The cloister, to the north, is a flower-filled haven of calm.

⑤ ✏️
Villa Rotonda

🏠 Via della Rotonda 45
📞 0444 32 17 93 🕐 10am-noon, 3-6pm Tue-Sun (24 Nov-mid-Mar: 10am-noon, 2:30-5pm) 🌐 villala rotonda.it

With its regular, symmetrical forms, this villa, also known as the Villa Capra Valmarana, is the epitome of Palladio's architecture and the most famous of all his villas, being the most widely copied. The design is simple yet satisfying, as is the contrast between the green lawns, white walls and

⑥
San Lorenzo

🏠 Piazza San Lorenzo
📞 0444 32 19 60 🕐 7am-noon, 3:30-7pm daily

This church's portal is a splendid example of Gothic stone carving, decorated with figures of the Virgin and Child, and St Francis and St Clare. The frescoes inside are damaged, but

⑦ ✏️ 🛍️
Palazzo Leoni Montanari

🏠 Contrà Santa Corona 25
🕐 10am-6pm Tue-Sun
🌐 gallerieditalia.com

This Baroque building, completed around 1720, was commissioned by Giovanni Leoni Montanari, who had made his fortune producing and selling cloth. Today the palazzo houses an art gallery renowned for its unique collections of Venetian paintings and Russian icons.

Elegant colonnaded exterior of Andrea Palladio's Villa Rotunda *(inset)* ↓

> **The wide avenue linking the city to the Basilica di Monte Berico on top of the hill features shady colonnades with many shrines along the route.**

↑ The grand entrance hall of the ornately decorated Villa Valmarana ai Nani

⑧
Casa Pigafetta

🏠 Contrà Pigafetta

This breathtaking Spanish Gothic building of 1481 has clover-leaf balconies, gryphon brackets and Moorish windows. The owner, Antonio Pigafetta, sailed round the world with Magellan in 1519–22, being one of only 20 men who survived the voyage. The palace's extraordinary exterior can be admired from the street, but there is no public access to the interior

---

⑨
Monte Berico

🏠 Basilica di Monte Berico, Viale X Giugno 87 ☎ 0444 55 94 11 ⏰ 6am–12:30pm, 2:30–7:30pm daily (to 8pm Sun)

Monte Berico is the green, cypress-clad hill to the south of the city to which wealthy Vicenzans once escaped in the summer to enjoy cooler air and bucolic charms. The wide avenue linking the city to the spectacular Basilica di Monte Berico on top of the hill features shady colonnades with many shrines along the route. The Baroque basilica was built in the 15th century and is dedicated to the Virgin who is said to have appeared during the 1426–8 plague to declare that the city of Vicenza and all who live there would be spared.

Many pilgrims travel to this charming church, where Bartolomeo Montagna's moving *Pietà* fresco (1572) makes an impact within the ornate interior. Other attractions include a fossil collection in the cloister, and Veronese's fine painting *The Supper of St Gregory the Great* (1572) in the refectory. The large canvas was violently cut to ribbons by bayonet-wielding soldiers during the revolutionary outbursts of 1848 and has since been painstakingly restored to its former glory

---

⑩ ♿
Villa Valmarana ai Nani

🏠 Via dei Nani 8 ⏰ 10am–6pm daily 🌐 villavalmarana.com

The wall alongside the Villa Valmarana ai Nani, built in 1688 by Antonio Muttoni, is topped by the figures of dwarfs, which give this building its somewhat unusual name – *ai Nani* translates as "at the Dwarfs". Legend has it that a young dwarf girl, Princess Layana, once lived here, and her parents ensured that the servants and custodians of the villa were also dwarfs.

Inside the villa, the walls are covered with frescoes by Tiepolo, in which pagan gods float on clouds watching scenes from the epics of Homer and Virgil. In the separate Foresteria (guest house), the frescoes with themes of peasant life and the seasons, painted by Tiepolo's son, Giandomenico, are equally decorative but more earthily realistic.

The villa can be reached by a 10-minute walk from the basilica on Monte Berico. Head downhill along Via M d'Azeglio to the high-walled convent on the right where the road ends, then take the Via San Bastiano.

> **THE CITY OF GOLD**
>
> Producing around 70 per cent or Europe's gold and precious metal jewellery, Vicenza has long been Italy's capital of jewellery-making. The VicenzaOro *(www.vicenzaoro.org)* gold trade fair takes place twice a year in January and September, when local and international jewellers peddle their glamorous wares. Check out the glittering exhibits at Museo del Gioello inside the Basilica Palladiana on Piazza Signori *(p190)*.

⑪ ⬨ 🏛

TEATRO OLIMPICO

🏠 Piazza Matteotti 🚍 Piazza Matteotti 🕐 9am–5pm Tue–Sun
(Jul & Aug to 6pm) 🌐 teatrolimpicovicenza.it

The Teatro Olimpico was Palladio's final masterpiece and is a
remarkable piece of work, a showcase of his mastery of style and
perspective. The façade has all the typical Palladian hallmarks; and
the interior an extravaganza of columns, sculptures and ornamentation.
Tread the boards while marvelling at the beauty of it all.

Europe's oldest surviving indoor theatre, the Teatro Olimpico
is a remarkable structure. Andrea Palladio began work on
the Teatro in 1579, but he died without finishing it. His pupil,
Vincenzo Scamozzi, completed it in time for its ambitious
opening of Sophocles' tragic drama, *Oedipus Rex*, on 3 March
1585, with the addition of his famous trompe-l'œil scenery.

The Teatro hosts a number of events throughout the year.
In early May it's the turn of Vicenza Jazz, followed by Musical
Weeks, with an emphasis on classical music, from mid-May
to early June. September sees Vicenza in Lirica take to the
stage, while the Vicenza Opera Festival is held in October.

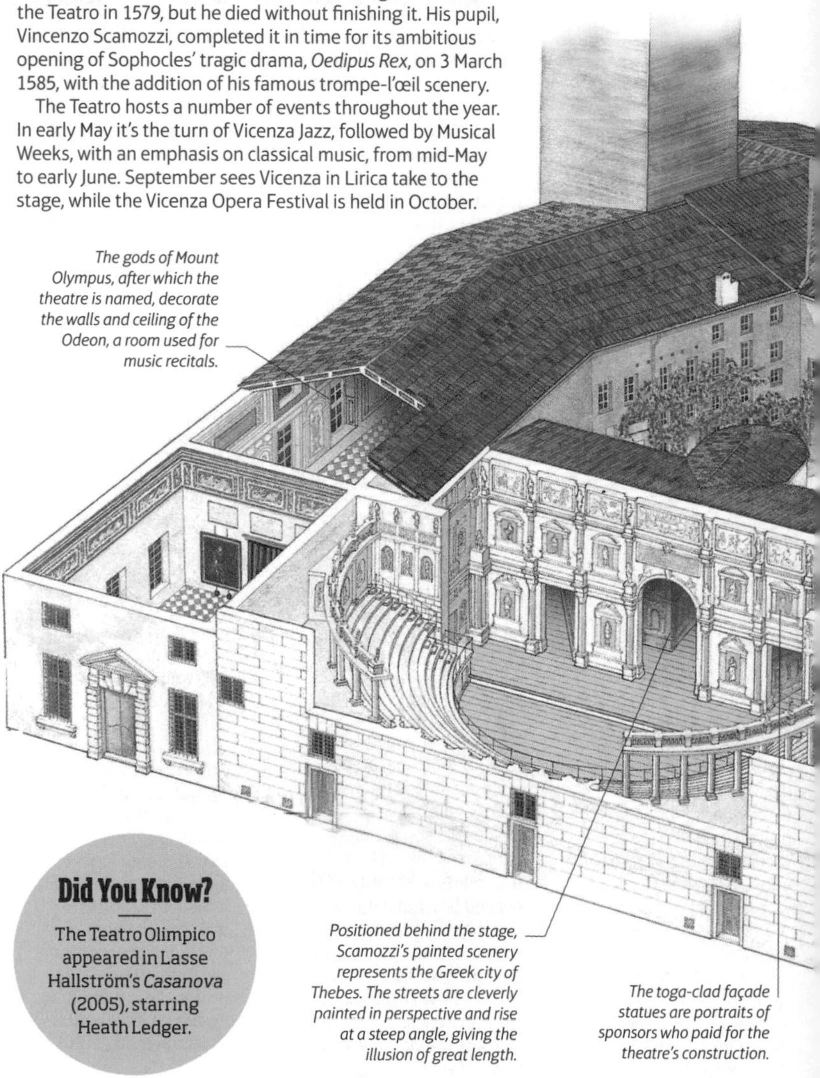

*The gods of Mount
Olympus, after which the
theatre is named, decorate
the walls and ceiling of the
Odeon, a room used for
music recitals.*

Did You Know?

The Teatro Olimpico
appeared in Lasse
Hallström's *Casanova*
(2005), starring
Heath Ledger.

*Positioned behind the stage,
Scamozzi's painted scenery
represents the Greek city of
Thebes. The streets are cleverly
painted in perspective and rise
at a steep angle, giving the
illusion of great length.*

*The toga-clad façade
statues are portraits of
sponsors who paid for the
theatre's construction.*

① The walled entrance to the Teatro Olimpico.

② Visitors strolling through the pristine grounds in the Olympic Theatre courtyard.

③ The theatre's ornate interior, with its frescoed ceiling, was designed to look and feel like an outdoor Roman amphitheatre.

< Illustration of the Teatro Olimpico interior and grounds

The armoury gateway, with its military-style carvings, leads from Piazza Matteotti into the picturesque theatre courtyard.

The courtyard of the former castle is adorned with sculptures donated by members of the Olympic Academy, the learned body that built the theatre.

ANDREA PALLADIO

Andrea Palladio was perhaps the most sought-after architect of the 16th century. Inspired by the treatises of ancient authors such as Vitruvius and Virgil, Palladio designed elegant palaces and villas for his clients that harked back to the Classical Golden Age. His own architectural treatise *The Four Books of Architecture* gained him widespread international recognition.

A SHORT WALK
VICENZA

Distance 3.5 km (2 miles) **Time** 35 minutes
Nearest Bus Vicenza Piazza Matteotti

Vicenza, the fourth-largest city in the Veneto, is packed to the brim with painstakingly precise buildings that combine classical sophistication and rugged simplicity. Walking around this great Palladian city, one can see the evolution of Andrea Palladio's distinctive style. In the centre is the monumental basilica he adapted to serve as the town hall, while all around are the palaces he built for Vicenza's wealthy citizens.

Contrà Porti is home to some of the most elegant palazzos in the city.

START

FINISH

*Palladio's impressive **Palazzo Valmarana**, built in 1566, was originally intended to be three times larger. It was not completed until 1680, 100 years after the architect's death.*

Loggia del Capitaniato *is a covered arcade designed by Palladio in 1571.*

CORSO ANDREA PALLADIO

CONTRA CAVOUR

C MUSCHERIA

VIA BATTISTI

CONTRA GARIBALDI

CONTRA PES VECC

CONTRA LAMPERTICO

CONTRA SAN ANTONIO

PIAZZA DEL DUOMO

↑ The Duomo, heavily restored and rebuilt after World War II

*The **Duomo**, Vicenza's cathedral, was rebuilt after bomb damage during World War II left only the façade and choir intact.*

0 metres	150
0 yards	150

N
↑

Encircled by grand 15th-century buildings, **Piazza dei Signori** (p190) is a lively spot, with a bustling market and busy cafés.

The **Torre di Piazza** is 82 m (269 ft) high. Begun in the 12th century, its height was increased in 1311 and 1444.

The 15th-century **basilica** has a magnificent loggia built by Palladio in 1549.

↑ Statue of the famous italian architect Andrea Palladio in the Piazzetta

The **Quartiere delle Barche** contains numerous attractive palaces built in the 14th-century Venetian Gothic style.

The elegant **Ponte San Michele** affords scenic views of the surrounding town.

Piazza delle Erbe, the city's market square, is overlooked by a 13th-century torture chamber, the Torre del Tormento.

Casa Pigafetta (p193) was the birthplace of Antonio Pigafetta, who in 1519 set sail round the world with Magellan.

This memorial to Vicenza's most famous citizen, Andrea Palladio, is often surrounded by busy market stalls.

Did You Know?

The city of Vicenza was officially designated a UNESCO World Heritage site in 1994.

↑ Ponte dei Quattro Papi crosses Padua's canal at dusk

②

PADUA

🚌 Piazzale Boschetti 🚉🛈 Piazzale della Stazione; www.turismopadova.it

Padua (Padova) is a university town with an illustrious academic history. Rich in art and architecture, it has two particularly outstanding sights. The magnificent Cappella degli Scrovegni (p204), north of the city centre, is famous for Giotto's lyrical frescoes, and forms part of the complex incorporating the Eremitani church and museums. The Basilica di Sant'Antonio is one of the most popular pilgrimage destinations in Italy.

① 🏛 🕙

La Specola

🏠 Vicolo dell'Osservatorio 5
📞 0498 29 34 49 🕙 For guided tours only; Oct-Apr: 4pm Sat, Sun & pub hols; May-Sep: 6pm daily

This attractive medieval tower on the river was turned into an observatory in 1761. The guided tour leads you around antique telescopes, charts and sextants before reaching the octagonal chamber with life-size depictions of eminent astronomers.

②

The Ghetto

The area known as "the Ghetto" was cordoned off in 1603 and gates were erected to enclose Padua's Jewish inhabitants. They were forced to live there until the segregation order was dropped in 1797, when Napoleon's army arrived and took control of the area. It is now a lovely neighbourhood with pedestrianized cobbled streets full of bars and shops. A plaque on the synagogue in Via Solferino commemorates

the 46 Paduan Jews who died in the Holocaust, reminding passers-by of the Ghetto's recent tragic history.

③ 🕙

Caffè Pedrocchi

🏠 Via VIII Febbraio 15
🕙 Daily (Jun-Oct: Tue-Sun)
🌐 caffepedrocchi.it

Grand cafés have long played an important role in the intellectual life of northern Italy, and many philosophical

GALILEO GALILEI

Often called "the father of modern science", Galileo (1564-1642) made his home in Padua, where he taught at the university. His astronomic discoveries supported Copernicus's theory that the Earth revolves around the sun. Accused of heresy and forced to recant, he spent the rest of his life under house arrest, though this did not stop his research.

issues have been thrashed out at the Caffè Pedrocchi since it first opened in 1831. Politics superseded philosophy when it became a centre of the Risorgimento movement, dedicated to liberating Italy from Austrian rule; it was the scene of uprisings in 1848, for which several student leaders were sadly executed. Later it became famous as the café that never closed its doors. These days people come to talk, read, play cards or watch the world go by as they eat and drink tempting cuisine from the varied menu.

The beautiful upstairs rooms, decorated in Moorish, Egyptian and Greek styles, are now the premises of the **Museum del Risorgimento e dell'Età Contemporanea**. On display here are historical artifacts from WWII.

Museum del Risorgimento e dell'Età Contemporanea

⊗ ☎049 820 50 07
🕘9:30am–12:30pm & 3:30–6pm Tue–Sun 🚫Aug

---

④ ⊗ Ⓜ

Palazzo del Bo (University)

🏠Via VIII Febbraio 2
☎0498 27 33 15 ⏰For guided tours only; call ahead

Named after a tavern called *Il Bo* (the ox), Padua's main university building is mostly used today for graduation ceremonies. Originally it housed the medical faculty, renowned throughout Europe. Among its famous teachers and students was Gabriele Fallopio (1523–62), after whom the Fallopian tubes are named. Elena Lucrezia Cornaro Piscopia was the first woman in the world to receive a university degree. She graduated in 1678 – long before women could study at many of Europe's other universities. Her statue can be found on the grand staircase leading to the upper gallery of the 16th-century courtyard.

On the tour, you can expect to see the pulpit that Galileo used when he taught here from 1592 until 1610. It also takes in the world's oldest surviving anatomy theatre, which dates back to 1594.

DRINK

Antonio Ferrari
Sophisticated and modern wine bar with friendly staff. Specializes in divine sparkling wines.

🏠Via Umberto I, 15
🌐antonioferrari.it

Enoteca Da Severino
Wide selection of wines with knowledgeable staff. Sample a glass with a selection of cheese, or buy a bottle to take home.

🏠Via del Santo 44
☎049 650 697 🕘2–5pm Mon–Sat & Sun

Gran Caffe Diemme
Drinks range from cappuccinos to beer and wine. Cool vibe, friendly atmosphere, and a brilliant location make this a great drinking den.

🏠Piazza dei Signori 17
🚫Mon 🌐grancaffe diemme.it

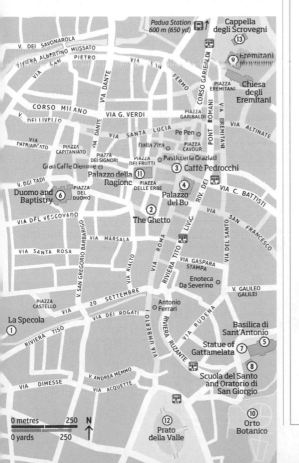

⑤
Basilica di Sant'Antonio

🏠 Piazza del Santo 📞 049 822 56 52 🕐 6:20am–6:45pm daily

This exotic church, with its minaret-like spires and Byzantine domes, is also known as Il Santo. It was begun in 1232 to house the remains of St Anthony of Padua, a preacher who modelled himself on St Francis of Assisi. Although he was a simple man who rejected worldly wealth, the citizens of Padua constructed one of the most lavish churches in Christendom to serve as his shrine.

The outline of the Basilica di Sant'Antonio reflects the influence of Byzantine architecture; a cone-shaped central dome is surrounded by a further seven domes, rising above a façade that combines Gothic with Romanesque elements. The interior is more conventional, however. Visitors are kept away from the high altar, which features Donatello's magnificent reliefs (1444–5) on the miracles of St Anthony, and his statues of the Virgin, the Crucifixion and several Paduan saints. There is access to St Anthony's tomb in the north transept, and it's hung with offerings and photographs of people who have survived serious illness or car crashes with the saint's

help. The walls around the shrine are decorated with large marble reliefs depicting St Anthony's life, carved in 1505–77 by various artists, including Jacopo Sansovino and Tullio Lombardo. These are rather cold by comparison with Altichiero da Zevio's *Crucifixion* fresco (1380s) in the opposite transept. This pageant-like painting of everyday scenes from medieval life depicts people, animals and plants.

---

⑥ ♿
Duomo and Baptistry

🏠 Piazza Duomo 📞 049 65 69 14 🕐 10am–6pm daily

Padua's grand Duomo was commissioned from Michelangelo in 1552, but his designs were altered during the construction. Of the 4th-century cathedral which stood on the site, the domed Romanesque Baptistry still survives, with its frescoes by Giusto de' Menabuoi (c 1376). The

> ### The outline of the Basilica di Sant'Antonio reflects the influence of Byzantine architecture; a cone-shaped central dome is surrounded by a further seven domes.

frescoes cover biblical stories, such as the Creation, Crucifixion and Resurrection and the Last Judgment.

---

⑦
Statue of Gattamelata

Near the entrance to the basilica stands one of the great Renaissance works. This gritty portrait of the mercenary soldier Gattamelata (whose name means "Honey Cat") was created in 1443–52, honouring a man who in his life did great service to the Venetian Republic. Donatello won fame for the monument, the first equestrian statue made of this size since Roman times.

---

⑧ ♿
Scuola del Santo and Oratorio di San Giorgio

🏠 Piazza del Santo 11 📞 049 822 56 52 🕐 9am–1pm & 2–6pm Tue–Sun

These two linked buildings contain excellent frescoes, including the earliest

←
The statue of Gattamelata stands beside the fine Basilica di Sant'Antonio

documented paintings by Titian. These comprise two scenes from the life of St Anthony in the Scuola del Santo, executed in 1511. The delightful saints' lives and scenes from the life of Christ in the San Giorgio Oratory are the work of two artists, Altichiero da Zevio and Jacopo Avenzo, who painted them in 1378–84.

Eremitani Museums

📍 Piazza Eremitani 8
🚌 ⏰ Museums: 9am-7pm Tue-Sun ⏱ 1 Jan, 1 May, 25 & 26 Dec 🌐 padovacultura. padovanet.it

This museum complex occupies a group of 14th-century monastic buildings attached to the church of the Eremitani, a reclusive Augustinian order. The admission ticket includes entry to the nearby Cappella

↑ Admiring the Eremitani Museums' rich collection of paintings and sculpture

degli Scrovegni (p204) which overlooks the city's Roman amphitheatre, and to the Archaeology Museum, the Medieval and Modern Art Museum, and the Bottacin Museum, housed in the Palazzo Zuckerman across the road.

The main highlight of the rich archaeological collection is the temple-like tomb of the Volumni family, dating from the 1st century AD. Among several other Roman tombstones from the Veneto region is one to the young dancer Claudia Toreuma – sadly, a fairly dull inscribed column rather than a portrait. The collection also includes some fine mosaics, along with several impressive life-size statues depicting muscular Roman deities and toga-clad dignitaries.

The massive Medieval and Modern Art Museum is well worth a visit. It covers the history of Venetian art, with paintings from Giotto to the 1700s. Another section looks at Giotto and his influence on local art, using the Crucifix from the Cappella degli Scrovegni as its centrepiece. The Crucifix is flanked by an army of angels (late 15th century) painted in gorgeous colours by the artist Guariento. Alongside the museum

complex is the Eremitani church (1276–1306), with its magnificent roof and wall tombs. Interred here is Marco Benavides (1489–1582), a professor of law at the city university whose mausoleum was designed by Ammannati, a Renaissance architect from Florence. Sadly missing from the church are Andrea Mantegna's celebrated frescoes of the lives of St James and St Christopher (1454–7), which were destroyed during a bombing raid in World War II. Two scenes from this magnificent work survive in the Ovetari Chapel, south of the sanctuary. The Martyrdom of St James was reconstructed from salvaged fragments, and The Martyrdom of St Christopher was removed carefully and stored elsewhere before the bombing. Otherwise only photographs on the walls remain to hint at the quality of the lost works.

TOP 3 ERMITANI MUSEUMS HIGHLIGHTS

Coin Collections
The Bottacin Museum houses an almost complete set of fine Venetian coinage and rare Roman medallions.

Renaissance Bronzes
The most appealing feature in the brilliant Archaeology Museum is the comical Drinking Satyr bronze by Il Riccio (1470-1532).

Molinari's Depiction
The Medieval and Modern Art Museum's painting of Elena Lucrezia Cornaro Piscopia, though not artistically special, is significant for depicting the first woman to graduate in the world.

3,000

The number of paintings housed in the monumental Medieval and Modern Art Museum.

Orto Botanico

📍 Via Orto Botanico 15
🕐 Tue-Sun (Apr-May: daily)
🚫 1 Jan, 25 Dec 🌐 orto botanicopd.it

Founded in 1545, Padua's botanical garden is the oldest in Europe, and it retains much of its original appearance; one of the palm trees dates to 1585. Originally intended for the cultivation of medicinal plants, the pathways now spill over with exotic foliage, shaded by ancient trees. The gardens were used to cultivate the first lilacs (1565), sunflowers (1568) and potatoes (1590) grown in Italy.

The original garden was expanded in 2014 with five biodiversity gardens on the site where the Benedictine vegetable gardens once grew. Containing a variety of microcosms, including a tropical rainforest and arid climates, the biodiversity garden building has been designed to be as environmentally friendly as possible, using natural solar energy and rainwater collection. The biodiversity garden is a great source of

> **PICTURE PERFECT**
> **Orchids Abound**
>
> The tropical green-house in the Orto Botanico has a large selection of orchids. Photograph those with large, bright flowers up close, and save a wider shot for the species with tiny flowers.

information, telling the stories of important plants from around the world that are used for a variety of purposes from medicine to construction.

THE BRENTA CANAL

The River Brenta, between Padua and the Venetian Lagoon, was canalized in the 16th century. Flowing for a total of 36 km (22 miles), its potential as a transport route was quickly realized, and fine villas were built along its length. Today, three of these elegant buildings open their doors to the public: the Villa Foscari at Malcontenta, the Villa Widmann-Foscari at Mira, and the Villa Pisani at Stra. They can be visited either on an eight- to nine-hour guided tour from Padua to Venice (or vice versa) along the river on a motor launch, or by bus, a cheaper and faster alternative. Booking is necessary through a local travel agent or online at *www.ilburchiello.it*. A ticket includes a bus between Padua and Stra, a boat tour and guide, and entrance to two villas.

Palazzo della Ragione

📍 Piazza delle Erbe (via the town hall) 📞 049 820 50 06
🕐 9am-7pm Tue-Sun (Nov-Jan: to 6pm) 🚫 Mon and pub hols

The "Palace of Reason", also known as the "Salone" by locals, was built to serve as Padua's law court and council chamber in 1218. The vast main hall was originally frescoed by the celebrated artist Giotto, but fire

Walking through the lush gardens at the beautiful Orto Botanico

EAT

PePen

A popular lunchtime spot, PePen has pizzas as well as a selection of traditional local dishes.

⌂ Piazza Cavour 15
🕐 3-6pm Mon-Sat
🔲 pepen.it

€€€

Dalla Zita

Loved by locals, this hole-in-the-wall eatery has a cornucopia of sandwiches.

⌂ Via Gorizia 12
☎ 049 664 992

€€€

Pasticceria Graziati

Though ostensibly a cake shop, Graziati serves meals in its wine-cellar restaurant.

⌂ Piazza della Frutta 40
🔲 graziati.com

€€€

destroyed his work in 1420. The frescoes that survive today are by the relatively unknown Nicola Miretto, though their astrological theme is fascinating.

The Salone is breathtaking in its sheer size. It is Europe's biggest undivided medieval hall, 80 m (260 ft) long, 27 m (90 ft) wide and 27 m (90 ft) high. The scale is reinforced by the wooden horse displayed at one end – a massive beast, copied from Donatello's Gattamelata statue (p200) in 1466 and originally made to be pulled in procession during Paduan festivities. It makes for an impressive photograph.

The walls are covered in Miretto's frescoes (1420–25), a total of 333 panels depicting the months of the year with appropriate gods, zodiacal signs and seasonal activities.

Also within the palazzo is the Stone of Shame, on which bankrupts were exposed to ridicule before they were sent into exile.

---

⑫

Prato della Valle

The Prato (field) claims to be the largest public square in Italy, and its elliptical shape reflects the form of the Roman theatre that stood on the site. St Anthony of Padua used to preach sermons

← Statue of Pope Alexander VIII in Prato della Valle

to huge crowds here, but subsequent neglect saw the area turn into a malaria-ridden swamp. The land was drained in 1767 to create the canal that now encircles the Prato. Four stone bridges cross the picturesque channel, which is lined on both sides by statues of 78 eminent citizens of Padua. These depict a range of figures, from Pope Alexander VIII to Gustavus Adolphus of Sweden.

The green area is a popular spot for locals and visitors to relax, catch up and bask in the sun. On Saturdays there is a market, selling everything from footwear to plants and fruits and vegetables.

Giotto's frescoes
covering the walls of
the Scrovegni Chapel ↑

⑬ ⚔

CAPPELLA DEGLI SCROVEGNI, PADUA

📍 Piazza Eremitani 8 (entrance Eremitani Museums) 🚎 To Piazzale Boschetti 🕐 9am-7pm daily; advance booking compulsory 🚫 Pub hols 🌐 cappelladegliscrovegni.it

Enrico Scrovegni built this chapel in 1303, hoping thereby to spare his dead father, a usurer, from the eternal damnation in hell described by the poet Dante in his *Inferno*. The interior of the chapel is covered with beautiful frescoes of scenes from the life of Christ, painted by Giotto between 1303 and 1305. As works of great narrative force, they exerted a powerful influence on the development of European art.

↑ The fine exterior of the Cappella degli Scrovegni

Giotto's Frescoes

The Florentine artist Giotto (1266–1337) is regarded as the father of the Renaissance, the great revival in the Classical traditions of Western art. His frescoes in this chapel – with their sense of pictorial space, naturalism and narrative drama – mark a decisive break with the Byzantine tradition of the preceding 1,000 years. In such scenes as *Lament over the Dead Christ* figures are naturalistic and three-dimensional, not stylized, and emotions are clearly expressed. He is the first Italian master whose name has passed into posterity, and, although Giotto was considered a great artist in his lifetime, few of the works attributed to him are fully documented. The famous frescoes inside the Chapel, nonetheless, are rare exceptions where his authorship is in no doubt.

← Giotto's *Mary is Presented at the Temple*

VISITING THE CHAPEL

It is compulsory to book your visit on the website in advance as there are strict limits on the number of visitors allowed in to the Chapel at any one time. Before entering, visitors must spend 15 minutes in a decontamination chamber, where an explanatory film on the chapel and its famous frescoes is provided. The visit itself is restricted to 15 minutes.

↑ Figures expressing grief in Giotto's *Lament over the Dead Christ*

A SHORT WALK
PADUA

Distance 1.5 km (1 mile) **Time** 20 minutes
Nearest Bus Piazza delle Erbe

The city centre of Padua (known as Padova in Italian) is one of the liveliest in northern Italy, thanks to a large student population and to the two street markets, one specializing in fruit and the other in vegetables. These take place every day except Sunday around the vast Palazzo della Ragione, the town's medieval law court and council chamber. The colonnades round the exterior of the palazzo shelter numerous bars, restaurants and shops selling meat, game, cheeses and wine.

Palazzo del Capitaniato, *built between 1599 and 1605 for the head of the city's militia, incorporates an astronomical clock made in 1344.*

Piazza dei Signori *is bordered by attractive arcades which house small speciality shops, interesting cafés and old-fashioned wine bars.*

START ▶ PIAZZA CAPITANIATO

VIA SAN CLEMENTE

PIAZZA DEI SIGNORI

Palazzo Liviano, *a 14th-century arts faculty, contains frescoes and a rare portrait of Petrarch.*

Now used as a conference centre, the elegant **Loggia della Gran Guardia,** *dating from 1523, once housed the Council of Nobles.*

VIA MONTE DI PIETÀ

VIA MANIN

PIAZZA DEL DUOMO

VIA SONCI

VIA VANDELLI

The **Palazzo del Monte di Pietà** *has 16th-century arcades and statues enclosing a medieval building.*

The 12th-century baptistry of the **Duomo** *(p200) contains one of the most complete medieval fresco cycles to survive in Italy, painted by Giusto de' Menabuoi in 1378 and now restored.*

← Winged lion and clock tower of Palazzo del Capitaniato

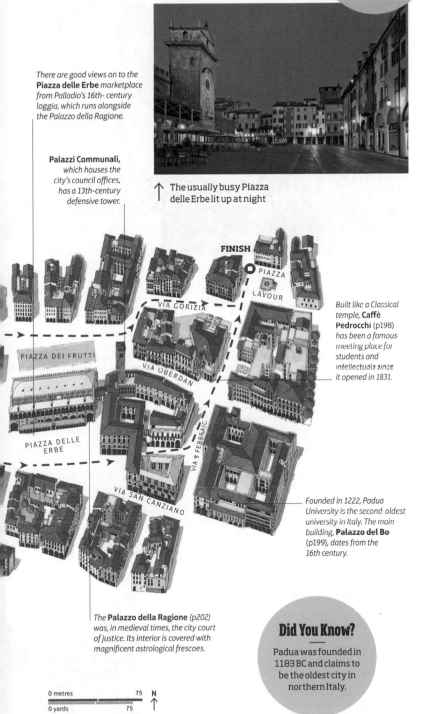

There are good views on to the **Piazza delle Erbe** marketplace from Palladio's 16th-century loggia, which runs alongside the Palazzo della Ragione.

Palazzi Communali, which houses the city's council offices, has a 13th-century defensive tower.

↑ The usually busy Piazza delle Erbe lit up at night

FINISH

PIAZZA CAVOUR

Built like a Classical temple, **Caffè Pedrocchi** (p198) has been a famous meeting place for students and intellectuals since it opened in 1831.

VIA GORIZIA

PIAZZA DEI FRUTTI

VIA UBERDAN

PIAZZA DELLE ERBE

VIA 9 FEBBRAIO

VIA SAN CANZIANO

Founded in 1222, Padua University is the second-oldest university in Italy. The main building, **Palazzo del Bo** (p199), dates from the 16th century.

The **Palazzo della Ragione** (p202) was, in medieval times, the city court of justice. Its interior is covered with magnificent astrological frescoes.

Did You Know?

Padua was founded in 1183 BC and claims to be the oldest city in northern Italy.

| 0 metres | 75 |
| 0 yards | 75 |

N ↑

↑ Visitors looking out from the Ponte degli Alpini in Bassano del Grappa

EXPERIENCE MORE

③
Bassano del Grappa

🚉🚌 ℹ Piazza Garibaldi 34; www.commune.bassano.gov.it

This town is synonymous with Italy's favourite after-dinner drink (*grappa* is not named after the town, but after *graspa*, the Italian term for the lees used to distil the liquor). Information on this and on the role played by Bassano during both world wars is given at the **Museo degli Alpini**, across the Ponte degli Alpini bridge. Designed in 1569 by Palladio, the current bridge dates from 1948: its timber allows it to flex when hit by spring meltwaters.

Bassano is also famous for the majolica wares at **Palazzo Sturm**. The works of locally born artist Jacopo Bassano (1510–92) and the sculptor Canova (1757–1822) are celebrated in the **Museo Civico**.

Museo degli Alpini
🔗📷🏛 🚗 Via Angarano 2 ☎0424 50 36 62 🕘9am-8pm Tue-Sun

Palazzo Sturm
🔗 🚗 Via Schiavonetti 40 ☎0424 51 99 40 🕘9am-1pm, 3-6pm Mon-Sat, 10:30am-7pm Sun & pub hols

Museo Civico
🔗 🚗 Piazza Garibaldi 🕘10am-7pm Wed-Mon 🌐museibassano.it

④
Thiene

🚌 ℹ Piazzetta Rossi 17; 0445 80 48 37

Thiene is one of the area's many historic textile towns, manufacturing jeans and

---

GRAPPA DISTILLERIES

Grappa is a hugely popular drink in Italy, with around 40 million bottles produced every year. Essentially a hard liquor, it is made from almost every part of the grape left over after the initial pressing to make wine. Italians like it after dinner but will also add it to an espresso to produce the *caffè corretto* - an alcoholic pick-me-up (that is, hair of the dog). There are thousands of labels, but some of the best in Bassano are produced at distinguished distilleries such as Nardini (nardini.it) and De Poli (poligrappa.com), both of which offer fascinating tours and tastings.

sweatshirts for sale all over Europe. Two grand villas nearby are certainly worth a visit. Of these, the **Castello Porto-Colleoni** stood in open countryside at the time it was built. Its impressive defences were a precaution against bandits and raiders. Inside there are 16th-century frescoes by Giambattista Zelotti that add a lighter note, and many portraits of horses remind the visitor that the villa's owners, the Colleoni family, were employed by the Venetian cavalry.

Zelotti also frescoed the **Villa Godi Malinverni**, which was the first villa designed by Palladio (p194). The garden is charming and the frescoes are magnificent. Inside the villa are works by Italian Impressionists and a lovely portrait by Pietro Annigoni (1910–88) called *La Strega* (The Sorceress).

Castello Porto-Colleoni
⊗ ⊗ ⊠ Corso Garibaldi 12
⊙ Mid-Mar–mid-Nov: Tue–Fri, Sun & pub hols (for tours only)
ⓦ castellodithiene.com

Villa Godi Malinverni
⊗ ⋒ Via Palladio 44
⊙ Times vary, check website
ⓦ villagodi.com

5
Marostica

⊠ 🛈 Piazza degli Scacchi; 0424 721 27

Marostica is an almost perfect medieval fortified town, with town walls built in 1370 by the Scaligeri (p233). The rampart walk from the **Castello Inferiore** (lower castle) to the Castello Superiore (upper castle) has fine views.

The lower castle exhibits costumes worn by participants in the town's human chess tournament, the Partita a Scacchi, which is held on a magnificent marble chess board in the piazza every other September. Up to 650 people participate in this colourful re-enactment of a game first played here in 1454.

Castello Inferiore
⊛ ⊠ Piazza degli Scacchi
⊙ 9am–noon, 3–6:30pm daily
⊠ 1 Jan, 25 Dec ⓦ marostica scacchi.it

↓ Cyclists in the checkered piazza in Marostica

(p233)

EAT

Antico Ristorante Cardellino
Expect a focus on seasonal fare; asparagus served with tagliatelle is a speciality in spring.

⋒ Via Bellavitis 17, Bassano del Grappa
ⓦ ristorantecardellino.it

€€€

Osteria Trinità
An elegant eatery with a strong line in grilled meats, and an excellent wine list.

⋒ Via Contrà San Giorgio 17, Bassano del Grappa
ⓦ osteriatrinita bassano.it

€€€

Ristorante Trevisani
This pretty restaurant is housed in a 14th-century building and offers traditional dishes.

⋒ Vicolo Jacopo da Ponte 37 Bassano del Grappa
⊙ Noon–11pm daily (to 10:30pm Sun)
ⓦ ristorantetrevisani.it

€€€

6

Cittadella

FS 🚌 ℹ️ **Porte Bassanesi 2;**
0499 40 44 85

This attractive town is the twin of Castelfranco. Both were fortified and Cittadella still preserves its 13th-century moated walls. These are interrupted by four gates and 16 towers. The Torre di Malta near the southern gate was used as a torture chamber by Ezzelino de Romano, who ruled in the mid-13th century. Far more pleasant is the *Supper at Emmaus* in the Duomo, a masterpiece by local Renaissance artist Bassano.

7

Valdobbiadene

🚌 ℹ️ **Piazza Marconi 1;**
0423 97 69 75

Valdobbiadene, surrounded by vine-covered hills, is a centre for the sparkling white wine called Cartizze, a type of prosecco. To the east, the Strada del Vino Bianco (white wine route) stretches 34 km (21 miles) to the town of Conegliano (p212), passing vineyards offering wine to try and to buy.

About 10 km (8 miles) northeast of Valdobbiadene is the small town of Follina, known for its well-preserved Romanesque abbey.

8

Treviso

🚌 **FS** ℹ️ **Via Fiumicelli**
30, Piazza Borsa; www.
visittreviso.it

Full of attractive balconied houses, Treviso is a rewarding city for visitors. Comparisons are often made with Venice, but Treviso has its own distinctive character. A good place to explore the architecture is the main street, Calmaggiore. The tradition of painting the exterior of the houses dates back to the medieval period, when this form of decoration compensated for the lack of suitable stone. The modern fish market also has medieval origins. It is held on an island in the middle of Treviso's River Sile so that the remains of the day's trading can be flushed away instantly.

Treviso's Duomo, founded in the 12th century, was reconstructed in the 15th, 16th and 18th centuries. Inside is Titian's *Annunciation* (1570), but it is upstaged by the *Adoration of the Magi* fresco (1520) of his arch rival, Il Pordenone. Other works of note are *The Adoration of the Shepherds* fresco by Paris Bordone, and the monument to Bishop Zanetti (1501) by Pietro Lombardo and his sons.

Did You Know?

A fresco in Treviso's Church of San Nicolò contains the first ever depiction of someone wearing glasses.

The **Museo Civico** houses an archaeology collection and a picture gallery in the restored convent of Santa Caterina dei Servi. Lorenzo Lotto's *Portrait of a Dominican* (1526), Titian's *Portrait of Sperone Speroni* (1544) and Bassano's *Crucifixion* are highlights.

Nestled near the 16th-century town wall is the bulky Dominican church of San Nicolò, full of tombs and frescoes, including some by Lorenzo Lotto. There is a gigantic painting of St Christopher by Antonio da Treviso.

Museo Civico – Sede
Santa Caterina
♿ 🏛️ **Piazzetta Mario Botter**
1 🕐 **Tue–Sun** 🚫 **Pub hols**
🌐 **museiciviitreviso.it**

Sunset over the green hills of Valdobbiadene, a renowned wine region

9
Castelfranco Veneto

FS 🚌 🛈 Via Riccati 14; 0423 49 50 00

Fortified in 1199 by rulers of Treviso, the historic core of this town lies within the well-preserved walls. **Casa di Giorgione**, the birthplace of artist Giorgione (1478–1511), houses a museum devoted to his life. He created such works as *The Tempest (p143)*. His *Virgin and Child with Saints Liberal and Francis* (1504) is displayed in the Duomo. Tuzio Costanza commissioned it to stand above the tomb of his son, Matteo, killed in battle in 1504.

At Fanzolo, northeast of Castelfranco, is Palladio's **Villa Emo**, designed in 1564. Here, Zelotti's frescoes show the love lives of Greek deities.

> **Valdobbiadene, surrounded by vine-covered hills, is a centre for the sparkling white wine called Cartizze, a type of prosecco.**

The imposing façade *(inset)* and period interiors of the Villa Barbaro outside Asolo ↑

Casa di Giorgione
🏛 🚪 Piazza San Liberale
🕐 9:30am–12:30pm Tue–Sun (also 2:30–6:30pm Fri–Sun)
🚫 1 Jan, Easter, 25 Dec
🌐 museogiorgione.com

Villa Emo
🏛 🏠 🚪 Via Stazione 5, Fanzolo **FS 🚌** 🕐 10am–6pm daily (Oct–Mar: to 5:30pm)
🚫 1 Jan, 25 & 31 Dec
🌐 villaemo.org

10
Asolo

🚌 🛈 Piazza Garibaldi 73; www.asolo.it

Asolo is beautifully situated among the cypress-clad foothills of the Dolomites. Queen Caterina Cornaro (1454–1510) once ruled this tiny walled town, and the poet Cardinal Pietro Bembo coined the verb *asolare* to describe the bittersweet life of enforced idleness she endured. Others who have fallen in love with these narrow streets include poet Robert Browning, who named a volume of poems after the town, and travel writer Freya Stark, who lived here until her death in 1993.

Just east of Asolo is the Villa Barbaro at Masèr, while to the north is the village of Possagno, birthplace of Antonio Canova. Canova's remains lie inside the huge temple-like church that he designed himself. Nearby is the family home, the **Casa di Canova**. The Gypsoteca here houses the plaster casts and clay models for many of Canova's sculptures.

Casa di Canova
🏛 🚪 Via Canova 74
🕐 9:30am–6pm Tue–Sun (to 7pm Sun) 🚫 1 Jan, Easter, 25 Dec 🌐 museocanova.it

⑪ Caorle

🚌 *i* Rio Terrà 3; 0421 810 85 🌐 turismo venezia.it/ Bibione-e-Caorle

Like Venice, Caorle was built among the swamps of the Venetian Lagoon by refugees fleeing the Goths in the 5th century. Today it is a bustling fishing village perched on the edge of an expanse of purpose-built lagoons, carefully managed to encourage fish to enter and spawn. The young are then fed and farmed.

The area is also of great interest to naturalists for its abundant birdlife. The town's 11th-century Duomo is worth a visit for its Pala d'Oro, a gilded altarpiece made up of Byzantine panel reliefs.

⑫ Mestre

🚌 *i* Via Antonio Lazzari 32

Mestre, the industrial offspring of Venice, is often favoured by visitors as a relatively less expensive base than Venice or other towns for exploring the region.

Mestre's M9 museum is highlight of the town itself. As well as interactive exhibits about the 20th century, the ultra-contemporary building houses exhibition space, an auditorium, and a hugely popular restaurant and bar.

> **Mestre, the industrial offspring of Venice, is often favoured by visitors as a relatively less expensive base for exploring the region than Venice or other towns.**

⑬ Conegliano

🚌 FS *i* Via XX Settembre 132; 0438 21 230

Conegliano lies between the prosecco-producing vineyards and those that produce fine red wine. Winemakers from both areas learn their craft at Conegliano's renowned wine school. The town's winding and arcaded main street, Via XX Settembre, is lined by 15th- to 18th-century palazzos, some decorated with external frescoes, some in Venetian Gothic style. The Duomo contains a gorgeous altarpiece by Cima da Conegliano (1460–1518) showing the *Virgin and Child with Saints* (1493).

Reproductions of Cima's paintings are displayed in the **Casa di Cima**, the artist's birthplace. His detailed landscapes were based on the hills around the town; they can still be seen from the gardens surrounding the **Castelvecchio** (old castle). A small museum of local history is housed in the castle.

Casa di Cima
⊛ ⌂ Via Cima 24 ☎ 0438 224 94 🕐 4–7pm Sat & Sun (Oct–Mar: 3–6pm)

Castelvecchio
⊛ ⌂ Piazzale Castelvecchio 8 ☎ 0438 228 71 🕐 10am–12:30pm, 4–7:30pm Tue–Sun (Nov–Mar: 2:30–6pm)

⑭ Euganean Hills

i Via Euganea Treponti 98, Teolo; 049 859 50 02

The Euganean Hills rise abruptly out of the Veneto Plain and offer plenty of walking opportunities. Hot springs bubble up out of the ground at Abano Terme and Montegrotto Terme, where scores of establishments offer thermal treatments. These spa cures date back to Roman

← A woman walking through the steep, narrow streets of Caorle's Old Town

times, and visitors can see extensive remains of the Roman baths and theatre at Montegrotto.

Abbazia di Praglia, the Benedictine monastery at Praglia, 6 km (4 miles) west of Abano Terme, is a peaceful haven in the tree-clad hills. The monks have long been growing herbs commercially and there is a shop selling aromatic wares. They also lead guided tours of parts of the abbey and the Renaissance church (1490–1548), with its beautiful cloister.

The picturesque town of Arquà Petrarca, south of the Euganean Hills, was once simply Arquà. Its name changed in 1868 to honour the medieval poet Francesco Petrarca, or Petrarch (1303–74), who lived here in his old age in a house frescoed with scenes from his poems. **Casa di Petrarca** still contains the poet's desk, chair, bookshelves and mummified cat. His sarcophagus sits in the piazza in front of the church.

To the north of Arquà is the **Villa Barbarigo**. The villa itself is only open to groups, but the real attraction is its outstanding Baroque garden. Planted from 1669, it is full of variety, with fountains, statues and lakes.

Abbazia di Praglia

🕙 🚪 Via Abbazia di Praglia, Bresseo di Teolo 🕐 Times vary, check website 🌐 praglia.it

↑ Villa Barbarigo, a spectacular 17th-century villa in the Euganean Hills

Casa di Petrarca

🕙 🕙 🚪 Via Valleselle 4, Arquà Petrarca 📞 0429 71 82 94 🕐 Tue–Sun 🚫 Most pub hols

Villa Barbarigo

🕙 🕙 🚪 Valsanzibio 🕐 Feb–Dec: 10am–1pm, 2pm–sunset daily 🌐 valsanzibiogiardino.it

15
Portogruaro

🚉 🚆 ⓘ Piazza della Repubblica 1; 0421 27 72 11; www.portogruarove.it

Situated on the main road linking Venice to Trieste, Portogruaro is the medieval successor to the Roman town of Concordia Sagittaria. Finds from Concordia, including statues and mosaics, are displayed in the town's **Museo Concordiese**. These were unearthed in the village

←
A striking statue on display in Portogruaro

of Concordia, 2 km (1 mile) to the south, where the ruined Roman buildings can be seen around the church and baptistry.

Museo Concordiese

🕙 🚪 Via Seminario 26 📞 0421 726 74 🕐 8:30am–7:30pm daily

LA STRADA DEL PROSECCO

Perched in the foothills of the Dolomites, the Strada del Prosecco connects Conegliano and Valdobbiadene (p210), meandering past crumbling farmhouses and quaint cantinas en route. This road is not for the faint-hearted, particularly in winter, but your bravery will be rewarded with fabulous views, hospitable hillside villages and, of course, rivers of delicious bubbly goodness.

⑯
Este

**FS 🚌 ℹ Via Guido Negri 9;
0429 600 462**

Excavations at Este have uncovered impressive remains of the ancient Ateste people, who flourished from the 9th century BC until they were conquered by the Romans in the 3rd century BC. The archaeological finds, including funerary urns, bronze vases and jewellery, are on display in the excellent **Museo Nazionale Atestino**, set within the walls of the town's 14th-century castle. The museum also displays examples of Roman and medieval art, and pieces of local pottery, renowned since the Renaissance period, and still produced.

Museo Nazionale Atestino
🛇 🄰 Via Guido Negri 9c
🕐 Daily 🗓 1 Jan, 1 May, 25 Dec
🌐 atestino.beniculturali.it

⑰
Montagnana

**FS 🚌 ℹ Piazza Trieste 15;
0429 813 20**

Medieval brick walls encircle this town, pierced by four gateways and defended by 24 towers. Just inside the castellated Padua Gate is the town's archaeological museum. The Gothic-Renaissance Duomo contains Paolo Veronese's *Transfiguration* (1555). Outside the city walls is Palladio's Villa Pisani (c 1560).

> 💬 INSIDER TIP
> **Chioggia by Boat**
>
> Rather than enduring the long drive from Venice to Chioggia, why not catch the ferry? The scenic boat journey from Venice Lido to the fishing port of Chioggia takes around 70 minutes.

Now rather neglected, its façade features the original owner's name (Francesco Pisani) in bold letters below the pediment.

⑱
Chioggia

FS 🚌 🚃 ℹ Lungomare Adriatico 101; www.lididichioggia.it

Chioggia is the principal fishing port on the lagoon, and the bustling fish market is a good reason to come here early in the day (it's open every morning except Monday). Many visitors enjoy the gritty character of the port area, with its smells, its vibrantly coloured boats and the tangle of nets and tackle.

For those looking to museum-hop, the **Museo Civico della Laguna Sud** is a good place to start. It offers a solid introduction to the lagoon and has a large model boat collection. Art fans should head for the **Museo Diocesano**, where a large collection of religious art, including two Paolo Veneziano polyptychs, is housed.

The town also has many inexpensive restaurants that serve fresh fish in almost every variety. Eel, crab and cuttlefish are the local specialities. There is a beach area at Sottomarina, and also worth seeking out is Carpaccio's *St Paul* (1520), the artist's last known work, which is permanently housed in the church of San Domenico.

Museo Civico della Laguna Sud
🛇 🛇 🄰 Campo Marconi 1
🕐 Times vary, check website
🌐 museo.chioggia.org

Museo Diocesano
🛇 🄰 Via Sagrato 🕐 Times vary, check website 🌐 amei.biz/musei/museo-diocesano-darte-sacra-d-chioggia

⑲
Monselice

**FS 🚌 ℹ Via del Santuario 2;
0429 78 30 26**

The town of Monselice stands at the foot of two hills, one of which has been quarried extensively for rich deposits of crystalline minerals. The other is topped by the ruined Castle Rocca, now a nature

→ The towering walls and gilded period interiors *(inset)* of Castello di Monselice

reserve. It's worth walking up the cobbled Via del Santuario as far as San Giorgio, to admire its exquisite inlaid marble work.

Other features on the way up are the 13th-century cathedral and the statue-filled Baroque gardens of the Villa Nani, which can be glimpsed through the gates. Nearby is **Castello di Monselice**, a 14th-century castle complete with period furnishings, suits of armour, frescoes and tapestries.

Castello di Monselice
⊕ ⊗ 🏠 Via del Santuario
🕐 For guided tours only, check website for times
🌐 castellodimonselice.it

㉔
Polesine and Rovigo
🚉 🚌 **𝒊 Piazza Ciceruacchio 1, Porto Tolle; 042 68 11 50**

Polesine is the flat expanse of fertile agricultural land, crisscrossed by canals and subject to flooding, between the River Adige and the Po. The Po Delta is now a national park and has a wealth of fascinating birdlife, including egrets, herons and bitterns.

The most scenic areas are around Scardovari and Porto Tolle, on the south side of the Po. Companies in Porto Tolle offer canoe and bicycle hire and half-day boat cruises.

The modern city of Rovigo has one outstanding monument: the splendid octagonal church called La Rotonda (1594–1602), decorated with paintings and statues in niches.

Adria, 22 km (14 miles) east of Rovigo, gave its name to the Adriatic Sea and was once a Greek and later an Etruscan port. A programme of silt deposition, undertaken to increase Adria's agricultural potential, left the city dry, apart from a 24-km (15-mile) canal. Among the exhibits on display in the **Museo Archeologico** is a complete

↑ Boats moored on a lake near the town of Polesine

iron chariot dating back to the 4th century BC.

Museo Archeologico
⊗ 🏠 Via Badini 59, Adria
📞 0426 21 61 2 🕐 8:30am–7:30pm daily 🚫 1 Jan, 1 May, 25 Dec

VERONA AND LAKE GARDA

Set within the curves of the Adige river, Verona has been a prosperous and cosmopolitan city since the Romans colonized it in 89 BC. It stands astride two important trade routes – the Serenissima, connecting the great port cities of Venice and Genoa, and the Brenner Pass, used by commercial travellers crossing the Alps from northern Europe. This helps to explain the Germanic influence in Verona's magnificent San Zeno church, or the realism of the paintings in the Castelvecchio museum, owing more to Dürer than to Raphael. Verona's passion and panache, however, are purely Italian. Stylish shops and cafés sit amid the impressive remains of Roman monuments. The massive Arena amphitheatre fills with crowds of 20,000 or more, who thrill to opera beneath the stars. All over the city, art galleries and theatres testify to a crowded calendar of cultural activities.

Italy's largest lake, Lake Garda, is renowned for its beautiful scenery. The southern end of the lake, with its waterfront promenades, is very popular with Italian and German visitors. The Monte Baldo mountain range rises high above the eastern shore, the ridge marking the western edge of the mountainous region north of Verona. Here is the great plateau of Monti Lessini, with its little river valleys that reach southwards to join the Adige.

VERONA AND
LAKE GARDA

TRENTINO-
ALTO ADIGE

Ballino

Drena

Arco

237

45b

Riva del Garda

Ronzo-
Chienis

Tiarno
di Sopra

Pieve di Ledro

Torbole

240

249

Lóppio

240

Me

Pregasina

Limone Sul Garda

Brentonico

Ponte Caffaro

240

△ Monte Caplone
1,977 m (6,486 ft)

45b

△ Monte Altissimo di Nag
2,078 m (6,817 ft)

Lago
d'Idro

Vesta

Cádria

Campione
del Garda

Malcesine

Avio

A22

Anfo

Vantone

△ Monte Manos
1,517 m (4,977 ft)

Sommavilla

Monte Baldo
2,200 m (7,218 ft)

Lavenone

237

Lago di
Valvestino

Castelletto

Belluno Veronese

Barghe

LOMBARDY

Cecino

Gargnano

249

Pai

Corno d'Aquilio
1,546 m (5,070 ft)

SANT'ANNA
D'ALFAEDO

Fornaci

237

Vobarno

Bogliaco

S. Zeno di
Montagna

Brentino
Belluno

Breonio

7

Toscolano-
Maderno

45b

Lumini

Caprino
Veronese

12

Paroletta

Fasano

Gardone Riviera

Castion
Veronese

Corrubbio

Tormini

Salò

Isola
del Garda

Torri del
Benaco

Costermano

Rivoli Veronese

Marano di
Valpolicella

Gavardo

45b

Portese

San Vigilio

Garda

A22

12

116

Puegnago
del Garda

S. Felice
del Benaco

Bardolino

249

Affi

Volargne

Sant'
Ambrogio
di Valpolicella

Soiano del Lago

572

Manerba
del Garda

❷
LAKE
GARDA

Cisano

Cavaion
Veronese

12

Santa
Maria

45b

Padenghe
sul Garda

Moniga
del Garda

Lazise

450

Pastrengo

Pescantina

11

Desenzano del
Garda

Sirmione

Adige

Bussolengo

VERONA

Lonato

Colombare

Pacengo

Sandrà

12

Rivoltella

S. Benedetto

249

Castelnuovo
del Garda

11

Lugagnano

12

Montichiari

San Martino
della Battaglia

11

Peschiera
del Garda

27

A4

Sommacampagna

Castel Venzago

Pozzolengo

Ponti sul
Mincio

Verona Villafranca
Airport

Ca' di David

Castiglione
delle Stiviere

18

Monzambano

249

Custoza

25

62

Castellaro
Lagusello

Mincio

Povegliano
Veronese

SOLFERINO

8

15

Carpenedolo

236

Cavriana

Valeggio
sul Mincio

24

Villafranca
di Verona

A22

Guidizzolo

Volta
Mantovana

28

Quaderni

Grezzano

343

Mozzecane

3

Acquafredda

Cerlongo

249

62

Pradelle

Tione

Ceresara

Roverbella

Castiglione
Mantovano

Gúito

VERONA AND LAKE GARDA

Must Sees
1 Verona
2 Lake Garda

Experience More
3 Soave
4 Montecchio Maggiore
5 Valdagno

6 Grezzana
7 Sant'Anna d'Alfaedo
8 Solferino
9 Bolca
10 Bosco Chiesanuova
11 Giazza

THE VENETO PLAIN p186

Dusk descends on Verona and the Adige river which bisects the city ↑

❶

VERONA

✈ Villafranca 14 km (9 miles) ⬛🚌 Piazzale 25 Aprile
ℹ Via degli Alpini 9; www.turismoverona.eu

Vibrant Verona is the second-largest city in the Veneto after Venice, and one of the most prosperous in northern Italy. A UNESCO World Heritage Site, its ancient centre boasts many Roman remains, second only to those of Rome itself, and palazzos, built of rosso di Verona, the local pink-tinged limestone. Verona has two main focal points: the massive 1st-century AD Arena and the Piazza delle Erbe with its colourful market, separated by a maze of narrow lanes lined with elegant boutiques.

① ⊘ 🎒

Castelvecchio

🏛 Corso Castelvecchio 2
🕐 1:30am–7:30pm Mon.
8:30am–7:30pm Tue–Sun;
last adm 45 mins before
closing 🚫 1 Jan, 25 & 26 Dec
🌐 museodicastelvecchio.
comune.verona.it

This spectacular castle, built by Cangrande II between 1355 and 1375, has been transformed into one of the Veneto's finest art galleries. Various parts of the medieval structure have been linked together using aerial walkways and corridors, designed by Carlo Scarpa to give striking views of the building itself, as well as the exhibits contained within.

The first section contains a wealth of late Roman and early Christian material. The martyrdom scenes depicted on the marble sarcophagus of SS Sergius and Bacchus (1179) are gruesomely realistic.

The following section, which is devoted to medieval and early Renaissance art, vividly demonstrates the infuence of Verona's Alpine neighbours on local links with Verona's neighbours across the Alps. Here, instead of the serene saints and virgins of Tuscan art, the emphasis is on brutal realism. This is summed up in the 14th-century *Crucifixion*

0 metres 400 N
0 yards 400 ↑

VIALE C. COLOMBO
Ponte Cate
VIA PORTA CATENA
VIA TOMASO DA VICO
VIA LEGA VERONESE
Ponte Risorgimen
VIA PONTIDA
San Zeno Maggiore ⑱
PIAZZA S. ZENO
PIAZZA CORRUBBIO
CIRCONVALLAZIONE
V.A. SCARSELLINI
V. ANTONIO ROSMIN
VIALE COLONNELLO GALLIANO
CIRCONVALLAZIONE PIETRO MARONCELLI
VIA AURELIO SAFFI

Timeline

1301
Dante is welcomed to the Scaligeri court, and dedicates the final part of his epic *Divine Comedy* to the ruler Cangrande I

1866
The Veneto is reunited with Italy

1913
▽ First Arena di Verona Festival

1263
△ The Scaligeri family begins their 124-year rule of Verona. They use ruthless tactics to rise to power but once established, the family brings peace to the city

1387
Verona falls to the Visconti of Milan, and then a succession of outsiders - Venice, France, and Austria - rule the city

1597
△ Shakespeare sets *Romeo and Juliet* in "fair Verona"

---

with *Saints*, depicting the tortured musculature of Christ and the racked faces of the mourners in painful detail. Far more lyrical is a 15th-century painting by Stefano da Verona called *The Madonna of the Rose Garden*.

After the armour room, take the walkway that leads out along the river flank of the castle, with its dizzying views of the swirling waters of the River Adige and the Ponte Scaligero. Turn the corner to reveal Cangrande I, a 14th-century statue that once

graced Cangrande's tomb. Beyond lie some of the museum's celebrated paintings, notably Paolo Veronese's *Deposition* (1565) and a portrait attributed by some to Titian, by others to Lorenzo Lotto.

---

②
Ponte Scaligero

This medieval bridge was built by Cangrande II between 1354 and 1376. The people of Verona love to stroll across it

to ponder the River Adige in all its moods, or to admire summer sunsets and distant views of the Alps. Such is their affection for the bridge that it was rebuilt after the retreating Germans blew it up in 1945, an operation that involved dredging the river to salvage the irreplaceable medieval masonry. The bridge leads from Castelvecchio to the Arsenal on the north bank of the Adige, built by the Austrians between 1840 and 1861 and now fronted by serene public gardens.

EAT

Enocibus
Close to the Arena lies
this friendly eatery
serving no-frills dishes
at bargain prices.

📍 Vicolo Pomodoro 3
🌐 enocibus.com

€€€

Locanda 4 Cuochi
Inventive dishes and
seasonal menus, plus
fresh pasta made on
the premises and an
impressive wine cellar.

📍 Via Alberto Mario 12
🌐 locanda4cuochi.it

€€€

Ristorante Torcolo
Hearty food in lovely
surroundings. Dishes
include the Veronese
classic *bollito misto*.

📍 Via Carlo Cattaneo 11
🌐 ristorantetorcolo.it

€€€

San Fermo Maggiore

📍 Stradone San Fermo
🕐 Times vary, check
website 🌐 chieseverona.it

San Fermo Maggiore consists
of not one but two churches.
This can best be appreciated
from the outside, where the
eastern end is a jumble of
rounded Romanesque arches
below with pointed Gothic
arches rising above. The lower
church, now rather dank due
to frequent flooding, dates
from 1065, but the upper
church (1313) is more
impressive. It has a splendid
ship's-keel roof and medieval
frescoes by Stefano de Zevico.
They show the fate of four
Franciscan missionaries who
journeyed to India in the mid-
14th century.

④

San Lorenzo

📍 Corso Cavour 28 📞 045
805 00 00 🕐 Daily
🕐 During Mass

San Lorenzo is one of Verona's
lesser-known churches, but
it is one of the city's most
beautiful. Built in 1117 on the
remains of a Paleo-Christian
basilica, the Romanesque
exterior, with alternate strips
of stone and bricks, is typical
of Veronese churches. The bell
tower dates from the 15th
century and inside there are
13th-century frescoes. The
church has two unusual
cylindrical towers.

---

⑤

Arco dei Gavi and Corso Cavour

Dwarfed by the massive
brick walls of Castelvecchio,
the monumental scale of
this Roman triumphal arch
is now hard to appreciate.
Originally the arch straddled
the main Roman road into
the city, today's Corso Cavour.
But French troops who were
occupying Castelvecchio
in 1805 damaged the
monument so much that a
decision was made to move
it to its present position just
off the Corso in 1933.

Continue up Corso Cavour
to see some fine medieval
and Renaissance palaces to
see (especially Nos. 10, 11
and 19) before reaching the
Roman town gate, the Porta
dei Borsari, which dates back
to the 1st century BC.

←

The decorative interior of the upper church at San Fermo Maggiore

⑥ ✍

Museo Lapidario Maffeiano

📍 Piazza Brà 28 📞 045 590 087 🕐 8:30am–2pm Tue–Sun

This "museum of stone" is home to all kinds of architectural fragments

that hint at the last splendour of this Roman city. There are many intricately carved funerary monuments, and a large part of the collection consists of Greek inscriptions collected by the museum's 18th-century founder, Scipione Maffei.

___

⑦ ✍

The Arena

📍 Piazza Brà 🕐 8:30am–7:30pm daily (from 1:30pm Mon; last adm 6:30pm); closes early on performance days 📅 1 Jan, 25 Dec 🌐 arena.it

Dominating the eastern side of the piazza is the Roman Arena, Verona's most important monument, still in use today for operatic performances. Verona's amphitheatre, completed around AD 30, is the third largest in the world, after

Exterior walls of Verona's ancient Roman Arena

Rome's Colosseum and the amphitheatre at Capua, near Naples. Originally, the Arena could hold almost the entire population of Roman Verona, and visitors came from across the Veneto to watch mock battles and gladiatorial combats. In the centuries to follow, the Arena has been the setting for public executions, fairs, theatre performances, bullfighting and opera productions.

The interior has survived virtually intact, maintained by the Arena Conservators since 1580.

The elliptical amphitheatre is 139 m (456 ft) long and 110 m (361 ft) wide.

Gladiators and wild beasts entered the Arena from both sides.

Stone seats in 44 tiers

Below ground were cages for lions, tigers and other wild beasts, and a maze of passages.

Illustration of the Arena, Verona's most important monument

⑧
Duomo

🅰 Piazza Duomo ⏰ Daily (pm only Sun) 🌐 chiese verona.it

Verona's cathedral was begun in 1139 and is fronted by a Romanesque portal carved by Nicolò, one of two master masons responsible for the façade of San Zeno Maggiore (*p228*). The highlight of the interior is Titian's *Assumption* (1535–40). Outside is a cloister in which the excavated ruins of earlier churches are visible. The 8th-century baptistry San Giovanni in Fonte (St John of the Spring) was built from Roman masonry; the marble font was carved in 1220.

⑨
Santa Maria Antica and Scaligeri Tombs

This tiny Romanesque church is almost swamped by the bizarre Scaligeri tombs built up against its entrance wall. Because Santa Maria Antica was their parish church, the Scaligeri rulers of Verona chose to be buried here, and their tombs speak of their military prowess.

Over the entrance to the church is the impressive tomb of Cangrande I, or Big Dog (d 1329), topped by his equestrian statue. This statue is a copy; the original is now in the Castelvecchio (*p221*). The other Scaligeri tombs are next to the church, surrounded by an intricate wrought-iron fence featuring the ladder motif of the family's original name (*della Scala*, meaning "of the steps"). Towering above the fence are the spire-topped tombs of Mastino II, or Mastiff (d 1351), and Cansignorio, meaning Noble Dog (d 1375).

> In the centre of Piazza dei Signori is a 19th-century statue of Dante, who surveys the surrounding buildings with an appraising eye.

These tombs are decorated with Gothic pinnacles. In terms of their craftsmanship and design there is nothing else in European funerary architecture quite like these spiky, thrusting monuments.

⑩
Piazza dei Signori

In the centre of Piazza dei Signori is a 19th-century statue of Dante, who surveys the surrounding buildings with an appraising eye. His gaze is fixed on the grim Palazzo del Capitaniato, home of Verona's military commander, and the equally intimidating Palazzo della Ragione, the Palace of Reason, or law court, both built in the 14th century. On the first floor of the Palazzo della Ragione is the Galleria d'Arte Moderna Achille Forti, a private collection of Veronese art ranging from 1840 to 1940. Fine views of the Alps can be had by climbing the Torre dei Lamberti, which rises from the western side of the courtyard.

↑ Cobbled medieval streets near the Arche Scaligeri in central Verona

CASA DI GIULIETTA

Crowds throng to visit Juliet's house at Via Cappello 23, though it was almost certainly a den of iniquity back in her day, and the balcony was added in 1928. But why quibble in the face of romance? Get your quill and parchment out with the letter-writing Juliet Club *(www. julietclub.com)* or grab tickets for the Estate Teatrale Veronese, a summer theatre festival inspired by the star-crossed lovers *(www.estateteatrale veronese.lt).*

Behind the statue of Dante is the pretty Renaissance Loggia del Consiglio, or council chamber, with its frescoed upper façade and statues of Roman worthies born in Verona, including Catullus the poet, Pliny the natural historian and Vitruvius the architectural theorist.

The piazza is linked to Piazza delle Erbe by the Arco della Costa, or the arch of the rib, whose name refers to the whale rib hung beneath it, put up here as a curiosity in the distant past.

⑪

Piazza delle Erbe

Once the site of the Roman forum, Piazza delle Erbe is named after the city's old herb market. Today's stalls, shaded by huge umbrellas, sell everything from vegetables and lunchtime snacks to clothes and souvenirs.

The Venetian lion that stands on top of a column to

→

The winged Venetian lion of St Mark takes pride of place in Piazza Delle Erbe

the north of the square marks Verona's absorption in 1405 into the Venetian empire. The statue-topped building that completes the north end of Piazza delle Erbe is the Baroque Palazzo Maffei (1668), now converted to shops and luxury apartments.

The fountain that splashes away quietly in the middle of the piazza is often overlooked amid the market's colourful stalls. Yet the statue at its centre dates from Roman times, a gentle reminder that the piazza has been in almost continuous use as a market-place for some 2,000 years.

⑫ 🅿️

Sant'Anastasia

🏛️ Piazza di Sant'Anastasia
☎ 045 59 28 13 ⏰ Time vary, check website
🌐 chieseverona.it

Sant'Anastasia was built in 1290 to hold the massive congregations who came to listen to the rousing sermons preached by members of the fundamentalist Dominican Order. Most interesting is the Gothic portal, with its faded 15th-century frescoes and carved scenes from the life of St Peter Martyr. Inside, the two holy water stoups are supported on realistic figures

↑ The ornate interior of the enormous Basilica Sant'Anastasia

of beggars, known as *i gobbi*, the hunchbacks (the one on the left carved in 1495, the other a century later).

Off the north aisle is the sacristy, home to Antonio Pisanello's fresco, *St George and the Princess* (1433–8). Despite being badly damaged, the fresco still conveys the aristocratic grace of the Princess of Trebizond as St George prepares to mount his horse in pursuit of the dragon.

↑ Manicured lawns, elegant statues and clipped hedgerows at Giardino Giusti

Parco Giardino Sigurtà

A short bus ride from Verona lies the Parco Giardino Sigurtà, a haven of ponds, wooded walks and literally millions of flowers. Visit in spring when the garden is in full bloom *(www.sigurta.it)*.

⑮
San Giorgio in Braida

⌂ Piazzetta San Giorgio, 7

San Giorgio is a rare example in Verona of a domed Renaissance church. It was begun in 1477 by Michele Sanmicheli, an architect best known for his military works. Sanmicheli also designed the classically inspired altar, which is topped by Paolo Veronese's *Martyrdom of St George* (1566). This celebrated painting is outshone by the calm and serene *Virgin Enthroned* between St Zeno and St Lawrence (1526) by Girolamo dai Libri.

⑬
Giardino Giusti

⌂ Via Giardino Giusti 2
☏ 045 803 40 29 ⌚9am-7pm daily 🚫 25 Dec

Hidden among the dusty façades of the Via Giardino Giusti is the entrance to one of Italy's finest Renaissance gardens, laid out in 1580. Artifice and nature are deliberately juxtaposed, as with other gardens of the same period, with the lower garden of clipped box hedges contrasting with the upper area of wild woodland.

Past visitors have included the English traveller Thomas Coryate, who, writing in 1611, called this garden "a second paradise". The diarist John Evelyn, visiting 50 years later, thought it the finest garden in Europe. Today the garden makes an excellent, picturesque spot for a quiet picnic.

⑭
Santo Stefano

⌂ Vicolo Santo Stefano 2 ☏ 045 834 85 29
⌚10am-5:30pm Thu-Sun & during Mass and religious ceremonies

This is one of the city's oldest churches; the original, long-demolished building was built in the 6th century. It served as Verona's cathedral until the 12th century when the Duomo was built on the opposite bank of the Adige. Visitors can enjoy a striking view of the Duomo across the river, taking in the Romanesque apse and the bishop's palace. Santo Stefano was rebuilt by Lombard architects and given its octagonal red-brick campanile, but the original apse survives.

Towering above the church to the east is Castel San Pietro, fronted by flame-shaped cypress trees.

⑯ 🖉 📷
Museo Civico di Storia Naturale

⌂ Lungadige Porta Vittoria 9 ☏ 045 807 94 00 ⌚9am-5pm Tue-Fri, 2-6pm Sat, Sun & pub hols 🚫 1 Jan, Easter, 1 May, 25 Dec

Verona's natural history museum contains an outstanding collection of fossils. Whole fish, trees, fern leaves and dragonflies, found in rock in the foothills of the Little Dolomites, are captured in extraordinary detail.

Human prehistory is represented by finds from ancient settlements around Lake Garda, and there are reconstructions of original lake villages. On the upper floor, cases full of stuffed birds, animals and fish provide an extensive account of today's living world.

---

(17) 🖾

Teatro Romano and Museo Archeologico

📍 Rigaste Redentore 2
☎ 045 800 03 60 🕐 8:30am-7:30pm daily (from 1:30pm Mon)

When this theatre was built, in the 1st century BC, the plays performed would have included satirical dramas by such writers as Terence and Plautus. The tradition continues here with open-air performances at the annual summer Shakespeare festival.

The theatre is built into a bank high above the Adige river and the spectacular views over the city must have been as entrancing to Roman theatre-

> **The spectacular views over the city must have been as entrancing to Roman theatre-goers as the events on stage.**

goers as the events on stage. Certainly it is for the views that the theatre is best visited today, since little is left of the original stage area, though the semicircular seating area remains largely intact.

A lift carries visitors from the Teatro Romano up through the cliffs to the monastery above, which has been converted into an archaeological museum. The first part of the museum displays well-restored mosaics, one of which depicts the kind of gory gladiatorial combat that once went on in Verona's amphitheatre (p223). Such barbaric performances, seen as a legitimate way of disposing of criminals and prisoners of war, came to an end in the early 5th century following a decree from the Christian emperor Honorius.

In the little monastic cells to the side of this room, visitors can see a bronze bust of the first Roman emperor, the young Augustus Caesar (63 BC–AD 14), who succeeded in overcoming his opponents, including Mark Antony and Cleopatra, to become the sole ruler of the Roman world in 31 BC.

↑ Verona's Teatro Romano and Castel San Pietro overlook the city

(18) 🚋

SAN ZENO MAGGIORE

📍 Piazza San Zeno 🚌 31, 32, 33 from Castelvecchio
🕐 Mar-Oct: 9am-6pm daily, 12:30pm-6pm Sun; Nov-Feb:
10am- 5pm Mon-Sat, 12:30pm-5pm Sun 🚫 1 Jan, 25 Dec
🌐 chieseverona.it

Worth visiting for Andrea Mantegna's glorious altarpiece alone, this magnifent church is brimming with trinkets, treasures and priceless artworks.

One of the most spectacular examples of Romanesque architecture in Italy, San Zeno Maggiore is also the most revered in Verona, housing the shrine of the city's patron saint, San Zeno. Built between 1120 and 1138 , the façade is embellished with marble reliefs of biblical scenes, matched in vitality by bronze door panels showing the miracles of San Zeno. Beneath an impressive rose window, a graceful porch canopy rests on two slim columns. A brick campanile soars to the south, while a squat tower to the north is said to cover the tomb of King Pepin of Italy (777–810).

Did You Know?

Saint Zeno is the patron saint of anglers and is often depicted with fish or fishing rods.

The nave has a ship's-keel ceiling, so called because it resembles the inside of an upturned boat. It was constructed in 1386, when the apse was rebuilt.

Striped brickwork is typical of Romanesque buildings in Verona. Courses of local pink brick are alternated with ivory-coloured tufa.

Andrea Mantegna's three-part altarpiece (1457–59) depicts the Virgin and Child with various saints. The painting served as an inspiration to local artists.

BRONZE DOOR PANELS

The 48 bronze panels of the west doors are primitive but forceful in their depiction of stories and scenes from the life of San Zeno. Those on the left date from 1030; those on the right were made 100 years later. Huge staring eyes and Ottoman-style hats feature prominently, and the meaning of some scenes remains unknown - such as that of the woman suckling two crocodiles.

North of the church the fine, airy cloister (1293–1313) has rounded Romanesque arches on one side and pointed Gothic arches on the other.

↑ Illustration of the church and grounds of San Zeno Maggiore

↑ The three distinct structures of San Zeno Maggiore

The campanile, started in 1045, reached its present height of 72 m (236 ft) in 1173.

↑ Entrance to the vaulted crypt that contains the tomb of San Zeno

The sanctuary rood screen has marble statues of Christ and the Apostles, dating from 1250, ranged along it.

The nave of the church is modelled on an ancient Roman basilica, the Hall of Justice. The main altar is situated in the raised sanctuary where the judge's throne stood.

The rose window symbolizes the Wheel of Fortune: figures around the rim show the rise and fall of human fortunes.

Marble side panels, carved in 1140, depict events from the life of Christ to the left of the doors, and scenes from the Book of Genesis to the right.

The vaulted crypt contains the tomb of San Zeno, appointed eighth bishop of Verona in AD 362, who died in AD 380.

Each of the western wooden doors has 24 bronze plates joined by bronze masks, nailed on to the wood to look like solid metal. A bas-relief above the doors depicts San Zeno vanquishing the devil.

↑ Still waters of Lake Garda, viewed from Limone sul Garda

❷

LAKE GARDA

🚉Peschiera del Garda, Desenzano del Garda 🚌🚌To all towns 🛈Viale Marconi 8, Sirmione; 0303 748 722

Garda, the largest and easternmost of the Italian lakes, is a favourite summer playground for sports lovers. Strong winds make ideal conditions for windsurfing and sailing, there are numerous yacht harbours and artificial beaches, and luxury hotels offer tennis and horse-riding facilities. The less energetic can explore the lake and shore by steamer, while the magnificent scenery of craggy peaks and spectacular sunsets will appeal to every visitor.

①

Garda

🚌 🛈Mar–Oct Piazza Donatori di Sangue 1; www.tourism.verona.it

This ancient fishing village is packed with visitors in the summer months. But it's still worth a lunch stop. Numerous pavement cafés brighten the streets around the central Palazzo dei Capitani, built in the 15th century for the use of the Venetian militia. Prehistoric rock engravings feature along the Strada dei Castei, an old route above the town. Stroll along shingle beaches, or head to the scenic Punta San Viglio, just 3km (2 miles) out of town.

②

Peschiera

🚌🚉 🛈Piazzale Bettelone 15; www.tourism.verona.it

At Peschiera, the Mincio river flows out of Lake Garda to join the Po river. The main site of interest is a fortress built in the 19th century. Named Fortezza del Quadrilatero because of its square shape, it replaced a 15th-century stronghold. Just outside town is **Gardaland®**, a theme park with roller coasters, carnival rides, a waterpark, a jungle safari and medieval shows.

Gardaland®
♿🚻 🚗Via Derna 4 🕐Apr–Sep: daily 🌐gardaland.it

> **LAKE TRIPS**
>
> Lake Garda's steamers serve the major towns around the southern rim of the lake. All have jetties where visitors can buy tickets for a leisurely cruise. Gardens and villas that are otherwise hidden from view can be seen from the water. A trip from one end of the lake to the other takes around two hours 20 minutes by hydrofoil, and four hours by steamer. Catamarans also serve the southern end of the lake.

③
Salò

🚌 🛈 Piazza Sant'Antonio; 0365 214 23

Locals prefer to associate this elegant town with Gaspare da Salò (1540–1609), the inventor of the violin, rather than with Mussolini, the World War II dictator. Mussolini set up the so-called Salò Republic in 1943 and ruled northern Italy from here until 1945, when he was executed by the Italian resistance firing squad.

Happier memories are evoked by Salò's buildings, including the cathedral with its unusual wooden altar piece (1510) by Paolo Veneziano. The main appeal of the town derives from its pastel-waterfront buildings, picturesque squares and alleyways, and a long pedestrian promenade with beautiful views of the lake. Salò marks the beginning of the Riviera Bresciana, where the shore is lined with lovely villas and grand hotels set in semi-tropical gardens.

④
Gardone Riviera

🚌 🛈 Corso Repubblica 8; 0365 203 47

Gardone's most appealing feature is the terraced public park that cascades down the hillside. Planted with all manner of noble trees, it is the perfect spot for a picnic. Equally impressive are the Mediterranean and African plants in the lush **Giardino Botanico Hruska**, founded in 1910, which benefit from the town's mild winters. Gardone has long been a popular resort – the magnificent 19th-century Villa Alba (now a congress centre) was built for the Austrian emperor to escape the bitter winters of his own country. However, the Art Deco Grand Hotel on the waterfront was built for those seeking fun, frolicks

and fortune in this beautiful lakeside setting.

High above the town is the **Villa il Vittoriale**, built for the poet Gabriele d'Annunzio. His Art Deco villa has blacked-out windows (he professed to loathe the world) and is filled with curiosities.

Giardino Botanico Hruska

♿ 🚻 Via Roma 2 ⏰ Mar–Oct: 9am–7pm daily 🌐 hellergarden.com

Villa il Vittoriale

♿ 🚻 🛈 🅿 Via Vittoriale 12 ⏰ Times vary, check website; ticket office closes 1 hour earlier 🚫 1 Jan, 24 & 25 Dec 🌐 vittoriale.it

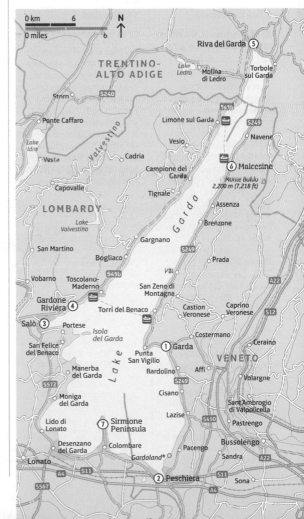

⑤
Riva del Garda

🚌 *ℹ* **Largo Medaglie d'Oro;**
www.gardatrentino.it

Riva's waterfront is
overlooked by the moated
Rocca di Riva, a former
Scaligeri fortress. Inside is a
museum with exhibits from
the region's prehistoric lake
villages, which were built by
driving huge wooden piles
into the lake bed to support
platforms. This point on the
lake is particularly popular
with windsurfers, with
equipment available for hire
during the summer months.
Lessons and guided tuition
is also available.

Rocca di Riva
🏛 ⊗ 🅰 Piazza Cesare
Battisti 3/a 🕐 10am–6pm
Tue–Sun 🅦 museoalto
garda.it

> 🔺 GREAT VIEW
> **Rocca Scaligera**
>
> On a clear day, the high
> central tower of the
> Rocca Scaligera castle
> commands spectacular
> views over the castle,
> its grounds and the
> whole of the Sirmione
> Peninsula, as well as
> Lake Garda.

⑥
Malcesine

🚌 *ℹ* **Via Gardesana 238**

German visitors who come to
Malcesine trace the journey
taken by the poet Goethe in
1788. His travels were full of
mishaps, and at Malcesine he
was accused of spying and
was locked up.

From Malcesine, visitors can
take the rotating cable car up
to the broad ridge of Monte
Baldo (1,745 m/ 5,725 ft). The
journey takes 15 minutes, and
on a clear day it is possible
to see the distant peaks of
the Dolomites, including the
Brenta range. Footpaths for
walkers are signposted at the
top. The lower slopes are
designated nature reserves;
a good place to see the local
flora is the Riserva Naturale
Gardesana Orientale, just to
the north of Malcesine, on
the western side of
Monte Baldo.

Piazza Castello

*Rocca Scaligera
was built in the 13th
century by the Scaligeri
of Verona. It is designed
to trap invading ships,
leaving them vulnerable
to missiles dropped
from the castle walls.*

*The moat, originally a
complex defence system, is
today home to schools of carp.*

←

A lakefront café with spectacular mountain views at Riva del Garda

⑦
Sirmione Peninsula

🚃🚢 *i* Viale Marconi 8; www.sirmionebs.it

Visitors have waxed lyrical about the Sirmione Peninsula since Roman times, when Catullus described it as a "gem". With its thermal spas, Roman ruins and breathtaking views, it remains a jewel despite the deluge of tourists. Head out of town to enjoy quieter charms. Sirmione is a finger of land extending into the southern end of the lake, connected to the mainland by a bridge. The Roman poet Catullus (b 84 BC) allegedly owned a villa here: the ruins of the **Grotte di Catullo** lie among ancient olive trees at the northern tip. The **Rocca Scaligera** castle stands guard at the base of the peninsula, and beyond, the narrow stone-paved streets of the village give way to peaceful lakeside walks and elegant spa hotels.

Grotte di Catullo

📞 030 91 61 57 🕐 8:30am-7:30pm Tue-Sat (Nov-Feb: to 5:pm), 9:30am-6:30pm Sun & pub hols 📅 1 Jan, 1 May, 25 Dec.

Rocca Scaligera

♿ 📞 030 91 64 68
🕐 8:30am-7:30pm Tue-Sat, 9:15am-5:45pm Sun 📅 1 Jan, 1 May, 25 Dec

---

THE SCALIGERI

The Rocca Scaligera is one of many castles built throughout the Verona and Lake Garda region by the Scaligeri family. During the 13th and 14th centuries, powerful military rulers fought each other in pursuit of riches and power. Despite the autocratic nature of their rule, the Scaligeri brought a period of peace and prosperity to the region, fending off attacks by the predatory Viscontis who ruled Lombardy.

The main keep tower was used for bombarding attackers trapped below.

The inner harbour provided a haven for fishermen during lake storms and an anchorage for the castle fleet.

←

The heavily fortified castle of Rocca Scaligera

The drawbridge is heavily fortified, linking the castle to the mainland and offering an escape route to the castle's inhabitants.

EXPERIENCE MORE

EXPERIENCE Verona and Lake Garda

3

Soave

 Piazza Foro Boario 1; **045 619 07 73**

Soave is a heavily fortified town ringed by 14th-century walls, and it is known all over Europe because of the light and dry white wine that is produced and exported from here in great quantity. Visitors will spot few vineyards around the town, since they are mainly located in the hills to the north, but evidence of the industry can be seen in the gleaming factories on the outskirts, where the Garganega grapes are crushed and the fermented wine bottled. Cafés and wine cellars throughout the town centre provide plenty of opportunity for sampling the excellent local product.

Beyond its wine, Soave is also known for its historic buildings. The city walls rise up the hill to the best known of these, the dramatically sited **Rocca Scaligera**. An ancient castle that was enlarged by the Scaligeri rulers of Verona in the 14th century, it has been furnished in period style. The route to

the castle makes for a scenic drive, or an exhilarating – though steep –hike. From here, you can take in extraordinary views across the Veneto countryside.

Rocca Scaligera

Via Castello Scaligero **045 768 00 36** **Mar-Sep: 9am-noon, 3-6:30pm daily; Oct-mid-Feb: 9am-noon, 2-4pm Tue-Sun**

4

Montecchio Maggiore

Via Pietro Ceccato 88, Alte Montecchio; 0444 69 65 46

Visitors to industrialized Montecchio Maggiore come principally to see the two 14th-century castles that stand guard on the hill above the town. Although these are known as the **Castello di Romeo** and the **Castello di Giulietta** (which includes a restaurant), there is no evidence that they belonged

53 million
_____

The number of bottles of Soave produced here annually.

to Verona's rival Capulet and Montague families (*p224*), but they look romantic and offer lovely views over the vineyard-clad hills to the north.

Castello di Romeo

Via Castelli 4 **Daily**

Castello di Giulietta

Via Castelli 4 **0444 40 09 79** **Sat & Sun**

5

Valdagno

comune.valdagno.vi.it

A scenic drive of 20 km (12 miles) from Montecchio

←

The frescoed interiors of Villa Allegri-Arvedi, located just outside Grezzana

Maggiore leads to Valdagno, a town of woollen mills and 18th-century houses. Just northwest is the Montagna Spaccata, its rocky bulk split by a dramatic 100-m- (330 ft) deep gorge and waterfall. The fissure is wreathed in evocative local legends, and is open to the public who can take in great views from the site's walkway platforms.

6

Grezzana

In Grezzana itself, seek out the 13th-century church of Santa Maria, which (though it was frequently rebuilt over the years) retains its robustly carved Romanesque font and its beautifully coloured campanile of pink, white and gold limestone.

Grezzana is in the foothills of the scenic Piccole Dolomiti or Little Dolomites. Close to the town, at nearby Cuzzano, is the 17th-century Baroque **Villa Allegri-Arvedi**, which is decorated with beautiful frescoes by Ludovico Dorigny. To the south, in Santa Maria in Stelle, there is a striking Roman nymphaeum (a shrine to the nymphs who guard the freshwater spring) next to the church (known as the Pantheon).

Villa Allegri-Arvedi
 ⓐ Via Conti Allegri
ⓒ Groups only (book ahead)
ⓦ villarvedi.it

←

Rolling, vineyard-lined hills, overlooking the fortified town of Soave

7

Sant'Anna d'Alfaedo

📧 ⓦ commune.santanna
dalfaedo.verona.it

Distinctively Alpine in character, Sant'Anna d'Alfaedo is noted for the stone tiles used to roof local houses. The hamlet of Fosse, immediately to the north, is a popular base for walking excursions up the Corno d'Aquilio (1,546 m/ 5,070 ft), a mountain that boasts one of the world's deepest potholes: the Spluga della Preta, which plunges to 850 m (2,790 ft) deep.

Just south of Sant'Anna and more accessible is another natural wonder – the Ponte di Veia, a great stone arch bridging the valley. Prehistoric

> ### Did You Know?
>
> The Ponte Veia is the remains of a karst cave which collapsed between 80,000 and 120,000 years ago.

finds have been excavated from the caves at either end. This spectacular natural bridge is one of the largest of its kind in the world.

8

Solferino

The allied armies of France and Sardinia under Napoleon III met the Austrian army at the small village of Solferino in 1859, as part of what was the wider battle for the unification of the Italian peninsula. The bloody Battle of Solferino left more than 6,000 dead and 40,000 wounded. All of them were completely abandoned without medical care or burial. Shocked by such neglect, a Swiss man named Henri Dunant began a campaign for better treatment. The result was the first Geneva Convention, signed in 1863, and the establishment of the International Red Cross. In 1901, Dunant was jointly awarded the first ever Nobel Peace Prize for his efforts.

In the town of Solferino there is a war museum

THE BATTLE OF SOLFERINO

The Battle of Solferino took place on 24 June 1859 and was a decisive episode in the struggle for Italian independence. The battle saw Emperor Franz Joseph's Austrian troops defeated by the Franco-Sardinian Alliance, which consisted of Napoleon III's French Army and Victor Emanuel II's Sardinian Army. The clash was a bloody one, resulting in over 6,000 dead, over 40,000 wounded and thousands more missing or captured. It was the last time in history that armies were led onto the battlefield by their monarchs.

and an ossuary chapel, lined with bones from the battlefield. There is also a memorial to Dunant built by the Red Cross with donations from member nations.

The Ponte di Veia, an impressive natural bridge near Sant'Anna d'Alfaedo

> **Pretty Bolca sits at the centre of the Monti Lessini plateau, looking down the valley of the River Alpone and encircled by fossil-bearing hills.**

⑨ Bolca

📧 **ℹ Via Villa Bolca; 045 656 00 13**

Pretty Bolca sits at the centre of the Monti Lessini plateau, looking down the valley of the River Alpone and encircled by fossil-bearing hills. The most spectacular finds have been transferred to Verona's Museo Civico di Storia Naturale (*p226*), but the local **Museo di Fossili** still has an impressive collection of plants, reptiles and particularly fish perfectly preserved in the local basalt stone. The museum first opened in 1971, but interest in the region and the size of the collection increased, so much so that a new building was inaugurated in 1996. Most of the specimens are thought to be some 49 million years old. A circular tour just outside the town (details available from the museum) takes in the quarries where the fossils were found.

Museo di Fossili

⊛ 🚪 **Via San Giovanni Battista Vestenanova** 🕒 Mar–Oct: 9am–noon, 2–6pm daily; Nov–Feb: 10am–noon, 2–5pm daily 🌐 museofossilibolca.eu

---

⑩ Bosco Chiesanuova

📧 🌐 **comunebosco chiesanuova.vr.it**

One of the principal ski resorts of the region, Bosco Chiesanuova is well supplied with hotels, ski lifts and cross-country routes. In summer, there are a number of bicycle routes from which to explore the area. To the east, near Camposilvano, is the picturesque Valle delle Sfingi (Valley of the Sphinxes), so called because of its landscape of large and impressive rock formations.

---

⑪ Giazza

The small town of Giazza has an almost Alpine appearance. Its **Museo dei Cimbri** was inaugurated in the 1970s and covers the history of the Tredici Comuni (Thirteen Communes). In reality there are far more than 13 little hamlets dotted about the plateau, many of them settled by Bavarian farmers who migrated from the German side of the Alps in the 13th century. Cimbro, their unique, German-influenced dialect, has now almost completely disappeared, but other traditions survive, such as their huge mountain horns, known as *tromboni*, which still play an important part in the town's local festivities.

Museo dei Cimbri

⊛ 🕐 🚪 **Via dei Boschi 62** 🕒 3–7pm Sat & Sun (Jul–Aug: also Fri) 🌐 cimbri.it

↑ Pretty whitewashed buildings in the alpine town of Giazza

A DRIVING TOUR
VALPOLICELLA WINE TOUR

Length 45 km (28 miles) **Stopping Points** The main village of the Valpolicella region, San Pietro in Cariano, has numerous cafés and restaurants.

This circular tour takes in the undulating hills and remarkably varied scenery of the famous wine district that lies between Verona and Lake Garda. On the shores of Lake Garda itself, deep and fertile glacial soils provide sustenance for the grapes that are used to make Bardolino, a wine that is meant to be drunk young. Inland, the rolling foothills of the Lessini mountains shelter tiny, unassuming hamlets where lives and working rhythms are astutely atuned to the needs of the vines. These particular vines are grown to produce the equally famed Valpolicella, a distinctive red wine that varies from light and fruity to full-bodied.

*The wine-producing village of **Affi** is surrounded by vineyards planted in the sheltered basin of the Adige Valley.*

Caprino Veronese

Costermano

Garda

8

Albarè

Rivoli Veronese

9

A22

Affi

Cavaion Veronese

11

Bardolino

31

249

*Famous for its light red wine of the same name, the town of **Bardolino** hosts a grape festival in September and has numerous cellars offering tastings.*

Cisano

450

Calmasino

Sega

Lazise

__Lazise__ has long been the chief port of Garda's eastern shore, its picturesque harbour and medieval church guarded by a 14th-century castle.

5

Pastrengo

Lake Garda

Colà

Sandrà

Pacengo

249

450

27

Castelnuovo del Garda

11

A4

← Pastel-coloured buildings line the entrance to Lazise harbour on the banks of Lake Garda

↑ Vineyards line the hillsides surrounding the town of Sant Ambrogio di Valpolicella

Locator Map
For more detail see p218

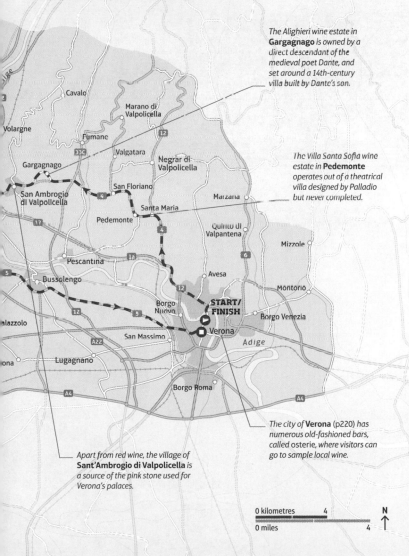

The Alighieri wine estate in **Gargagnago** *is owned by a direct descendant of the medieval poet Dante, and set around a 14th-century villa built by Dante's son.*

The Villa Santa Sofia wine estate in **Pedemonte** *operates out of a theatrical villa designed by Palladio but never completed.*

The city of **Verona** *(p220) has numerous old-fashioned bars, called osterie, where visitors can go to sample local wine.*

Apart from red wine, the village of **Sant'Ambrogio di Valpolicella** *is a source of the pink stone used for Verona's palaces.*

0 kilometres   4
0 miles   4

N
↑

THE DOLOMITES

The name of the Dolomites conjures up a vision of spectacular mountains, as noble and awe-inspiring as the Alps. To the south of the region lie the cities of Feltre, Belluno and Vittorio Veneto. To the north is the renowned ski resort of Cortina d'Ampezzo. In between, travellers will encounter no more cities – just spectacular panoramas unfolding endlessly before them and pretty hamlets tucked into remarkably lush and sunny south-facing valleys.

The Dolomites cover a substantial portion of the Veneto's landmass, yet it is easy to forget when visiting the cities of the flat Veneto Plain that behind them lies this range of mountains rising to heights of more than 2,000 m (6,500 ft). Italian is the region's principal language, but in the northwest a German influence can sometimes be heard, reflecting the region's strong historic links with the Austrian Tyrol. Once ruled by the Habsburgs, certain areas of the region only became part of Italy in 1918, after the break-up of the Austro-Hungarian empire at the end of World War I. Some of that war's fiercest fighting took place in the Dolomites, as both sides tried to wrest control of the strategic valley passes linking Italy and Austria-Hungary. Striking war memorials in many villages and towns provide a sad reminder of that time.

THE DOLOMITES

Must See
1 The Dolomite Mountains

Experience More
2 Cortina d'Ampezzo
3 Misurina
4 Pieve di Cadore
5 Belluno
6 Val di Zoldo
7 Vittorio Veneto
8 Feltre

THE DOLOMITES

AUSTRIA

Moos

Passo di Monte Croce
di Comélico

52

Passo
Cimabanche

Tre Cime di Lavaredo
2,999 m (9,839 ft)

Monte Rinaldo
2,473 m (8,113 ft)

51

Santo Pietro
di Cadore

355

Monte Cristallo
3,221 m (10,567 ft)

3 MISURINA

Giralba

48

Auronzo
di Cadore

Sappada

Sauris
di Sopra

Tofana
3,244 m (10,645 ft)

48

2 CORTINA D'AMPEZZO

Stabiziane

Santo Stefano
di Cadore

Monte Cimon
2,415 m (7,923 ft)

48

Zuel

638

Tondi di Faloria
3,205 m (10,515 ft)

Cimon del Froppa
2,932 m (9,619 ft)

Lozzo
di Cadore

Monte Terza Grande
2,585 m (8,481 ft)

52

51

1

THE DOLOMITE
MOUNTAINS

San Vito
di Cadore

Domegge
di Cadore

Forni
di Sopra

Selva di Cadore

251

Borca
di Cadore

Antelao
3,264 m (10,709 ft)

Calalzo
di Cadore

4 PIEVE DI CADORE

51b

52

Cima Monfalcon
2,548 m (8,359 ft)

Forni
di Sotto

Passo
Staulanza

M. Pelmo
3,108 m (10,394 ft)

Valle di
Cadore

Piave

M. Civetta
3,220 m (10,564 ft)

Boite

41

347

6 VAL DI
ZOLDO

Sasso Cibiana
2,413 m (7,917 ft)

Rivalgo

Cima dei Preti
2,703 m (8,868 ft)

La Fratta di Barbin
2,233 m (7,326 ft)

M. Moiazza
2,865m (9,400 ft)

Forno
di Zoldo

Maè

Ospitale di Cadore

Passo Duran

Passo di
S. Osvaldo

Cimolais

Claut

Agordo

347

M. Tamer
2,546 m (8,353 ft)

251

Castellavazzo

Longarone

Erto

251

Rivamonte
Agordino

La Muda

203

Monte Schiara
2,563 m (8,409 ft)

91

Provagna

Col Nudo
2, 472 m (8,110 ft)

Barcis

Maniago

La Stanga

Monte Serva
2,132 m (6,995 ft)

Soverzene

Alpago

251

ena

Gioz

Polpet

Pieve
d'Alpago

Chies d'Alpago

Sospirolo

Ponte
nelle Alpi

Mas

204

A27

Bastia

Aviano

251

Sedico

5 BELLUNO

Visome

31

Farra d'Alpago

Meano

50

1

Lago di
Santa Croce

29

Santa
Giustina

Trichiana

Novegal

Santa Croce

Mel

Tassei

Col Visentin
1,761 m (5,777 ft)

Polcenigo

Piave

1

Carve

Pranolz

Fregona

Fontanafredda

Lentiai

Col de Moi
1,358 m (4,455 ft)

Passo di
S. Boldo

7 VITTORIO
VENETO

A28

635

Tovena

2

Tarzo

Sacile

13

Pordenone

VENETO

Follina

Cozzuolo

A27

51

A28

M. Ceseo
1,570 m (5,151 ft)

Formeniga

86

35

Combai

4

A28

THE VENETO
PLAIN

p186

Pieve
di Soligo

Conegliano

15

N

0 kilometres   10

0 miles   10

Colfosco

77

248

1

THE DOLOMITE MOUNTAINS

🄸 Piazza Duomo 2, Belluno; www.infodolomiti.it

A striking mountain range in northeastern Italy, the Dolomites are home to bubbling springs, thick tangles of forest, cool glacial lakes, swathes of lush green fields and sunny south-facing valleys. It's the perfect place for some adrenaline-pumping activities. Snow covers the peaks from October to May, and it is possible to ski all year round on Marmolada, the highest peak in the range. However, the solitude of these stunning mountains also appeals to those looking to escape and unwind in one of the areas many alpine spas or mountain retreats.

The Dolomites are the most distinctive and arguably most beautiful mountains in Italy. Unlike the glacier-eroded saddles and ridges of the main body of the Alps, they were shaped by the corrosive effects of ice, sun and rain, sculpting the cliffs, spires and "organ pipes" that we see today. The eastern section is the more dramatic, especially the Catinaccio (or Rosengarten) range, which famously turns rose pink at sunset.

Outdoor activities in the area include skiing in winter, and walking and rambling along marked footpaths to picnic sites in summer. Chair lifts from the main resorts provide visitors with easy access up into the mountains themselves, transporting you to some breathtaking view points.

GREAT VIEW
Freccia nel Cielo

Take the cable car to the highest peak of Cortina: the imposing Tofana, where a platform affords 360-degree views of the surrounding landscape from this dizzying height.

① An overcast afternoon at Lake Misurina in the Tre Cime di Lavaredo Natural Park.

② Alpine ibex roam freely on steep mountainsides.

③ A snowboader, mid-jump as they descend the snowy Dolomite slopes.

Did You Know?

Dolomite rocks are known for their cleansing properties, and are used in many toothpastes.

HIKING IN THE DOLOMITES

The Dolomites were hit by devastating storms in October 2018, felling trees, washing away paths and blocking major access routes. It is essential to check with the local tourist board that routes are safe and accessible before you attempt to hike them. For the more difficult climbs and *vie ferrate*, make sure you have insurance as mountain rescue is expensive. This may seem alarmist, but it's important to respect these wild and wonderful mountains.

←

The village of Santa Maddalena sits below dramatic peaks

EXPERIENCE MORE

❷ Cortina d'Ampezzo

🚃 **ℹ** Corso Italia 81;
www.cortinadolomiti.eu

Italy's top ski resort, much favoured by the smart set from Turin and Milan, is well supplied with restaurants and bars. The reason for its popularity is the dramatic scenery, which adds an extra dimension to the pleasure of speeding down the slopes. Guests are encircled by crags and spires, which rise skyward, thrusting their weather-sculpted shapes above the trees.

As a consequence of hosting the 1956 Winter Olympics, Cortina has above-average sports facilities. There is a ski jump and a bobsleigh run, the Olympic ice stadium holds skating discotheques, and there are swimming pools, tennis courts and riding facilities. During the summer months, Cortina becomes an excellent base for walkers. Information on the many trails is available from the tourist office.

Visitors can also take the cable car Freccia nel Cielo (Arrow in the Sky), which ascends to a height of 3,243 m (10,639 ft) above sea level.

❸ Misurina

🚃 **ℹ** Via Monte Piana 2;
www.auronzomisurina.it

Smaller and quieter than Cortina, Misurina nestles by the exquisite Lake Misurina. The lake's mirror-like surface reflects the peaks of Monte Sorapiss and the Cadini group. Take the toll road that climbs northeast for 8 km (5 miles) to the Auronzo mountain refuge and to the base of the Tre Cime di Lavaredo peaks, which rise to 2,999 m (9,840 ft).

Did You Know?

Cortina d'Ampezzo stars as a glamorous location in the 1981 James Bond film *For Your Eyes Only*.

❹ Pieve di Cadore

🚃 **🌐** commune.pievedi
cadore.bl.it

For centuries the Cadore forests supplied Venice with its timber. The main town of this vast mountainous region is Pieve di Cadore, primarily known as the birthplace of Titian. The humble **Casa di Tiziano** can be visited, and the nearby **Museo Archeologico** has exhibits of finds from the pre-Roman era.

Principally, though, this is a base for touring the scenic delights of the region. North of Pieve the valley narrows to a dramatic ravine, and the road north to Comelica and Sesto is noted for its Alpine scenery and its traditional balconied houses. It also winds alongside the Piave river.

Casa di Tiziano
⊗ 🏠 Via Arsenale 4 📞 0435 322 62 🕐 Jul–Aug: 10am–7pm daily

Museo Archeologico Cadorino
⊗ 🏠 Palazzo della Magnifica Comunità Cadorina, Piazza Tiziano 2 📞 0435 322 62 🕐 May–Sep: 10am–12:30pm, 3:30–6:30pm daily; Jan–Apr: Sat & Sun

←

Tourists walking along the main street in the ski town of Cortina d'Ampezzo

↑ Gorgeous autumn foliage framing an Alpine village near Belluno

⑤

Belluno

FS◫ *i* Piazza Duomo 2; www.infodolomiti.it

Picturesque Belluno serves as a bridge between the two very different parts of the Veneto, with flat plains to the south and the Dolomite peaks to the north. Both are encapsulated in the picture-postcard vistas to be seen from the 12th-century Porta Rugo at

the southern end of Via Mezzaterra. Even more spectacular are the views from the 16th-century Duomo, designed by Tullio Lombardo, but rebuilt twice after damage by earthquakes.

The nearby baptistry contains a font cover carved by Andrea Brustolon (1662–1732). Close by is the 12th-century Torre Civica and the city's most elegant building, the Renaissance Palazzo dei Rettori (1491), once home to Belluno's Venetian rulers.

The **Museo Civico**, housed in the Baroque splendour of the Palazzo Fulcis, is worth visiting for the paintings by Bartolomeo Montagna (1450–1523) and Sebastiano Ricci (1659–1734). Beside it is the Piazza del Mercato, with arcaded Renaissance palaces and a fountain built in 1410.

South of the town are the ski resorts of the Alpe del Nevegal. It is worth taking the chair lift in the summer to the Rifugio Brigata Alpina Cadore, which has superb views and a

← A bronze statue of Titian that stands in Pieve di Cadore, the town of his birth

botanical garden specializing in Alpine plants.

Museo Civico

⊘⊘ 🕐 🅰 Via Roma 28
🕐 Times vary, check website
🆆 mubel.comune.belluno.it

EAT

El Zoco
A romantic, wood-panelled restaurant serving generous mountain-style dishes.

🅰 Località Cademai 18, Cortina d'Ampezzo
🕐 Tue–Sun 🆆 elzoco.it

€€€

Pizzeria Ristorante Croda Café
Expect great value pizza and pasta, plus excellent local wine.

🅰 Piazza Pittori Fratelli Ghedina 28, Cortina d'Ampezzo 🕐 Wed–Mon
🆆 crodacortina.it

€€€

⑥
Val di Zoldo

🚌 From Longarone 🛈 Pecol;
0437 78 91 45

The wooded Zoldo Valley
is a popular destination for
walking holidays. Its main
resort town is Forno di Zoldo
and the surrounding villages
are noted for their Tyrolean-

style Alpine chalets and
haylofts. Examples built in
wood on stone foundations
can be seen at Fornesighe, 2
km (1 mile) northeast of Forno
di Zoldo, and on the slopes of
Monte Penna at Zoppe di
Cadore, 8 km (5 miles) north.

If you have time, a circular
tour is a good way to explore
the area. Drive north on the
S251, via Zoldo Alto to Selva di
Cadore, then west via Colle di
Santa Lucia (a favourite
viewpoint for photographers).
From here take the S203 south
through the lakeside resort
of Alleghe. The route passes
through wonderful woodland
scenery dotted with pretty
mountain hamlets that
complement the splendour
of the rocky crags.

The southernmost town of
the area is Agordo, nestling in
the Cordevole Valley. From
here, a spectacularly scenic
route follows the S347 northeast to the Passo Duran,
descending to Dont, close to
the starting point of the tour.
Wayside shrines mark the
route and it is worth stopping
to visit village shops selling
local woodcarving. Take care
when driving along this
narrow and winding road.

VITTORIO VENETO AT WAR

Vittorio Veneto was
the site of a significant
battle at the tail end of
World War I, ending on
3 November 1918 with
the Italians defeating
the Austro-Hungarian
troops and effectively
ending the war on the
Italian front. Over
350,000 troops from
across the empire were
captured. The Veneto
saw many battles and
the area is strewn with
cemeteries and monu-
ments that bear witness
to the awful fighting
that took place in these
peaceful surroundings.

Did You Know?

Not all of the Dolomites
are composed of dolo-
mite rock. Marmolada,
the highest peak, is in
fact limestone.

⑦
Vittorio Veneto

🚆🚌 🛈 Viale della Vittoria
110; 0438 572 43

Two separate towns, Ceneda
and Serravalle, were merged
and renamed Vittorio Veneto
in 1866 to honour the
unification of Italy under King
Vittorio Emanuele II. The town
later gave its name to the last
decisive battle fought in Italy
in World War I. The **Museo
della Battaglia** in the Ceneda
quarter commemorates this.
Serravalle is much more
picturesque, with many fine

→

Visitors strolling
through colonnaded
arcades in scenic Feltre

←

The lakeside town of Alleghe near Val di Zoldo, encircled by mountains

15th-century palazzos and pretty arcaded streets. Franco Zeffirelli shot scenes for his film *Romeo and Juliet* in this town, which sits at the base of the rocky Meschio gorge. To the east, via Anzano, the S422 climbs up to the Bosco del Cansiglio, a wooded plateau.

Museo della Battaglia

⊗ ⊗ 🏛 Piazza Giovanni Paolo I 🕐 9:30am–12:30pm Tue–Fri; 10am–1pm, 3–6pm Sat & Sun 🌐 museo battaglia.it

❽ Feltre

 🌐 commune.feltre.bl.it

Feltre owes its good looks to the vengeful Holy Roman emperor Maximilian I. He sacked the town twice, in 1509 and in 1510, at the outbreak of the war against Venice waged by the League of Cambrai (*p52*). Despite the destruction wreaked, Feltre remained stoutly loyal to Venice, and in return Venice rebuilt the town after the war, thus the main street of the old town, Via Mezzaterra, is lined with arcaded early 16th-century houses. At the striking Piazza Maggiore it is possible to see the remains of Feltre's medieval castle, the church of San Rocco and a fountain by Tullio Lombardo (1520).

On the eastern side of the square is Via L Luzzo, a lovely street lined with Renaissance palaces, one of which houses the **Museo Civico**. The museum displays a fresco by the local artist Lorenzo Luzzo, who was known as Il Morto da Feltre (The Dead Man of Feltre) due to the deathly pallor of his skin.

Museo Civico

⊗ 🏛 Palazzo Villabruna, Via Luzzo 23 📞 0439 88 52 41 🕐 Fri–Sun & pub hols 🔒 1 Jan, 25 & 26 Dec

NEED TO KNOW

Busy canal on the island of Murano

BEFORE
YOU GO

Forward planning is essential to any successful trip. Be prepared for all eventualities by considering the following points before you travel.

AT A GLANCE

CURRENCY
Euro (EUR)

AVERAGE DAILY SPEND

SAVE	SPEND	SPLURGE
€50	€100	€200+

BOTTLED WATER	COFFEE	BEER	DINNER FOR TWO
€1.50	€1.50	€5.00	€60

ESSENTIAL PHRASES

Hello	Buongiorno
Thank you	Grazie
Please	Per favore
Goodbye	Arrivederci
Do you speak English	Parla inglese?
I don't understand	Non ho capito

ELECTRICITY SUPPLY
Power sockets are type F and L, fitting two- and three-pronged plugs. Standard voltage is 220-230v.

Passports and Visas

EU nationals and citizens of the UK, US, Canada, Australia and New Zealand do not need visas for stays of up to three months. Consult your nearest Italian embassy or check the **Polizia di Stato** website if travelling from outside these areas.
Polizia di Stato
W poliziadistato.it

Travel Safety Advice

Visitors can get up-to-date travel safety advice from the UK Foreign and Commonwealth Office, the US State Department, and the Department of Foreign Affairs and Trade in Australia.
Australia
W smartraveller.gov.au
UK
W gov.uk/foreign-travel-advice
US
W travel.state.gov

Customs Information

An individual is permitted to carry the following within the EU for personal use:
Tobacco products 800 cigarettes, 400 cigarillos, 200 cigars or 1 kg of smoking tobacco.
Alcohol 10 litres of alcoholic beverages above 22% strength, 20 litres of alcoholic beverages below 22% strength, 90 litres of wine (60 litres of which can be sparkling) and 110 litres of beer.
Cash If you plan to enter or leave the EU with €10,000 or more in cash (or the equivalent in other currencies) you must declare it to the customs authorities prior to departure.
If travelling from outside the EU, limits vary so check restrictions before travelling.

Insurance

It is wise to take out an insurance policy covering theft, loss of belongings, medical problems, cancellation and delays. Emergency medical care in Italy is free for all EU and Australian citizens. EU citizens should ensure they have an **EHIC** (European Health Insurance Card) and

Australians should be registered to **Medicare** to receive this benefit. It is advisable for visitors from outside these areas to arrange their own private medical insurance before arriving in Italy.

EHIC

Ⓦ gov.uk/european-health-insurance-card

Medicare

Ⓦ humanservices.gov.au/individuals/medicare

Vaccinations

No inoculations are needed for Italy.

Booking Accommodation

Book hotels in advance, especially during peak season (Carnival, Easter, June to September, and over Christmas and New Year). For those visiting Venice on a budget, consider staying in Mestre, or on the Lido across the lagoon.

Hotels throughout Italy charge overnight guests a small tourist tax (*imposta di soggiorno*) on top of room price. The amount varies. Under Italian law, hotels are required to register guests at police headquarters and issue a receipt of payment (*ricevuta fiscale*), which you must keep until you leave Italy.

Money

Most places accept major credit, debit and pre-paid currency cards, but carry cash for smaller items and for *traghetti* fares. Exchange foreign currency at a *cambio* exchange booth or at banks, which tend to offer better rates. Cash machines (*bancomat*) can be found at banks, at the train station and in various locations around town.

Travellers with Specific Requirements

Venice has made real effort to improve access for travellers with specific requirements, with 70 percent of the centre now accessible to those with impaired mobility and most sites reachable by public transport. However, many older buildings do not have wheelchair access or lifts. Some city museums offer free admission to disabled people and carers, as well as induction loops and audio guides for the hearing impaired and partially sighted. Many of the city's bridges are fitted with low steps but no stair lifts, while all vaporetto stops are accessible for people with impaired mobility. The main routes 1 and 2 can carry up to 4 wheelchairs and a discounted disabled ticket costs €1.50 including a carer.

Beyond Venice, all buses of the Mestre urban network and some of the Lido buses have extendable platforms and a designated area within them for wheelchairs.

The **Comune di Venezia** website includes a map of accessible Venice, plus itineraries designed for disabled travellers. **Sage Traveling** is a great resource for more indepth information.

Comune di Venezia

Ⓦ comunevenezia.it

Sage Traveling

Ⓦ sagetraveling.com

Language

Italian is the official language, though many people speak a Venetian dialect. English is widely spoken.

Closures

Mondays Some museums, restaurants and tourist attractions close.

Sundays Many shops close early or for the day. Some churches forbid tourists from visiting during services.

Public holidays Many shops, restaurants, museums and attractions close for the day.

PUBLIC HOLIDAYS	
1 Jan	New Year's Day
6 Jan	Epiphany
Mar/Apr	Easter
25 Apr	Liberation Day
1 May	Labour Day
2 Jun	Republic Day
15 Aug	Feast of the Assumption
1 Nov	All Saints' Day
8 Dec	Feast of the Immaculate Conception
25 Dec	Christmas Day
26 Dec	St Stephen's Day

GETTING AROUND

With its canals and waterways, and no cars or buses within the city limits, Venice is unlike many destinations when it comes to transportation.

AT A GLANCE

TRAVEL COSTS

VAPORETTO

€7.50

One way; valid for 75 minutes

TRAGHETTO

€2

Single trip

GONDOLA

€80

Max six people for 30 minutes

SPEED LIMITS IN VENETO

MOTORWAY

130 km/h (80mph)

DUAL CARRIAGEWAYS

100 km/h (60mph)

NATIONAL ROADS

80 km/h (50mph)

URBAN AREAS

50 km/h (30mph)

Arriving by Air

The main international airport, Aeroporto di Venezia Marco Polo (Venice Marco Polo Airport), is situated 14km (9 miles) from Venice on the shores of the Venetian Lagoon, just a short bus or boat ride away from the city. A secondary, much smaller airport, Aeroporto di Treviso Antonio Canova (Treviso Antonio Canova Airport) is located 40km (25 miles) north of Venice. This airport is popular for charter flights and some European budget airlines, including Ryanair, which offers a convenient connecting coach service with Piazzale Roma, Venice's major bus terminal at the entrance to the city.

To transfer to the city from Marco Polo Airport, you can travel by bus, airport shuttle or taxi, or go by boat from the airport boathouse, in a vaporetto or water taxi. There is little point in hiring a car from the airport, as Venice is a totally car-free city.

For those visiting the Veneto, Valerio Catullo Airport, in Verona, receives direct flights from the UK, other European countries and Africa. A bus service connects to Verona city centre, and costs around €5 each way. In summer a direct minibus shuttles visitors to Lake Garda.

Train Travel

International Train Travel

Italy's train network is operated by **Trenitalia**. Regular high-speed trains connect the main towns and cities of the Veneto to the rest of Italy, Austria, Germany, France and Eastern Europe. Reservations for these services are essential, and tickets get booked up quickly.

Trenitalia
🆆 trenitalia.com

Train Travel in Venice and the Veneto

The easiest and most convenient way to get around the Veneto is by rail. Trenitalia runs an extensive and efficient network throughout the region, and the cost of travel is very reasonable. Services range from the slow *reggionale*, which stops at every station en route, through the various intercity trains to the high-speed Freccia

GETTING TO AND FROM VENICE MARCO POLO AIRPORT

Public transport	Journey time	Fare
Airport Bus Express (ATVO)	35 mins	€8
Public Bus (ACTV)	21 mins	€15
Waterbus (Alilaguna)	30 mins	€15
Taxi	20 mins	€40
Water Taxi	20 mins	€110–125

and Eurostar, which link Venice with Verona Porta Nuova and beyond.

Direct lines serve **Venezia Santa Lucia** – Venice's main railway station – and **Venezia Mestre** from numerous northern Italian towns including Bologna, Florence, Milan and Verona. Both stations are extremely busy, with over 450 trains arriving in Venice daily.

Train tickets must be validated before boarding by stamping them in machines at the entrance to platforms. Heavy fines are levied if you are caught with an unvalidated ticket.

Venezia Mestre
W veneziamestre.it
Venezia Santa Lucia
W veneziasantalucia.it

Long-Distance Bus Travel

Eurolines offers international coach routes to Venice and other destinations throughout the Veneto from numerous European cities. Fares are very reasonable, with discounts available for students, children and seniors.

SITA Bus offer reasonably priced coach travel throughout Italy. You can buy tickets on board, and services usually depart from outside main railway stations or from the main piazza of smaller towns or cities.

FlixBus is a low-cost intercity coach network with direct services to Venice from Florence, Milan, Naples, Rome and Turin, as well as from international destinations. Coaches into Venice arrive at the main bus terminus in Piazzale Roma.

Eurolines
W eurolines.eu
FlixBus
W flixbus.com
Sitabus
W sitabus.it

Cruise Travel

Venice is one of the busiest cruise ports in the Mediterranean, with around 500 ships per year and over 700,000 cruise passengers. The city has two main cruise basins, Marittima (near the main Santa Lucia railway station) for large vessels, and San Basilio (in Giudecca canal) for smaller ships. Both passenger terminals are managed by the Venice Port Authority. An automated People Mover carries passengers from the central part of the terminal to Piazzale Roma in minutes. However, it is usually more convenient to travel by the shuttle buses that are provided by the individual cruise companies as they pull up at boarding points. Santa Marta and San Basilio are served by vaporetto line 6, which terminates at the Lido.

If you do choose to arrive in Venice by cruise ship, it's important to be aware of the issues that surround this increasingly popular mode of transport, and the detrimental effects it is having on the city and its lagoon. Venetians have a complicated relationship with cruising vessels. Although they do provide local jobs, the average cruise liner pollutes as much as 14,000 cars, damages the already fragile lagoon environment and brings in an unmanageable number of visitors to this tiny city. While their plight is often overlooked by the Italian government, the No Grandi Navi (no big ships) campaign – which calls for a ban on large cruise ships entering the lagoon – is gaining significant attention on the global stage. Their cause has been taken up by UNESCO, who have threatened to put Venice and its lagoon on their list of endangered heritage sites unless that ban goes ahead.

Venezia Terminal Passeggeri
W vtp.it

Public Transport

Each city in the Veneto has its own public transport provider. Verona is served by **ATV**, Padua by **APS Holding**, Vicenza by **AIM Mobilità** and Belluno and the surrounding area by **Dolimiti Bus**.

Venice has a unique transport system. No cars, buses or bicycles are allowed in the streets, and boats are the city's main mode of transportation. Venice's transit authority, the **ACTV**, operates three different types of waterbus (*vaporetti*, *motoscafi* and *motonavi*) , plus a network of buses on the Lido and the mainland. Most services run between 5am and midnight. Some modes of transport also offer hourly night services.

Belluno: Dolimiti Bus
w dolomitibus.it
Padua: APS Holding
w apsholding.it
Venice: ACTV
w actv.it
Verona: ATV
w atv.verona.it
Vicenza: AIM Mobilità
w aimmobilita.it

Waterbus

Vaporettos are the slow, single-storey waterbuses you will see chugging along the major canals. They are flat-decked and fully accessible for wheelchairs, prams and buggies, with plenty of seating and standing room. The most popular routes are lines 1 and 2. Faster, more stream-lined *motoscafi* travel beyond the sheltered waters of the city to outlying islands, as do the large double-decker *motonavi* ferries.

Waterbus stops are shown on most Venice maps and are clearly signposted around the city. Their yellow and white floating platforms are easy to spot. At stops with multiple platforms, check the boat number you require and the direction of travel. All the departure quays *(pontile)* have route maps and timetables.

Tickets are available from ACTV booths, from machines at larger stops and also at some newsstands and tobacconists. Validate your ticket at the white electronic ticket reader near the entrance to the platform prior to boarding. Note that green ticket readers are "read only" and will not validate your ticket. If the stop doesn't have a ticket machine, you can approach the conductor immediately after embarkation and ask for a *biglietto*. If you are caught travelling without a validated ticket, you may be fined.

Traghetti

These are large unadorned gondolas which cross the canal at seven points between San Marco and the railway station from early morning until around 7 or 8pm (although they are not all always in operation). They are rowed by oarsmen who ply backwards and forwards with no fixed timetable, and are a fun and convenient way of crossing the Grand Canal, as it only has four bridges. Simply wait on a *traghetto* pier for the boat to arrive. Pay cash (€2 per person) to the oarsman as you board or leave the gondola. It is customary to stand up for the crossing, but you can opt to sit if you prefer. (Note that these vessels are not suitable for wheelchair users. Instead, travel one stop on vaporetto Line 1 to cross, as it conveniently zig-zags the length of the Grand Canal.)

Gondola

Venice's traditional hand-built wooden gondolas are undoubtedly the most romantic way to see the city, but also the most expensive, used almost exclusively by tourists. There are a number of gondola ranks along the Grand Canal, including beside the Palazzo Ducale and Rialto, and also at busy pedestrian crossings along secondary canals. Each location offers a different type of gondola experience – choose whether you would prefer to experience the hustle and bustle of the Grand Canal or a quieter backwater before you start. Official tariffs should be available at the dock. Expect to pay around €80 for the first 40 minutes, then €40 for additional 20-minute increments. After 7pm, prices are hiked to around €100, and €50 for an extra 20 minutes. However, do not assume you will automatically pay the going rate: before boarding, agree a price with the gondolier to avoid being overcharged. Most gondoliers speak English and have a good knowledge of the main Venetian sights, art and history.

Water Taxi

Small, sleek motorboats, with highly polished wooden decking and stylish leather-upholstered cabins comprise Venice's water taxi fleet – an elite form of transport, which is reflected in the price. Expect to pay around €50–70 for a short hop within the city; and in excess of €110 to travel from the airport to a city centre abode. Water taxis can hold up to ten people, making it a viable option if you are splitting the fare with family or friends.

Bus

In Venice, buses serve the mainland and the Lido only. The main bus station in Venice is at Piazzale Roma near the main train station. On the Lido, route A serves the north of the island, while route B heads south.

City buses in the Veneto are cheap and regular. Tickets, which must be bought prior to travel, are available from newsstands, tobacconists, and shops that display the relevant bus company logo in the window. A flat fee usually covers the city centre and suburbs. Tickets must be validated upon boarding.

People Mover

This high-tech elevated **People Mover** tramway shuttles passengers cheaply and rapidly between the city's three main arrival points: Marittima cruise terminal, the Tronchetto parking island and Piazzale Roma. It runs 7am to 11pm Monday to Saturday, 8am to 10pm (9pm in winter) on Sundays and costs €1.50. Tickets are available at all three stations. You must scan your ticket to validate it at ground level before you can access the tramway.

Walking

Although it is very pleasant to sit on a vaporetto as you cruise down the Grand Canal or visit the outlying islands on one of the big *motonavi* ferries, Venice is a tiny city and all the main sights in the *centro storico* are accessible on foot within half-an-hour of each other, so remember to pack comfortable walking shoes. Beyond the main drag and the must-see sights, it is well worth taking time to explore the backwaters, with their hidden churches, monuments, squares and locals' bars and restaurants, for a taste of hidden Venice.

Bicycle Hire

Cycling is not allowed in Venice city centre, but bike hire is popular on the mainland and on some of the islands in the lagoon, including the Lido. The **BicinCittà** city bicycle scheme has a number of stations for bike hire in Marghera and Mestre, and three on the Lido (at Piazzale Santa Maria Elisabetta; Palazzo del Cinema/Via Candia; and Riva di Giovanni Diacono/Piazzale Malamocco). The first hour is free, the second hour costs €1, then €2 per hour thereafter.
BicinCittà
w bicincitta.com

Driving

Car rental

There are a number of car rental offices at Marco Polo, Treviso Antonio Canova and Valerio Catullo airports and at Piazzale Roma, including Avis, Europcar and Hertz, for those wishing to explore the Veneto or further afield. Some of the smaller towns and scenic drives are only accessible by private vehicle, and the rolling hills of the Veneto landscape make it perfect terrain for a scenic driving holiday.

To rent a car you must be over 21 and have held a valid driver's licence for at least a year. Driving licences issued by any of the EU member states are valid throughout the European Union, including Italy. If visiting from outside the EU, you may need to apply for an International Driving Permit.
Avis
w avis.com
Europcar
w europcar.com
Hertz
w hertz.com

Rules of the Road

Drive on the right, use the left lane only for passing, and yield to traffic from the right. Seat belts are required for all passengers, and heavy fines are levied for using a mobile phone while driving. A strict drink-drive limit *(p258)* is enforced. During the day dipped headlights are compulsory when you are driving on motorways, dual carriageways and on all out-of-town roads. A red warning triangle, spare tyre and fluorescent vests must be carried for use in an emergency. In the event of an accident or breakdown, switch on your hazard warning lights and place the warning triangle 50m (55yd) behind your vehicle. For breakdowns, call the ACI emergency number (116) or the emergency services. The ACI will tow any foreign-registered vehicle to the nearest ACI-affiliated garage free of charge.

VAPORETTO ROUTES

Line 1
Zigzag leisurely down the Grand Canal, calling at 20 stops between Piazzale Roma and the Lido.

Line 2
Take a circular route from San Zaccaria (one stop on from Piazza San Marco) via the Giudecca Canal and Tronchetto then back down the Grand Canal to Rialto or San Marco.

Line 4.1
Travel around Venice anti-clockwise on the outer side of the city, then to Murano and back via the Cannaregio Canal. (Line 4.2 does the same route clockwise.)

Line 12
From Fondamente Nuove, this line calls at a number of Venice's outlying islands including Murano, Torcello and Burano.

Line N
This night service runs 11.30pm–4.30am daily from San Marco and San Zaccaria to the Lido via the Giudecca Canal and the Grand Canal. It is a cheap and spectacular way to see the city sights lit up at night.

PRACTICAL
INFORMATION

A little local know-how goes a long way in Venice and the Veneto. Here you can find all the essential information you will need during your stay.

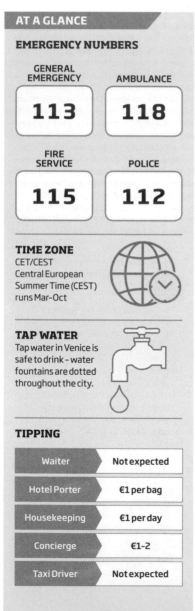

AT A GLANCE

EMERGENCY NUMBERS

GENERAL EMERGENCY	AMBULANCE
113	**118**

FIRE SERVICE	POLICE
115	**112**

TIME ZONE
CET/CEST
Central European
Summer Time (CEST)
runs Mar–Oct

TAP WATER
Tap water in Venice is safe to drink – water fountains are dotted throughout the city.

TIPPING

Waiter	Not expected
Hotel Porter	€1 per bag
Housekeeping	€1 per day
Concierge	€1–2
Taxi Driver	Not expected

Personal Security

Venice is one of the safest cities in Europe. Serious crime is rare. Nevertheless, it is wise to take a few simple precautions, particularly against pickpockets. Leave valuables and any important documents in the hotel safe and carry only the minimum amount of money necessary for the day. After dark, stick to main thoroughfares rather than gloomy alleyways.

If you have anything stolen, report the crime as soon as possible at the nearest police station and take ID with you. Get a copy of the crime report (denuncia) to claim on your insurance. Contact your embassy or consulate if your passport is lost or stolen, or in the event of a serious crime or accident.

Health

Seek medicinal supplies and advice for minor ailments from pharmacies (farmacia). You can find details of the nearest 24-hour service on all pharmacy doors.

Emergency medical care in Italy is free for all EU and Australian citizens (p252). If you have an EHIC card, be sure to present this as soon as possible. You may have to pay for treatment upfront and reclaim the money later.

For visitors from outside the EU or Australia, payment of medical expenses is entirely the patient's responsibility. It is therefore important to arrange comprehensive medical insurance prior to your visit.

Smoking, Alcohol and Drugs

Smoking and vaping are banned in enclosed public places, and the possession of illegal drugs is strictly prohibited and could result in a prison sentence.

Italy has a strict limit of 0.05 per cent BAC (blood alcohol content) for drivers. This means that you cannot drink more than a small beer or a small glass of wine if you plan to drive afterwards. For newly qualified drivers who have less than three years' driving experience, the limit is 0.

ID

By law you must carry identification at all times in Italy. A photocopy of your passport photo page (and visa if applicable) should suffice.

Responsible Tourism

In response to the high volume of tourists visiting Venice, the **#EnjoyRespectVenezia** campaign was launched in 2017 to raise awareness of tourist impact and to encourage responsible tourism in the city. The campaign asks that visitors follow certain rules to lessen their impact: walk on the right, do not linger on busy bridges, do not cycle in the city or lead bikes by hand. The steps of churches, bridges, wells, monuments and canalbanks are not picnic areas, nor are busy squares or *campi* – instead head to public gardens. Do not jump into the canals or attempt to swim in the lagoon, except at designated spots. Do not wear inappropriate clothing such as swimwear in the city. Don't drop litter – instead dispose of waste properly and recycle wherever possible. Do not feed pigeons, and respect the privacy of local residents. Camping is also prohibited in the city, as is attaching padlocks to buildings or bridges, or buying fake goods from illegal street vendors. **#EnjoyRespectVenezia**

w comune.venezia.it/en/content/enjoyrespectvenezia

Visiting Sacred Sights

When entering religious buildings, strict dress codes apply: cover your torso and upper arms, and ensure shorts and skirts cover your knees. Shoes must be worn.

Mobile Phones and Wi-Fi

Wi-Fi is generally widely available throughout Venice, and cafés and restaurants will usually give you the password for their Wi-Fi on the condition that you make a purchase. Much of the city has wireless hotspots.

Visitors travelling to Italy with EU tariffs are able to use their devices abroad without being affected by roaming charges. Users will be charged the same rates for data, SMS and voice calls as they would pay at home.

Post

Main post offices are found in the Rialto and on the Piazzale Roma. Stamps *(francobolli)* can be purchased from any tobacconist *(tabacchi)* displaying a black and white T sign.

Taxes and Refunds

VAT (called IVA in Italy) is usually 22 per cent, with a reduced rate of 4–10 per cent on some items. Non-EU citizens can claim an IVA rebate.

Discount Cards

Venice tourist office, **Venezia Unica**, offers a range of different discount cards to make visiting Venice easier on the purse strings. The silver, gold or platinum City Pass, which includes discounted museum, gallery and church entry, is available from €29.90, €58.90 and €70.90. For young people aged 16–29 years, the €6 Rolling Venice pass and ACTV 3 Day Youth Pass, provide a worthwhile travel discount (€22 for a three-day travel pass instead of €40) plus reduced entry to a number of city sights.

ACTV also offer a variety of discounted travel cards *(biglietti a tempo)*, valid on all ACTV water and land routes for 24 hours (€20), 48 hours (€30), 72 hours (€40) or seven days (€60). They can be purchased at ACTV ticket booths, tobacconists *(tabacchi)* or online. All discount passes can be purchased online from Venezia Unica.

Venezia Unica
w veneziaunica.it

INDEX

Page numbers in **bold** refer to main entries

PHRASE BOOK

IN EMERGENCY

Help!	Aiuto!	eye-*yoo*-toh
Stop!	Ferma!	fair-*mah*
Call a doctor	Chiama un medico	kee-*ah*-mah oon *meh*-dee-koh
Call an ambulance	Chiama un' ambulanza	kee-*ah*-mah oon am-boo-*lan*-tsa
Call the police	Chiama la polizia	kee-*ah*-mah lah pol-ee-*tsee*-ah
Call the fire brigade	Chiama i pompieri	kee-*ah*-mah ee pom-pee-*air*-ee
Where is the telephone?	Dov'è il telefono?	dov-*eheel* teh-*leh*-foh-noh?
The nearest hospital?	L'ospedale più vicino?	loss-peh-*dah*-leh pee-oovee-*chee*-noh?

COMMUNICATION ESSENTIALS

Yes/No	Sì/No	see/noh
Please	Per favore	pair fah-*vor*-eh
Thank you	Grazie	*grah*-tsee-eh
Excuse me	Mi scusi	mee *skoo*-zee
Hello/good morning	Buon giorno	bwon *jor*-noh
Goodbye	Arrivederci	ah-ree-veh-*dair*-chee
Good evening	Buona sera	*bwon*-ah *sair*-ah
morning	la mattina	lah mah-*tee*-nah
afternoon	il pomeriggio	eel poh-meh-*ree*-joh
evening	la sera	lah *sair*-ah
yesterday	ieri	ee-*air*-ee
today	oggi	*oh*-jee
tomorrow	domani	doh-*mah*-nee
here	qui	*kwee*
there	la	*lah*
What?	Quale?	*kwah*-leh?
When?	Quando?	*kwan*-doh?
Why?	Perchè?	pair-*keh*?
Where?	Dove?	*doh*-veh

USEFUL PHRASES

How are you?	Come sta?	*koh*-meh stah?
Very well, thank you.	Molto bene, grazie	*moll*-toh *beh*-neh *grah*-tsee-eh
Pleased to meet you.	Piacere di conoscerla.	pee-ah-*chair*-eh dee coh-*noh*-shair-lah
See you soon.	A più tardi.	ah pee-*oo* tar-*dee*
That's fine.	Va bene.	va *beh*-neh
Where is/are ...?	Dov'è/Dove sono ...?	dov-*eh*/doveh *soh* noh?
How long does it take to get to ...?	Quanto tempo ci vuole per andare a ...?	*kwan*-toh *tem*-poh chee voo-*oh*-leh pair an-*dar*-eh ah...?
How do I get to ...?	Come faccio per arrivare a ...?	*koh*-meh *fah*-choh pair arri-*var*-eh ah...?
Do you speak English?	Parla inglese?	*par*-lah een-*gleh*-zeh?
I don't understand.	Non capisco.	non ka-*pee*-skoh
Could you speak more slowly, please?	Può parlare più lentamente, per favore?	pwoh par-*lah*-reh pee-*oo* len-ta-*men*-teh pair fah-*vor*-eh?
I'm sorry.	Mi dispiace.	mee dee-spee-*ah*-cheh

USEFUL WORDS

big	grande	*gran*-deh
small	piccolo	*pee*-koh-loh
hot	caldo	*kal*-doh
cold	freddo	*fred*-doh
good	buono	*bwoh*-noh
bad	male	*mal*-eh
enough	basta	*bas*-tah
well	bene	*beh*-neh
open	aperto	ah-*pair*-toh
closed	chiuso	kee-*oo*-zoh
left	a sinistra	ah see-*nee*-strah
right	a destra	ah *dess*-trah
straight on	sempre dritto	*sem*-preh *dree*-toh
near	vicino	vee-*chee*-noh
far	lontano	lon-*tah*-noh
up	su	*soo*
down	giù	*joo*
early	presto	*press*-toh
late	tardi	*tar*-dee
entrance	entrata	en-*trah*-tah
exit	uscita	oo-*shee*-ta
toilet	il bagno	eel ban-yo
free, unoccupied	libero	*lee*-bair-oh
free, no charge	gratuito	grah-*too*-ee-toh

MAKING A TELEPHONE CALL

I'd like to place a long-distance call.	Vorrei fare una interurbana.	vor-*ray* far-eh oona in-tair-oor-*bah*-nah.
I'd like to make a reverse-charge call.	Vorrei fare una telefonata a carico del destinatario.	vor-*ray* far-eh oona teh-leh-fon-*ah*-tah ah *kar*-ee-koh dell dess- tee-nah-*tar*-ree-oh.
I'll try again later.	Ritelefono più tardi.	ree-teh-*leh*-foh-noh pee-oo *tar*-dee.
Can I leave a message?	Posso lasciare un messaggio?	*poss*-oh lash-ah-reh oon mess-*sah*-joh?
Hold on	Un attimo, per favore	oon *ah*-tee-moh, pair fah-*vor*-eh.
Could you speak up a little please?	Può parlare più forte, per favore?	pwoh par-*lah*-reh pee-oo for-teh, pair fah-*vor*-eh?
local call	la telefonata locale	lah teh-leh-fon-*ah*-ta loh-*kah*-leh

SHOPPING

How much does this cost?	Quanto costa questo?	*kwan*-toh *cos*-stah *kweh*-stoh?
I would like ...	Vorrei ...	vor-*ray*...
Do you have ...?	Avete ...?	ah-*veh*-teh...?
I'm just looking.	Sto soltanto guardando	stoh sol-*tan*-toh gwar-*dan*-doh
Do you take credit cards?	Accettate carte di credito?	ah-chet-*tah*-teh *kar*-teh dee *creh*-dee-toh?
What time do you open/close?	A che ora apre/chiude?	ah keh or-ah *ah*-preh/*kee-oo*-deh?
this one	questo	*kweh*-stoh
that one	quello	*kwell*-oh
expensive	caro	*kar*-oh
cheap	a buon prezzo	ah bwon *pret*-soh
size, clothes	la taglia	lah *tah*-lee-ah
size, shoes	il numero	eel *noo*-mair-oh
white	bianco	bee-*ang*-koh
black	nero	*neh*-roh
red	rosso	*ross*-oh
yellow	giallo	*jal*-loh
green	verde	*vair*-deh
blue	blu	*bloo*
brown	marrone	mar-*roh*-neh

TYPES OF SHOP

antique dealer	l'antiquario	lan-tee-*kwah*-ree-oh
bakery	la panetteria	lahpah-net-tair-*ree*-ah
bank	la banca	lah *bang*-kah
bookshop	la libreria	lah lee-breh-*ree*-ah
butcher's	la macelleria	lah mah-chell-eh-*ree*-ah
cake shop	la pasticceria	lahpas-tee-chair-*ee*-ah
chemist's	la farmacia	lah far-mah-*chee*-ah
department store	il grande magazzino	eel *gran*-deh mag-gad-*zee*-noh
delicatessen	la salumeria	lah sah-loo-meh-*ree*-ah
fishmonger's	la pescheria	lah pess-keh-*ree*-ah
florist	il fioraio	eel fee-or-*eye*-oh
greengrocer	il fruttivendolo	eel froo-tee-*ven*-doh-loh
grocery	alimentari	ah-lee-men-*tah*-ree
hairdresser	il parrucchiere	eel par-oo-kee-*air*-eh
ice cream parlour	la gelateria	lah jel-lah-tair-*ee*-ah
market	il mercato	eel mair-*kah*-toh
news-stand	l'edicola	leh-*dee*-koh-lah
post office	l'ufficio postale	loo-*fee*-choh pos-*tah*-leh
shoe shop	il negozio di scarpe	eel neh-*goh*-tsioh dee *skar*-peh
supermarket	il supermercato	eel su pair mair *kah*-toh
tobacconist	il tabaccaio	eel tah-bak-*eye*-oh
travel agency	l'agenzia di viaggi	lah-jen-*tsee*-ah dee vee-*ad*-jee

SIGHTSEEING

art gallery	la pinacoteca	lahpeena-koh-*teh*-kah
bus stop	la fermata dell'autobus	lah fair-*mah*-tah dell ow-toh-booss
church	la chiesa	lah kee-*eh*-zah
	la basilica	lah bah-*seel*-i-kah
garden	il giardino	eel jar-*dee*-no
library	la biblioteca	lah beeb-lee-oh-*teh*-kah
museum	il museo	eel moo-*zeh*-oh
railway station	la stazione	lah stah-tsee-*oh*-neh

| tourist information | l'ufficio turistico | loo-**fee**-choh too-**ree**-stee-koh |
| closed for the public holiday | chiuso per la festa | kee-oo-zoh pair lah **fess**-tah |

STAYING IN A HOTEL

Do you have any vacant rooms?	Avete camere libere?	ah-**veh**-teh **kah**-mair -eh **lee**-bair-eh?
double room	una camera doppia	oona **kah**-mair-ah **doh**-pee-ah
with double bed	con letto matrimoniale	kon **let**-toh mah-tree-moh-nee-**ah**-leh
twin room	una camera con due letti	oona **kah**-mair-ah kon **doo**-eh **let**-tee
single room	una camera singola	oona **kah**-mair-ah **sing**-goh-lah
room with a bath, shower	una camera con bagno, con doccia	oona **kah**-mair-ah kon **ban**-yoh, kon **dot**-chah
porter	il facchino	eel fah-**kee**-noh
key	la chiave	lah kee-**ah**-veh
I have a reservation.	Ho fatto una prenotazione.	oh **fat**-toh oona preh-noh-tah-tsee-**oh**-neh

EATING OUT

Have you got a table for ...?	Avete un tavolo per ...?	ah-**veh**-teh oon **tah**-voh-loh pair ...?
I'd like to reserve a table.	Vorrei riservare un tavolo.	vor-**ray** ree-sair-**van**-reh oon **tah**-voh-loh
breakfast	colazione	koh-lah-tsee-**oh**-neh
lunch	pranzo	**pran**-tsoh
dinner	cena	**cheh**-nah
The bill, please.	Il conto, per favore.	eel **kon**-toh pair fah-**vor**-eh
I am a vegetarian.	Sono vegetariano/a.	**soh**-noh veh-joh-tar-ee-**ah**-noh/nah
waitress	cameriera	kah-mair-ee **air** ah
waiter	cameriere	kah-mair-ee-**air**-eh
fixed price menu	il menù a prezzo fisso	eel meh-noo ah **pret**-soh **fee**-soh
dish of the day	piatto del giorno	pee-**ah**-toh dell **jor**-no
starter	antipasto	un-tee-**pass**-toh
first course	il primo	eel **pree**-moh
main course	il secondo	eel seh-**kon**-doh
vegetables	il contorno	eel kon-**tor**-noh
dessert	il dolce	eel **doll**-che
cover charge	il coperto	eel koh-**pair**-toh
wine list	la lista dei vini	lah **lee**-stah day **vee**-nee
rare	al sangue	al **sang**-gweh
medium	a puntino	a poon-**tee**-no
well done	ben cotto	ben **kot**-toh
glass	il bicchiere	eel bee-kee-**air**-eh
bottle	la bottiglia	lah bot-**teel**-yah
knife	il coltello	eel kol-**tell**-oh
fork	la forchetta	lah for-**ket**-tah
spoon	il cucchiaio	eel koo-kee-**oye**-oh

MENU DECODER

apple	la mela	lah **meh**-lah
artichoke	il carciofo	eel kar-**choff**-oh
aubergine	la melanzana	lah meh-lan-**tsah**-nah
baked	al forno	al **for**-noh
beans	i fagioli	ee fah-**joh**-lee
beef	il manzo	eel **man**-tsoh
beer	la birra	lah **beer**-rah
boiled	lesso	**less**-oh
bread	il pane	eel **pah**-neh
broth	il brodo	eel **broh**-doh
butter	il burro	eel **boor**-oh
cake	la torta	lah **tor**-tah
cheese	il formaggio	eel for-**mad**-joh
chicken	il pollo	eel **poll**-oh
chips	patatine fritte	pah-tah-**teen**-eh **free**-teh
baby clams	le vongole	leh **von**-goh-leh
coffee	il caffè	eel kah-**feh**
courgettes	gli zucchini	lyee dzoo-**kee**-nee
dry	secco	**sek**-koh
duck	l'anatra	**lah**-nah-trah
egg	l'uovo	loo-**oh**-voh
fish	il pesce	eel **pesh**-eh
fresh fruit	frutta fresca	**froo**-tah **fress**-kah
garlic	l'aglio	**lahl**-yoh
grapes	l'uva	**loo**-vah
grilled	alla griglia	ah-lah **greel**-yah
ham cooked/cured	il prosciutto cotto/crudo	eel pro-**shoo**-toh **kot**-toh/**kroo**-doh
ice cream	il gelato	eel jel-**lah**-toh
lamb	agnello	la-**gnel**-lo

lobster	l'aragosta	lah-rah-**goss**-tah
meat	la carne	la **kar**-neh
milk	il latte	eel **laht**-teh
mineral water sparkling/still	l'acqua minerale gassata/naturale	**lah**-kwah mee-nair-**ah**-leh gah-**zah**-tah/nah-too-**rah**-leh
mushrooms	i funghi	ee **foon**-gee
oil	l'olio	**loll**-yoh
olive	l'oliva	loh-**lee**-vah
onion	la cipolla	lah chee-**poll**-ah
orange	l'arancia	lah-**ran**-chah
orange/lemon juice	succo d'arancia/ di limone	**soo**-kohdah-**ran**-chah/ dee lee-**moh**-neh
peach	la pesca	lah **pess**-kah
pepper	il pepe	eel **peh**-peh
pork	carne di maiale	**kar**-neh dee mah-**yah**-leh
potatoes	le patate	leh pah-**tah**-teh
prawns	i gamberi	ee **gam**-bair-ee
rice	il riso	eel **ree**-zoh
roast	arrosto	ar-**ross**-toh
roll	il panino	eel pah-**nee**-noh
salad	l'insalata	leen-sah-**lah**-tah
salt	il sale	eel **sah**-leh
sausage	la salsiccia	lah sal-**see**-chah
seafood	frutti di mare	**froo**-tee dee **mah**-reh
soup	la zuppa, la minestra	lah **tsoo**-pah, lah mee-**ness**-trah
steak	la bistecca	lah bee-**stek**-kah
strawberries	le fragole	leh **frah**-goh-leh
sugar	lo zucchero	loh **zoo**-kair-oh
tea	il tè	eel **teh**
herb tea	la tisana	lah tee-**zah**-nah
tomato	il pomodoro	eel poh-moh-**dor**-oh
tuna	il tonno	eel **ton**-noh
veal	il vitello	eel vee-**tell**-oh
vegetables	le verdure	leh vair-**du**-rah
vinegar	l'aceto	lah-**cheh**-toh
water	l'acqua	**lah**-kwah
red wine	vino rosso	**vee**-noh ross-oh
white wine	vino bianco	**vee**-noh bee-**ang**-koh

NUMBERS

1	uno	**oo**-noh
2	due	**doo**-eh
3	tre	treh
4	quattro	**kwat**-roh
5	cinque	**ching**-kweh
6	sei	**say**-ee
7	sette	**set**-teh
8	otto	**ot**-toh
9	nove	**noh**-veh
10	dieci	**dee**-eh-chee
11	undici	**oon**-dee-chee
12	dodici	**doh**-dee-chee
13	tredici	**treh**-dee-chee
14	quattordici	kwat-**tor**-dee-chee
15	quindici	**kwin**-dee-chee
16	sedici	**say**-dee-chee
17	diciassette	dee-chah-**set**-teh
18	diciotto	dee-**chot**-toh
19	diciannove	dee-chah-**noh**-veh
20	venti	**ven**-tee
30	trenta	**tren**-tah
40	quaranta	kwah-**ran**-tah
50	cinquanta	ching-**kwan**-tah
60	sessanta	sess-**an**-tah
70	settanta	set-**tan**-tah
80	ottanta	ot-**tan**-tah
90	novanta	noh-**van**-tah
100	cento	**chen**-toh
1,000	mille	**mee**-leh
2,000	duemila	**doo**-eh **mee**-lah
5,000	cinquemila	**ching**-kweh **mee**-lah
1,000,000	un milione	oon meel-**yoh**-neh

TIME

one minute	un minuto	oon mee-**noo**-toh
one hour	un'ora	oon **or**-ah
half an hour	mezz'ora	medz-**or**-ah
a day	un giorno	oon **jor**-noh
a week	una settimana	oona set-tee-**mah**-nah
Monday	lunedì	loo-neh-**dee**
Tuesday	martedì	mar-teh-**dee**
Wednesday	mercoledì	mair-koh-leh-**dee**
Thursday	giovedì	joh-veh-**dee**
Friday	venerdì	ven-air-**dee**
Saturday	sabato	**sah**-bah-toh
Sunday	domenica	doh-**meh**-nee-kah

ACKNOWLEDGMENTS

The publisher would like to thank the following for their kind permission to reproduce their photographs:

Key: a-above; b-below/bottom; c-centre; f-far; l-left; r-right; t-top

123RF.com: efired 108bl; fesus 19cb; Valentyn Volkov 47cla.

4Corners: Stefano Amantini 110-1t; Guido Baviera 148tl, 164t, 185b, 192b; Massimo Borchi 200b; Franco Cogoli 105c, 160-1t, 198t; Olimpio Fantuz 180-1t; Nicolò Miana 164-5b; Aldo Pavan 249b; Maurizio Rellini 13cr; Stefano Scatà 122t.

akg-images: De Agostini Picture Lib. / A. Dagli Orti 159br.

Alamy Stock Photo: AA World Travel Library 177cla; age fotostock / Andre Lebrun 121clb, / Carlo Morucchio 126tl, / Aldo Pavan 31cl; AGF Srl / Lorenzo De Simone 201tr; Duncan Anderson 192cr; Art Collection 2 141tc; Awakening Photo Agency 185tr, / Xianpix / Simone Padovani 47br; Azoor Photo Collection 141tr; B.O'Kane 81cr; Roman Babakin 229tr; Bailey-Cooper Photography 96bl, 125tl; Peter Barritt 112-3b; Bernard Bialorucki 225tr; FREESPACE / Riccardo Bianchini / *Bamboo Stalactite, 2018, installation bamboo 16. Mostra Internazionale di Architettura - La Biennale di Venezia* by Vo Trong Nghia Architects & Inexhibit 27br; Frank Bienewald 10c; Piere Bonbon 149clb, 181bl; Ceri Breeze 238bl; Eden Breitz 88-9t; Dalibor Brlek 207tl; John Burnikell 133br; John Cairns 135tr; Chronicle 51tl; Mary Clarke 49clb; ClickAlps Srls / Moreno Geremetta 245tr; Silvia Cozzi 215tr; Ian Dagnall 232t; Matteo Del Grosso 129br; Peter Delius 147t; FineArt 61tr; Kirk Fisher 184tl; Lois GoBe 97br; GoneWithTheWind 17bl, 116-7; Grant Rooney Premium 124b; Thierry GRUN - Aero 44-5b; Hackenberg-Photo-Cologne 214cr; hemis.fr / Gregory Gerault 140-1b, / Sylvain Sonnet 60clb; Heritage Image Partnership Ltd / Fine Art Images 58br, 141ca; Kate Hockenhull 90-1t; Peter Horree 141tl; imageBROKER / Barbara Boensch 127t, / Stefan Espenhahn 166cla; Independent Photo Agency Srl 48crb; Brian Jannsen 77clb; Jon Arnold Images Ltd 122cr; David Keith Jones 44tl; Andrew King 197cra; Art Kowalsky 27tr; Joana Kruse 248-9tl; Lebrecht Music & Arts / ColouriserAL 52br; Angel Manzano 159cla; Martin Thomas Photography 204; MB_Photo 193tr; Henk Meijer 66-7t; Hercules Milas 50t, 81bl, 92b, 103tr, 159cra; Mira 166t; Roberto Moiola 247t; Tim Moore 24clb; Russell Mountford 120-1t; Theo Moye 32-3t; nagelestock.com 43tr; North Wind Picture Archives 168tc; Samantha Ohlsen 202-3t; peizais 114clb; peterforsberg 182clb; Pictorial Press Ltd 41br; The Picture Art Collection 105cla, 105cra, 121crb, 142cr; Prisma Archivo 53clb, 78fcrb; Stefano Ravera 169br; Realy Easy Star / Maurizio Sartoretto 208t, / Toni Spagone 93t, 213bl, 214-5b, 224b; robertharding 131tl, / Nico Tondini 239tl; Stuart Robertson 171tl; Riccardo Sala 195tr; Scattolin 108-9t; Scenics & Science 226tl; Matthias Scholz 28cra, 177tr, 182b; Marco Secchi 170hl; Rastislav Sedlak 230t; Gordon Sinclair 48cl; Alan Skyrme 95br; Andrea Spinelli 46b; Slawek Staszczuk 57br,167bl; P Tomlins 43br; TRAVELSCAPES 45cb, 67cra, 87br, 104-5b, 109cla, 133tl,134bl,141br, / © Fondazione Musei Civici di Venezia 179crb; Jorge Tutor 229cra; Viennaslide 103br, 146bl, 150-1b; Richard Wayman 65crb; WENN Rights Ltd 49crb; Scott Wilson 94-5t; Jan Wlodarczyk 13br.

AWL Images: Alessia Bortolameotti 21, 240-1; Matteo Colombo 115br; Andrea Comi 45br; Francesco Iacobelli 10-1b, 70-1, 190-1t; Ken Scicluna 16c, 72-3.

Bridgeman Images: Cameraphoto Arte Venezia / Santi Giovanni e Paolo, Venice, Italy 121bc; De Agostini Picture Library 51cra, / A. Dagli Orti 51crb, 52-3t, / Veneranda Biblioteca Ambrosiana, Milan, Italy 29tr; Isabella Stewart Gardner Museum, Boston, MA, USA 53tr; Palazzo Ducale, Venice, Italy / *The Taking of Constantinople* Palma Il Giovane (Jacopo Negretti) 51bl; Private Collection 50bl; Luisa Ricciarini 142bl.

Da Fiore: 32bl.

Depositphotos Inc: Iakov 2-3; Isaac74 234-5b; Ody1988 221tc; Xantana 145br.

Dorling Kindersley: Roger Moss 247bl.

Dreamstime.com: Albmex 20tl, 186-7; Anton Aleksenko 56-7t, 65b, 151tr; Kuznetsov Andrey 159tr; Anyaivanova 103tl; Ivan Vander Biesen 60b; Brasilnut 179crb; Mauro Carli 203bl; Anna Chaplygina 48cra; Christophefaugere 153tl; Paul Cowan 162br; Crisfotolux 126bc; Robert Crum 162cra; Daliu80 245tl; Svetlana Day 90bl; Dimabl 178; Emicristea 8clb, 80b; Enzodebe 205cl; Erickn 11br; Fedecandoniphoto 53br; Giovanni Gagliardi 38-9t; Janos Gaspar 244-5b; Giuseppemasci 208-9b; GoranJakus 36br; Zbigniew Guzowski 46-7t; Anna Hristova 45tr; Mihail Ivanov 144cr; Javarman 8cla; Keko64 149b; Jan Kranendonk 86br; Lucianbolca 42b; Olga Lupol 250-1; Makasanaphoto 43cb; Marcorubino 130-1b; Alberto Masnovo 225br; Milosk50 111b; Minnystock 11crb, 17t, 98-9, 128-9t; Monysasi 195tl; Roland Nagy 106-7t; NatashaBreen 33cl; Neirfy 54; Njarvis5 31tr; Nullplus 6-7; Andrey Omelyanchuk 83t, 83cra; Ralph Paprzycki 221tl; William Perry 78crb; Photogolfer 19tl, 154-5, 162-3b; Enrico Della Pietra 123br; Pro777 42tl; Rndmst 196clb; Fesus Robert 172-3; Rosshelen 30-1b, 34-5b, 59t, 223tr; Rudi1976 8cl, 220t; Scaliger 84-5b, 158-9b; Jozef Sedmak 103cr; Michal Stipek 246bl; Toldiu74 11t, 20cb, 216-7; Vvoevale 206bl; Natalia Zakharova 12clb; александр макарскııко 236t.

Fondazione Musei Civici di Venezia: 84cla, 85tr, 88bl, 112cr.

Fondazione Teatro La Fenice: Michele Crosera 40-1b.

Getty Images: AFP / Andreas Solaro 211t; Alinari Archives 235tl; Awakening / Simone Padovani 39crb; Bloomberg 161br; Corbis Documentary / Sylvain Sonnet 22crb; De Agostini / DEA 39cla, 78cb, / Biblioteca Ambrosiana 26tr; DigitalVision / Matteo Colombo 62-3t, 86t; EyeEm / Chloé Boulos 33crb;

Penguin
Random
House

Main Contributers Jo-Ann Titmarsh,
Susie Bolton, Christopher Catling,
Gillian Price, Sally Roy

Senior Editor Alison McGill

Senior Designer Bess Daly

Project Editor Danielle Watt

Project Art Editor Ben Hinks

Designers Van Anh Le,
Ankita Sharma, Kitty Glavin

Factchecker Toni deBella

Editors Louise Abbott,
Zoë Rutland, Rachel Thompson

Proofreader Susanne Hillen

Indexer Hilary Bird

Senior Picture Researcher Ellen Root

Picture Research Manpreet Kaur, Sumita
Khatwani, Erica Martin, Vagisha Pushp,
Rituraj Singh

Illustrators Arcena Studios, Annabelle Brend,
Dawn Brend, Neil Bulpitt,
Donati Giudici Associati Srl, Richard Draper,
Nick Gabbard, Kevin Jones Associates,
John Lawrence, The Maltings Partnership,
Robbie Polley, Simon Roulestone, Sue Sharples,
Derrick Stone, Paul Weston, John Woodcock

Senior Cartographic Editor Casper Morris

Cartography Ashutosh Ranjan Bharti,
Jane Hanson, Phil Rose, Jennifer Skelley

Jacket Designers Van Anh Le,
Bess Daly, Maxine Pedliham

Jacket Picture Research Susie Watters

Senior DTP Designer Jason Little

DTP Rohit Rojal

Producer Samantha Cross

Managing Editor Rachel Fox

Art Director Maxine Pedliham

Publishing Director Georgina Dee

First edition 1995

Published in Great Britain by Dorling Kindersley Limited,
80 Strand, London, WC2R ORL

Published in the United States by DK Publishing,
1450 Broadway, Suite 801, New York, NY 10018

Copyright © 1995, 2020 Dorling Kindersley Limited
A Penguin Random House Company
20 21 22 23 10 9 8 7 6 5 4 3 2 1

A CIP catalog record for this book
is available from the British Library.

A catalog record for this book is available
from the Library of Congress.

ISSN: 1542 1554
ISBN: 978 0 2414 0770 7

Printed and bound in China.

www.dk.com

MIX
Paper from
responsible sources
FSC™ C018179
www.fsc.org

**The information in this
DK Eyewitness Travel Guide is checked regularly.**
Every effort has been made to ensure that this book
is as up-to-date as possible at the time of going to
press. Some details, however, such as telephone
numbers, opening hours, prices, gallery hanging
arrangements and travel information, are liable to
change. The publishers cannot accept responsibility
for any consequences arising from the use of this
book, nor for any material on third party websites,
and cannot guarantee that any website address
in this book will be a suitable source of travel
information. We value the views and suggestions
of our readers very highly. Please write to: Publisher,
DK Eyewitness Travel Guides, Dorling Kindersley,
80 Strand, London, WC2R ORL, UK, or email:
travelguides@dk.com